The Lords of Baseball

The Lords of Baseball

⊗⊗⊗⊗⊗

Harold Parrott

Praeger Publishers
New York

Published in the United States of America in 1976
by Praeger Publishers, Inc.
111 Fourth Avenue, New York, N.Y. 10003

Library of Congress Cataloging in Publication Data

Parrott, Harold.
    The lords of baseball.

    1. Baseball clubs—History.   I. Title.
GV875.A1P37   796.357′092′2   75-4152
ISBN 0-275-22570-4

Printed in the United States of America

To Josephine

This totally irreverent book is dedicated (with much reverence) to the most beautiful girl, inside and out, I've ever met. She so admired Branch Rickey for the love and family warmth he gave us in place of dollars. (*Why couldn't it've been both, B.R.?*) She still prays that Durocher, who even now carries the medal she gave him years ago, will come back to The Fold, because the Lip, in backing up my ghosted stuff that he'd never bothered to read, proved a stand-up guy even when brought to his knees by the MacPhail mob and Unhappy Chandler. This girl still believes we'll find another baseball owner as honest as Stoneham or Autry—and a baseball Commissioner who'll speak the truth, or at least speak, when you need him. But in a lump, she rates the players and their wives far above these windbags and admired Jackie Robinson and his Rachel far more than the stuffed shirts who made life tough for them. She thanks her saints that baseball brought us close to Eddie Brannick, Bill Terry, Bill Brandt, and Roscoe McGowen . . . and to Ray Hopper and John and Marie Martin who lived (and died) with us in those dear Dodger days. She loved Gil Hodges and Pee Wee and Rex Barney and the Lion because they helped our four boys with their homework on road trips and gave 'em Dodger suits and Hopalong Cassidy movies every other night in spring training and shielded them from a lot of the language you'll read in these pages. She sees some good in everybody, even the Big Oom and Peter Bavasi and yes, even in Harold Parrott.

Foreword

Once a year the New York baseball writers entertain a thousand or so diners with a show that does little permanent harm to the American theater but sends some members of the baseball establishment away in a hurry to have their shirts restuffed. Before World War II, when Larry MacPhail was throwing around money the Brooklyn Dodgers didn't have, the late Arthur Mann impersonated the demon promoter. Doing a sleight-of-hand act, Arthur sang:

> "When mortgage-holders squall,
> I introduce a yellow ball . . .
> I've got a pocketful of schemes."

And out of the air Arthur conjured the colored baseball Mac-Phail had employed in Ebbets Field on the theory that it would be more clearly visible than a white ball against a background of fans in shirt sleeves. Today Charley Finley of the Oakland A's is shouting for adoption of an orange ball and taking bows as a daring innovator.

As the champion of new ideas, Finley is more than thirty-five years behind MacPhail, and Charley is regarded in baseball as a dangerous radical. This should tell us something about the men who run the game. (An exception must be made for Bill Veeck now that this uninhibited character is back in the lodge. For imagination, initiative, enterprise, and originality, not even Mac-Phail could match the old new head of the Chicago White Sox.)

Still, MacPhail was no slouch. In three short years after taking over a dilapidated franchise in Cincinnati, then the smallest city in the major leagues, he revived a moribund box office, built a team that would win two National League pennants and one World Series, introduced night ball to the majors, had a fist fight with the house dick of a hotel, quarreled with Powel Crosley, his employer, and departed.

He moved on to Brooklyn for a four-year stretch that Eddie Murphy of the New York *Sun* called the Reign of Terror. With the club already in hock to the Brooklyn Trust Company, he borrowed a lot more money, installed lights in Ebbets Field, and, for Brooklyn's first night game, selected Johnny Vander Meer's second consecutive no-hitter. He signed Babe Ruth as a coach. With a team that finished next to last on merit, he pumped up home attendance from 450,000 to 750,000 in his first season.

He pioneered radio broadcasting in New York baseball and attuned the metropolitan ear to the cornpone accents of Red Barber. He enriched the cultural climate of Flatbush by creating the "Dodger Press Club," a semiprivate saloon that came to rival Madison Square Garden as a fight club, chiefly because of his presence. Another cultural contribution was the installation of a pipe organ with Miss Gladys Goodding at the controls.

MacPhail's Dodgers was the first team in the big leagues to travel regularly by air. Larry gave Leo Durocher his first job as manager, fired him before spring training began, and many times after that. He made the Dodgers a national institution and convinced Brooklyn residents that it was their civic duty to make sure attendance topped a million annually.

After a hitch as an army major in World War II, MacPhail returned to baseball as architect and beneficiary of the most profitable business deal the game has witnessed. He persuaded two rich men, Del Webb and Dan Topping, to buy the Yankees and cut him in as president and one-third partner. For $2.6 million they got Yankee Stadium and that part of the Bronx on which it stands, players like Joe DiMaggio, Charley Keller, Bill Dickey, and Tommy Henrich, the ball clubs and ball parks in Newark and Kansas City, and all other assets of the far-flung Yankee empire.

Two years later the Yankees won the world championship and MacPhail sold out in a touching valedictory. He wept and punched a long-time associate, John McDonald. Webb punched Larry.

MacPhail fired George Weiss, who had created and cultivated the most productive farm system in baseball. Webb and Topping immediately rehired Weiss, and in the next dozen years he made them well over $20 million before they sold the Yankees for $16 million.

When he retired, MacPhail left behind a club that dominated the game for another seventeen years. He made other contributions; namely, he brought Happy Chandler in as commissioner and had Leo Durocher kicked out for a year. No other man, living or dead, can make the same boast.

Today Finley makes headlines by dressing his athletes like a girls' softball team and quarreling with his players. Hell, MacPhail punched everybody, including the author of this book whom he outweighed by at least seventy-five pounds.

Chances are there is nobody in the world better fitted than Harold Parrott to write about MacPhail and Finley and Walter O'Malley and C. Arnholt Smith and other lords of baseball, past and present. As a Brooklyn newspaperman, Harold was close to the hurricane's eye when MacPhail was on the loose. Later he worked for O'Malley in Brooklyn and Los Angeles. He did turns in Anaheim with the California Angels and in San Diego with the Padres, and he drove the getaway car in the American League's one-year caper in Seattle.

Free now of entangling alliances in baseball, he can give the reader illuminating glimpses of men they know only by their public images. When big, genial Walter O'Malley was Gene Autry's landlord in Chavez Ravine, Harold relates, the Angels were billed for cleaning the windows of a ticket office that had no windows, and for toilet paper used by O'Malley's customers.

Like other owners in championship years, O'Malley rewarded his employees with rings as World Series mementoes. Unlike others, when the Dodgers won again their boss collected the old rings before distributing new ones. Then there was the time the Harry Hickeys wanted to accompany their friend Walter to Japan—but no, better let Harold tell the story.

During his years in baseball, Harold Parrott met more interesting people than he ever did as a reporter on the Brooklyn *Eagle*, and now in his memoirs he pays off some old scores. O'Malley isn't the only fascinating character in his tale; there is also the self-effacing Arnholt Smith, whose Padres had to wear brown because their owner wore brown suits, hats, and shoes, drove a brown Cadillac, and wrote on brown paper.

There is also Dewey Soriano, who played a prominent role in the sack of Seattle. As far as I know, Harold Parrott is the first to reveal that American League owners who could stomach Soriano refused to accept a group of civic leaders who had raised $11,500,000 to buy the bankrupt Pilots and keep them in Seattle.

Many years ago a wise man wrote that baseball must be a great game because it had survived the men who ran it. This book cites evidence that the situation has not changed. Not, at least, in the eyes of the Oakland fans who, weary of Charley Finley and his mule mascot, displayed a bedsheet banner reading: "Finley—Get your ass out of town."

Writing this foreword, I am relying on my memory as Harold relied on his when he wrote the book. They don't always agree. For example, I think it was John Drebinger of the *New York Times* who, helping George Phair out, composed that moving epitaph to Manning Vaughan, sports editor of the Milwaukee *Journal.*

That's nit-picking, however. Instead of quibbling over historical trivia, let us rejoice in Harold's special gifts. Who else could have written of Uncle Wilbert Robinson, who bumbled through almost two decades with the Dodgers, that he "was more a habit than a manager"?

There is no better way to describe the era when Brooklyn was managed by Casey Stengel, who had not yet come to glory with the Yankees, than Harold Parrott's way: "Stengel's jokes got better but the team didn't."

Ave!

RED SMITH

Contents

Part I

×××

Is This Any Way to Run a Business?

1. The Gate-Crashers: Finley, Veeck the Wreck, and Swindler Smith

"No box seats for this guy—he's against us."

Walter O'Malley's familiar Spencerian scrawl across the application for Dodger tickets fairly screamed in blue crayon. It hit me as I sifted through thousands of letters—most with fat checks attached—that seemed to land in our makeshift Los Angeles office almost as quickly as the refugee skeleton office staff from Brooklyn.

This was January 1958, and O'Malley and the rest of us in the Dodger front office didn't yet know where in Los Angeles the ball team he had kidnapped out of Brooklyn was going to perform: Wrigley Field, a minor league crackerbox in a rundown part of town, the dilapidated Rose Bowl in socialite Pasadena, or the bathtub-shaped Coliseum, which pitcher Ed Roebuck called at first sight a "Grand Canyon with seats."

The ticket request that had been pontifically nixed by the Big Oom, as we called him, was from C. Arnholt Smith, the very large wheeler-dealer of San Diego, a village just a two-hour drive south of us.

O'Malley told us vaguely that he had heard some bad, bad things about Arnholt, and when the big bank and tuna fish man's name came up again the next day, the Big Oom mumbled something about Blackjack Smith, Arnie's brother, and "the horse-race crowd." Even in those days Walter carried a grudge against the nags, for if they were allowed to run at night or on Sundays they could siphon dollars out of his boxoffice.

Anyway, Smith's check, along with some silly excuse O'Malley asked me to invent, couldn't have been shot back to San Diego faster had it carried cholera or the bubonic plague. This raised a few eyebrows in our office, for there is nothing the Big Oom loves more than money.

So Arnholt Smith couldn't buy into the ballgame. Not right then.

Not too long after Banker Smith got this brushoff, Dan Topping and Del Webb, who then owned the New York Yankees, were having lunch during a break in baseball's winter meetings with a funny, nonstop talker named Trader Frank Lane. The Trader swapped ballplayers like bubble gum cards, and he had a thousand stories, a few of which were true. The ballplayers and reporters called him motor-mouth, but he was part of the backdrop at this annual flap, and big shots like Topping and Webb ate up his gossip.

Passing a window of the restaurant where the three sat, Charles O. Finley—the "O" is for outrageous, some biographers insist—pulled up short. When he saw the empty chair at their table, his eyebrows went up hopefully.

Those eyebrows are an arresting feature of Finley's face, which has more readable lines than the front page of the New York Times. "Eyebrows like Brillo pads," Wells Twombly once wrote. The eyes beneath them pierce and probe as Finley stares inside you. His hair, once red and curly to top off a handsome face, is white now, giving him a Foxy Grandpa look. He likes to put on a half-smile, as if he's in on some joke you're missing. "He who mischief hatcheth, mischief catcheth," it said under his picture in a 1936 high-school yearbook.

But he can switch masks quickly and turn on the somber dignity. Not long ago Charley was a defendant in a lawsuit brought by one of the battalion of people he has fired. To impress the jury, he testified in rambling sentences that seemed to drip with pontifical knowledge, if you could decipher them. "Even without the robes," one court observer wrote, "Finley looked and sounded more like the judge than the judge."

Incidentally, Charley tried to settle that suit out of court for five thousand bucks and a pitcher named George Lauzerique. The guy who was suing him, Bill Cutler, owner of the Spokane Indians, would have loved to have the pitcher, but it was no go.

Finley's voice is as startling as his looks. He sounds like an auctioneer, and the tones are deep in texture, well modulated, and trained to the utmost for use by a supersalesman.

His philosophy is interesting, to say the least. Once when Cutler pleaded for a week off to visit his wife and twelve children, who were a continent away from Oakland, Finley commanded him to take fifty bucks out of the Oakland club's petty cash fund. "Go out and get laid," he ordered, "then you won't feel so lonesome."

He has been described as a combination of Machiavelli, Barnum, and Billy Graham. "He hollers the loudest when he's not sure of something," says an intimate. Another describes him as a "routinely offensive business tycoon who is exactly what baseball deserves." When this schemer kidnapped his ball team out of Kansas City and hustled it into Oakland, California, Missouri Senator Stuart Symington said, tongue in cheek, "Oakland will find it's the luckiest city since Hiroshima."

One more thing: The man's a striver, an around-the-clock worker, and the miles he has on him and the hard knocks he's taken show in the sunken cheeks on the once-handsome face. In beating a bad-health rap that included a perforated ulcer and a case of pneumonic tuberculosis that pulled his weight down to ninety-seven pounds and hospitalized him for two years, Finley joined a very exclusive club in baseball that included Branch Rickey, who was on his back for two years with TB; Larry MacPhail, who won two bouts with cancer and many more with the bottle and a bad heart; and of course Bill Veeck, who lost a leg to war injuries as a Marine, quit the White Sox in 1961 on doctor's orders, and is back again now tempting fate as he runs the same store.

Finley, who begged for a seat that day at lunch with Lane and the late Webb and Topping, is the most controversial man in baseball today, and privately envied as a winner by the very men who denounce him most.

"In many ways he is the most remarkable man I ever met," says Reggie Jackson, a superstar on Finley's Athletics. "We are the only team in the game on which the owner is discussed more than the players."

Was there a note of admiration in the remark? How does Reggie really feel about his boss?

"Fuck Charley Finley," said Jackson without the slightest hesitation. "We win despite him."

Mike Epstein, who once played for Finley, came up with an unusual thesis. "The man gave us unity of purpose. Every player on the team hated him, and we were together in that at least."

During the period in 1961 when Charley O. was maneuvering for a seat at lunch with Trader Lane and friends, he had already been annoying the big boys in baseball for months, even years, trying to buy into their game at cut-rate prices. He had made millions—dollars, not friends—working the medical side of the insurance street. It had been Charley's own idea to sell the big medical associations disability insurance for their members, and he pushed so hard he had written forty thousand policies inside the AMA alone, in seventeen states. Big companies like Fireman's Fund, Continental Casualty, and Lumbermen's did his bidding. "Every smart doctor in the United States insures with Charley Finley," he once boasted. It wasn't strictly so, but there was enough truth there to bring him more than a million bucks a year in profits.

Once inside baseball, Finley wore out the other owners with his nutty ideas. Charley always seemed to be tugging at one of their sleeves to yak about yellow baseballs, fag-white spikes, or three-ball bases on balls. He was an idea man, but the notions he had about managers, broadcasters, and front-office promotions were regarded by the establishment as very far out.

Now, when this pest flashed his pal Lane the sign he'd like to come in and sit down, the Trader, no shrinking violet himself, suggested the idea to the Yankee big shots.

Webb almost had a convulsion. Turning aside to cough so that the man outside the window couldn't read his lips, the Yankee owner hissed an emphatic "No!" under his breath. Then, with some emphasis, he added "The man's a nuisance, who needs *him?*"

So Charley Finley was shut out once more, and didn't get to sit down with the moguls. Not right then, but soon.

The stuffed shirts of baseball can be very snobbish and clannish, as they showed when they twice slammed their door in the face of Bill Veeck, the newest owner of the Chicago White Sox.

The last time they did that, in December of 1975, they locked Veeck out of the lodge for just a few weeks.

But much stranger was the time they locked Bill *in* baseball, refusing to let him escape with his St. Louis Browns to Baltimore in 1953. The Browns were starving in St. Louis, and Veeck was dying with them, financially.

In their eyes he had been a naughty boy, promoting freaks like Eddie Gaedel, a midget pinch hitter, so a bitter clique of American League owners, ignoring his plight, decided to make him go on suffering in St. Louis. This was something like tying your disobedient youngster to a bedpost and leaving his food just out of reach.

The leader of that torture-minded group was Del Webb, the same guy who wouldn't let Finley sit down to lunch.

The moment Veeck gave up in St. Louis and sold out, the American League bosses all changed their votes and moved the nearly dead franchise to Baltimore.

Because Veeck dared to write about this bitter experience in his book *Veeck as in Wreck,* they ganged up on him again in 1975. "He knocked the game, and now he wants to re-enter it," said Gene Autry. "I can't bring myself to vote for a man like that."

Autry and the other eggheads in the American League had voted down Veeck's first bid for the White Sox in November of 1975, saying he had too many flimsy notes and debentures in his offer, but they told him if he raised another million or so in cash, they'd let him in.

When the ex-bad boy came back with the exact change, the poobahs reversed themselves and voted him down again.

At this point, John Fetzer, the Detroit owner, made an impassioned plea against the personal prejudices they all held and begged for sanity. "This man has called me a son-of-a-bitch repeatedly," Fetzer revealed, "but now that he's done all that we asked, we must be honest and vote him in!"

It was backhanded praise by faint damning, but it worked. Veeck squeaked in by one changed vote.

The American has been a sick league for years now, being millions behind the National in attendance and showing a chronic rash of losers. One of the danger spots where the rash showed up worst was Chicago, and it has to be a perfect illustration of magnate muddleheadedness that the owners did not jump at the pill that Veeck represents and gulp it down, instead of twice spitting it out like stubborn children.

This man Veeck is a World War II hero from an old baseball family, and he has proved twice that he knows the ins and outs of the game, can put together winning teams, and can draw big crowds.

What more could the stuffed shirts want?

Veeck's first credentials were spelled out in 1948, when he won in Cleveland and pulled 2,620,000 through the turnstiles, still a record there.

He did it again with the 1959 White Sox, the first champion there in forty years, or since the Black Sox scandal.

Yet these American League dunderheads, just to spite Veeck, seemed willing enough to lose their very valuable TV exposure in the major Chicago market—and careless enough to throw overboard all the glorious tradition of the Comiskeys and the venerable White Sox franchise—by moving out of the Windy City. Or so they voted on their first few ballots.

The stuffed shirts will go on making it tough for Veeck, because he, like Charley Finley, is a rebel, a maverick in the lodge.

Veeck won't disappoint them. Hardly had they let him in when he offended them again by setting up a two-desk "field office" in the middle of the Diplomat East Hotel in Hollywood, Florida, where the 1975 winter meetings of the game were held. Not only that, but he hung above the desks a brash hand-made sign saying "Open for Business." And he swung some multiple-player deals right there in the lobby, making the Old Guard gasp. This smart-ass, they growled, was destroying all the time-honored mystique that went into the making of baseball trades.

Between them, Veeck and Finley are sure to liven up the stuffy old halls. They have started already, with Charley O. boasting in public that for the next three years Veeck will have to pay part of the salary of Chuck Tanner, the manager Finley hired right after Bill demoted him. There are sure to be dozens more wild pronouncements, a flood of biting exchanges as these two tune up.

Of course, neither of these two rebels cares one whit what the stuffed shirts in the establishment think. Both have been rebuffed too often to care about that. Both had clamored in vain at the front door for admission.

Finley was more raucous than Veeck, if possible. Charley had always been one to attract attention, even in the early days in insurance in Gary, Indiana, when he purposely parked in a no-parking zone to get talked about. He paid each ticket he got without a whimper, saying it was cheap advertising, good for business to have his ticketed car sitting there.

When Charley found he couldn't get in through the American League's front gate, he shoved his foot through the back door.

Finley submitted a sealed bid to the executors of the estate of Arnold Johnson, who had owned the American League's branch store in Kansas City. Charley picked up 52 percent of the franchise for $2 million, a bargain compared to what the Big Boys were asking up at their front counter.

The brothers of the American League Lodge were furious when they found that they had missed out on the bidding and that Charley had sneaked in. They wanted to get up more money among themselves to top his bid and squeeze him out right then. But a judge ruled that the bidding was closed.

This upstart was getting too close for comfort now, and the nervous lodge brothers decided something had to be done. They chose Joe Iglehart, a heavyweight on the boards at both Columbia Broadcasting and their own Baltimore Orioles, to get a profile on Finley.

The verdict came back loud, clear, and very fast. "Under no conditions," Iglehart told the brothers, "should this person be allowed into our league!"

But Charley O. bulled his way in while they all stood around and wrung their hands.

Before long Finley was ridiculing Joe Cronin, the lodge president at the time. He sassed the commissioner and threatened them all with lawsuits if they refused to let him move out of Kansas City, where he had started a war with the press that made his position untenable. Later still, he shook up the whole establishment with his Catfish Hunter fiasco, which put a bad crack in the cornerstone of baseball, the reserve clause in the standard player contract.

On top of that, Charley called O'Malley "senile" in the newspapers.

Meanwhile Arnholt Smith contrived the largest bank failure in the history of the United States. His schemes, in which he juggled millions like a modern-day Ponzi to stay a half-step ahead of the Securities and Exchange Commission, the IRS, and even the FBI while he kept his National League Padres on a poverty budget, sent thousands to the poorhouse. Banker Smith pleaded "no contest" when the case came up. It embarrassed all the moguls to sit down with a man like that: it was like discovering you'd invited a burglar into your parlor.

There's not an owner in baseball today who wouldn't give a twenty-game winner plus a .300 hitter and an option on a domed stadium to be rid of the stench caused by Banker Smith and Ferocious Finley.

Does all this bungling by the Lords of Baseball, as Dick Young lovingly calls them, surprise you?

Not me!

Their flip-flop on Finley was right in tune with the way the owners have orchestrated their Great Game, as they've kept on calling it for the forty years I've watched their didos from behind the scenes. They've had egg on their faces most of that time.

Why would O'Malley go full speed in reverse to persuade the gullibles in his National League to embrace Banker Smith, whom he had blue-crayoned and bad-mouthed earlier?

Because it suited the Big Oom's timetable just then to put his longtime lieutenant, Buzzie Bavasi, in bed with Banker Smith in San Diego, thereby neatly clearing the decks on the good ship *Dodger* for son Peter O'Malley to grab the helm.

There are cynics who insist that O'Malley knew from the start that the San Diego venture would sink, and that the Big Oom in fact tried to hasten the shipwreck by televising tempting Dodger games into San Diego homes on the very evenings and Sundays when Bavasi was trying to lure the villagers out to buy tickets to see his own Padre clown act in the flesh.

These gossips are mean enough to say that O'Malley had planned for Bavasi's franchise to go to the cleaners and be repackaged for delivery to some other sucker city—say, Washington, D.C.—long before it almost happened in the fall of 1973. The Big Oom, they tell you in knowing whispers, planned then to convert the baseball-hungry San Diego territory, its appetite whetted by crumbs from the poor Padres, into a rich farmland for pay TV. O'Malley's own pay TV network, of course.

Could O'Malley, shrewd as he is, possibly have blueprinted such a long-range disaster?

Would the man wish to thus doublecross a lifelong pal like Bavasi, who had steered the Dodgers so capably for him after he heaved Branch Rickey overboard in 1950?

Never, never would I start ugly rumors like those. But I do find it hard to disbelieve them.

You would too, if you'd been a bystander, as I was, when O'Malley similarly repaid another pal, Cowboy Gene Autry.

That shenanigan came up because Walter had been lucky enough to run into Phil Wrigley just when the chewing gum king was very angry at a whole city: Los Angeles. "A bush town," Wrigley called it, and swore he'd never have anything to do with the place again, as soon as he could get rid of his minor league franchise, the Pacific Coast League Angels.

O'Malley was drooling but trying hard to hide his interest.

I can just see the Irishman as he rolled up his sleeves and purred to Wrigley, "Tell you what I'm gonna do for you today, Phil," like a side show medicine man.

This put into the Big Oom's head the idea for the biggest snatch ever pulled off in baseball: the kidnapping of the Dodgers away from their loved ones in Brooklyn.

It didn't matter in the slightest that O'Malley was dickering even then with Mayor Bob Wagner of New York City for a free site for a new Ebbets Field. That was all a smoke screen.

All O'Malley did was con Wrigley into taking, in a straight swap—lock, stock, and ballpark—the Fort Worth franchise in the Texas League. Branch Rickey had picked up the Fort Worth package ten years before for a mere $75,000.

What the Irishman got, in addition to the franchise, was a square city block in Los Angeles.

There are no rules in the baseball lodge, you see, against snookering the other members; after all, where in the outside world could you find patsies like these?

As soon as he had landed in Los Angeles with the team he had whisked out of Brooklyn, O'Malley camped in the freakish Coliseum while he made plans to capture Chavez Ravine, the hilltop where his Dodger kingdom now sits.

A compliant Los Angeles mayor, Norris Poulson, and a buzz-saw councilwoman, with whom he was able to barter choice seat locations (I was the ticket manager who delivered the favors to Roz Wyman), gave Walter all the foothold he needed.

But the screams from the public were ear-splitting; and the editorials in the L.A. papers were calling Chavez Ravine the biggest land grab since Manhattan Island.

O'Malley needed help—loud help—to win a public referendum so he could move onto his choice hilltop, which overlooked the downtown City of the Angels.

He turned to the Cowboy and Horse, owners and operators of KMPC, which broadcast the play-by-play of all the Dodger games. The Cowboy was of course Autry; Horse was his partner, Bob Reynolds, a very large man who had earned that name as a sixty-minute tackle for Stanford in three straight Rose Bowls.

That's what pals were for, right? So would the Cowboy and Horse please turn on all their kilowatts for a friend in need?

They would, and they did. Radio KMPC pumped out an around-the-clock barrage of Dodger propaganda that tipped the scales.

The referendum was close enough to be scary for the Big Oom, although he won it.

The night of the triumph, he threw his arms around the Cowboy and Horse. "We'll be in business up there for years," said Walter, looking up with misty eyes at his new acres. "How can I ever repay you two?"

He found a way.

Not more than two months later Autry got a letter by certified mail announcing that the Dodgers were ditching KMPC, which had not bothered to press a pal like O'Malley to sign a contract. No sweet talk, no regrets—not even a phone call. In pursuit of still another buck, O'Malley was moving his valuable Dodger play-by-play to KFI, Autry's archrival. All the Cowboy and Horse had to show for their "partnership" with the Big Oom was a lot of unsold air time.

This drove the two gullibles up the wall—and to St. Louis, where baseball's winter meetings were going on. The American

League just happened to be taking in new members—for a $6 million fee that the brothers in the lodge would split up.

Seeking only the broadcast rights for the new franchise that the Big Boys were going to plant in Los Angeles, Autry got a surprise from Joe Cronin, the American League president.

"How'd you like the whole franchise?" said Cronin.

The amazed Autry sprang for it and wound up owning the Angels.

This was like buying the King Ranch to get a pony, but Autry didn't care. The only authentic sportsman to enter the owners' fraternity in years, the Cowboy was as excited as a kid in a candy factory.

By now the Cowboy and Horse should have discovered where the wolves and slickers lurked. Had they learned their lessons?

Hardly. They were now wandering unattended among the swifties in the unreal world of baseball, and soon they found themselves again in the clutches of O'Malley.

They became his tenants in the very Dodger Stadium they had won for him, the palace Walter had built without a single drinking fountain, the better to sell his beer and soda.

Before long Autry's auditors came up with proof that the emperor of the Dodgers was charging the infant Angels for fictitious items like "cleaning ticket office windows."

There were no windows whatever in the stadium cellars fifty feet underground, where the Smiling Irishman had stuck Autry's team and its staff. I know this for sure, because I was down there, with the fertilizer and the plumbing, as ticket manager of the new franchise.

Speaking of plumbing, Autry's bookkeeping beagles flushed out still another malodorous charge by the O'Malleys. Kindly old Walter, whose rich team was attracting thousands of fans compared to every sparse hundred Autry was drawing, was charging the Cowboy for half the restroom tissue used in the big ballpark each season.

They split over this tissue issue, which was just one more reason the Cowboy and Horse ran away to Anaheim, thirty-five miles to the south, where the folk in Disney City built them a shiny new stadium.

By this time Autry was a little poorer but much, much wiser.

However, the Cowboy, badly as he was ripped off, never came close to being the easiest mark in the halls of baseball.

That dubious honor is up for grabs between Phil Wrigley, who once proved to an incredulous Durocher (while Leo was managing his Cubs) that he carried more than a million bucks in his private checking account, and John Galbreath, the Pittsburgh Pirate owner, a very big man in skyscrapers and Derby winners, who once moved a whole city up the side of a mountain.

Another strong entry in the race for the dunce cap would be August Anheuser Busch, the medium-sized beer baron with the very large, profane voice.

Behind his back they call Gussie "Big Eagle" after the bird in the Busch trademark. Big Eagle has been enormously successful in ballooning his empire until it has grabbed off 23 percent of the nation's beer market, which absorbs enough suds to float all the ocean liners left today.

Big Eagle, when his brewery bought the Cardinals in 1953, trotted out some ideas that made veteran baseball magnates cringe. He made pets of his star players, entertaining them and their families on his sumptuous Grant's Farm Estates on the outskirts of St. Louis. He was going to reward them with beer distributorships, as he did sourpussed Roger Maris. His baseball ownership was a personal sales campaign, like the one Gussie had mounted to push his beer across the country. And Big Eagle told his players he wanted a quick pennant.

To help things along, he took personal charge of getting a few black players. He had noted how Jackie Robinson was filling the St. Louis park and others, and winning ballgames as well.

So Big Eagle agreed to pay $185,000 for Memo Luna and Tom Alston, two completely forgettable minor leaguers. When Manager Fred Hutchinson was asked by Busch why he wasn't playing Alston at first base, the brewer got a surprise answer: "If you wanted a clown, Mr. Busch, why didn't you buy Emmett Kelly?"

Busch's pets didn't win the pennant he wanted, and then they had the nerve to hit him up for more salary. Outraged, Gussie traded Curt Flood and Steve Carlton and Jerry Reuss away.

This was embarrassing when Carlton turned out to be the best pitcher in baseball, winning twenty-seven games for the 1971 Phillies.

It was even more embarrassing in 1975, when three pitchers who had been discarded by Busch's St. Louis organization—Rick Wise, Reggie Cleveland, and Jim Willoughby—pitched another team, the Boston Red Sox, to the American League pennant.

Busch has found out you can't treat a pitching staff the same as a sales staff.

Mixups like this moved Hy Zimmerman, the pundit of the Seattle *Times*, who has been writing baseball almost since the round ball was invented, to observe that owners of big league teams are a rare breed of creature apparently equipped with two totally different sets of brains. "One set they use in their outside businesses," says Hy, "but in baseball matters only the other set functions."

Like Busch, John Galbreath in Pittsburgh is an empire-builder who made his fortune scanning every acre and every blueprint with a hard eye to make sure the deal tilted his way. But inside baseball, Galbreath seemed to go into a daze. He'd have bought the Brooklyn Bridge from Branch Rickey had the Old Man been able to find a Dodger shirt large enough to drape around the old landmark.

Despite the childlike antics of Busch and Galbreath, Phil Wrigley of the Cubs has lately taken the lead in the race for the booby prize among the magnates.

The chewing gum tycoon achieved this by appointing an expert on popcorn and peanuts, E. R. Saltwell—appropriately known as "Salty"—to direct the managers, coaches, scouts, and ballplayers in his Chicago Cub organization.

⚾⚾⚾

2. Oom the Omnipotent and Room 40

The Chicago Cubs kept Salty Saltwell hidden for twenty years under the grandstand at Wrigley Field, where he ran the concessions with a hard hand.

To the average fan, a food-and-drink stand at the ballpark means long lines, last year's peanuts, and some slow-moving smartass in a trick hat who makes short change for an un-hot dog.

Apparently this was also Wrigley's vision when he brought Saltwell up from his dungeon and told him to "get tough" with the Cubs' "spoiled ballplayers."

"We've been too nice here," announced the chewing gum millionaire. "Nobody has as many player grievances as Oakland, but they keep winning for an owner they hate."

Wrigley delivered one last shot on the subject. "Everybody hated Durocher around here," he said, "but he came the closest to giving us a winner."

The Cubs haven't won in thirty years, but it hasn't been for lack of trying their owner's nutty ideas.

Saltwell is another brainstorm by the man who gave baseball the college of revolving coaches to replace a field manager for his Cubs. A different coach took his turn running the team each day.

During another bit of heavy thinking, Wrigley once removed a carping reporter-critic from a Chicago newspaper by hiring him to run the Cubs as general manager. Jim Gallagher, the surprised reporter, gave so many valuable Cub players away in bad deals that Wrigley abolished the position of GM along with Gallagher. The promotion of Saltwell makes him the first Cub GM in almost thirty years.

Wrigley is just dandy in Doublemint, but he should have a guardian with him when he starts making decisions in baseball. He could have used one the time he got talked into buying two first basemen, almost in the same breath, from super-spieler Branch Rickey. Dee Fondy couldn't hit, and Chuck Connors, who couldn't hit either, turned out to be TV's "Rifleman."

Getting two men for one position was something like buying two left shoes.

None of Wrigley's ideas has worked, not for Wrigley, at least. But this last one—"Get tough with 'em, Salty!"—will undoubtedly do extremely well for Marvin Miller, the head of the ballplayers' union.

Every blast at the hired help by an unthinking owner is just so much more wind in the sails of Miller, who has the ballplayers' union scudding along just fine.

At first glance Marvin is a slightly insipid-looking man with a waxed mustache and racetrack clothes. He has all the warmth of a bill collector. Even the players backed off from him at first because of his background; "steelworkers" and "union" were dirty words in the parlors of baseball.

Today Miller is the most powerful man in the game. He sits on top of them all with a salary of close to $100,000, which is paid by the players. The magnates and their commissioner make faces behind his back, but they quake when he speaks any words that even rhyme with "strike."

How did Marvin pull off this miracle?

"The owners did it for me," he confesses with a wry smile. "Not that they wanted to, of course, but they have been my biggest allies. When some of them tried to talk their players out of hiring me in 1966, the men simply concluded: Anybody the owners hate that much can't be all bad!"

Bill Veeck laughs in the same key as Miller. "Whenever Marvin needed help," Veeck grins, "these dunderheads seemed to do or say something that rallied his players behind him. Miller reminds me of a successful funeral director; he just sits back, wearing that sympathetic little smile of his, and waits for people to fall into his hands. And they always do."

In all of baseball, only one man has had the nerve to take potshots openly at Marvin Miller: Durocher. The Brassy One all but broke up a meeting of the players the labor leader was holding in the outfield at Leo's last Houston Astros training camp in Florida.

Like a little boy zipping spitballs at teacher, the Lip kept hitting fungo flies into the middle of the meeting. The angry Miller kept ducking and weaving like a man under a swarm of bees. Marvin filed an official protest. Durocher? He just laughed.

Toward the end of the next season, in August 1974, Bad Boy Durocher came within an inning or two of being hired back by the unpredictable O'Malley, it now can be revealed. Walter would forgive all his sins if Leo would just come back and pump some life into his stumbling Dodger team, which hadn't won a pennant in eight seasons under Automatic Walt Alston.

This was the same O'Malley who had been delighted to see Durocher ridden out of baseball on a sham by Unhappy Chandler in 1947; and the very same Smiling Irishman who had nudged his partner, Rickey, into canning Leo in the middle of the 1948 season.

Let Leo tell that strange story the way he gave it to me the day we were discussing his recent book, *Nice Guys Finish Last*. (Incidentally, Pee Wee Reese summed up that epic: "What the Lion left out of this," said Pee Wee, tapping the cover, "would make a good book!")

"O'Malley called me in Palm Springs in August 1974," Durocher revealed, "and asked me if I'd do something for him. I'd left the Houston club the year before, and I was really enjoying the summer, and I told Whalebelly as much."

Durocher had called the Dodger chief that for as long as I could remember. And the Lip has always enjoyed making cracks like, "When is the balloon going up?" when Walter entered the room.

"He asked me to drive up to the ballgame at Dodger Stadium that night and have dinner with him in his private box," Leo went on. "I wasn't crazy about the idea, but he said it was urgent, so I went."

"We'd just about finished dinner and the game was starting before O'Malley finally got to the point. He turned toward me in that big swivel chair he sits in and said, straight out, 'Could you be induced to come back to the game and take over a club that could win a pennant?'"

What happened?

"The club won that night," said Leo, "and they won the next couple, and the Fat Man stuck with Alston, an' they finally squeaked in. Shoulda win it by ten, though."

But what was your answer to O'Malley that night?

"You oughta know by now how I like to win," he said with an easy laugh. "I said, 'Yes, if you wanta win it that bad, I'll come.'"

"O'Malley was delighted," Leo chuckled. "And he promised to send me four strips of tickets to the World Series, no matter what happened. I told him I couldn't use 'em, because I was going on a trip with Frank about World Series time."

There is only one "Frank" in the whole world of Leo Durocher, and you are supposed to know that he means Sinatra.

There was an odd bottom line to Durocher's story. "O'Malley sent me four strips of tickets anyway," he said. "About four hundred bucks' worth. You know something? That was the first free tickets I ever got for *any* World Series!"

Why would O'Malley do a complete about-face like that on Durocher, after pushing to have him canned a couple of times?

And why would he promote the charade that his marriage to manager Alston has been one of unbroken happiness during twenty-four straight one-year contracts, when he knows full well that he was thinking of replacing the Quiet Man with the Loud One in 1974, and that he had actually uncoupled Alston in 1962, only to be blocked by Bavasi?

The late Joe E. Lewis had an apt story about a hotel man named Belden Katelman, who fought the flames the night his Rancho Hotel burned down in Las Vegas. Strangely, the story of those flames may cast some light on O'Malley.

Katelman owned the Rancho Vegas, and Joe E. Lewis had been his star attraction for years.

"When I saw Belden in the front ranks holding that hose," Lewis liked to tell it, "I said to myself, 'How courageous for the owner to be down there in the trenches with the troops, trying to save the joint.'

"Then I noticed," the veteran comedian went on, "that Katelman's hose was hooked up to the Texaco pump!"

That's Walter O'Malley: You're never sure whose hose he's holding, or what it's hooked up to.

The Big Oom had called me in during the first year his team was playing in their new stadium in L.A. and told me to move this same Katelman's seats away from the corner of the Dodger dugout.

"The man's got strong ties with gamblers," O'Malley said. "In fact, he's an out-and-out bleep, and I don't want him near our players!"

When I suggested it might not be easy to dislodge Katelman from these choice locations, the Irishman said, "Well, move him over behind the other team's dugout!"

It wasn't a month after that when O'Malley casually revealed that he had given Katelman the much-coveted parking contract for the new Dodger Stadium.

"But didn't you tell us the man was a bleep?" pressed Bavasi.

"He is," said O'Malley, "but he's a bleep with a lotta dough!"

The "Big Oom" moniker had been hung on Walter by his playmates in Room 40 at Brooklyn's Bossert Hotel, a private dining, drinking, and wheeling-and-dealing gymnasium where the inmates practiced practical jokes on each other. The Papa Bear in this ménage was ruddy-faced George V. McLaughlin, who had been police commissioner of New York City. He was called George the Fifth at the Brooklyn Trust Company, where he liked to roar through the marble halls frightening the secretaries.

O'Malley's principal cronies were Judge Henry Ughetta, who had succeeded in politics and the judiciary by marrying a shoe-polish heiress; George Barnewall, a suave officer at Brooklyn Trust; and Harry Hickey, who was big in insurance.

O'Malley had for years been a combination bodyguard, valet, and general right hand to the powerful George the Fifth, who had to be steered home and tucked in bed almost every night after an evening filled with orange blossom cocktails and oratory at the New York AC's clubhouse in Manhattan. The rewards Walter got for this faithful service will be detailed later; for one thing, he was let in on the Dodger deal when McLaughlin's bank foreclosed on the tipsy Ebbets heirs who had borrowed past the limit on the bankrupt Dodger corporation. O'Malley got in when they had to import Rickey, the master baseball mechanic; neither of them had to put up a nickel for one-fourth of the ball club until they started paying off their stock with club profits. McLaughlin had been kind enough to include John L. Smith, millionaire head of Pfizer chemicals, to bankroll the whole thing in return for an equal share with O'Malley and Rickey.

The "Big Oom," or Oom the Omnipotent as Ughetta liked to call him, could turn on the charm, the jokes, or the sarcasm from handy spigots in his many-faceted personality. Making jokes about Rickey was the main sport at Room 40, and sometimes it descended almost to the level of pin-the-tail-on-donkey with the Mahatma's picture, which was on the wall there with their own. They liked to ridicule the Old Man as a psalm-singing faker. Of

course, they were the ones who had lured him into a Brooklyn contract and got him started digging up the Duke Sniders and Carl
Furillos, the Carl Erskines and Gil Hodgeses who were to carry
the ball club for years.

Once Rickey was firmly hooked into a five-year contract (which
the Old Man honestly thought would be stretched to life, his last
stop in baseball), O'Malley began to nitpick and deplore almost
everything that went on in Rickey's office, which was only two
blocks down Montague Street from Room 40.

For his own part, Rickey would as soon have cultivated a cobra
as O'Malley, although he masked his feelings like the actor he
was. He was about as comfortable with these high rollers and
their boozy way of life as a country bumpkin at a fancy-dress
ball. Rickey's instincts were right, because it was here in the
Room 40 gas chamber that he one day would be roughed up and
kicked off the Dodgers.

Even while Rickey was still Dodger president, O'Malley liked
to entertain in the grand manner; a private railroad car for him
and his cronies was the way they liked to go to and from Vero
Beach, Florida, where the Dodgers did their spring training.

While this bunch was whooping it up, Rickey was very likely
puddle-jumping in a Beechcraft with a pilot who had to fly by
the seat of his pants and read from the rooftops below whether or
not this was the hamlet they were looking for to sign a young
ballplayer.

Rickey was painted as a tightwad by the press, and not without some reason.

One night the two of us were having a bite in Toots Shor's restaurant, the crossroads of the sports world. The Old Man liked me
to steer him in there so he could gape at the Beautiful People he
was always reading about.

It was a mild fall evening, and as we left I retrieved Rickey's
homburg from the hat-check girl and tossed her a dollar.

"Why did you do that, son?" he asked hoarsely as soon as we
were out in the street.

*I told him anybody watching knew it was his hat, not mine, and
Jimmy Powers was always calling him El Cheapo.*

The old gent nodded sadly and gave me a friendly squeeze on the shoulder. He understood.

Rickey had the widespread reputation as a skinflint, and O'Malley helped build that image. But I honestly feel that of the two, the Big Oom was tighter with a buck, although he would make the big grandstand giveaway if there was a photographer or writer in sight.

After Rickey was ousted, the Big Oom began making Dodger employees who were lucky enough to get World Series rings (a reward started by the Mahatma) turn back their previous rings before they could get the latest model. What could a scratched, dented, chipped old ring with a man's initials be used for, anyway? Melted down for the precious metal, perhaps? I never found out.

Anyway, O'Malley was most insistent on getting his trade-in rings.

When the Dodgers won their next pennant, Irving Rudd, a real Brooklyn-born hustler who had been brought in to help in publicity, was slow turning in his used ring. O'Malley sent Red Patterson to get it.

"It's gone, I ain't got it," said Rudd, who dearly prized it.

"Where did it go?" Patterson pursued.

"I dunno," said Rudd hopelessly. "Alls I know is, it rolled down a sewer!"

Completely unhorsed, Patterson retreated.

Red did not often retreat. When O'Malley brought him into the Dodger family (Patterson had had a fight with the late George Weiss and quit the Yankees), he joined the Dodger publicity department and fitted in like a Chinaman in a bull shop. Within a month Frank Graham, Jr., one of the gentlest people you could meet in a year's travel, had quit, and Patterson had a full-scale war going with Rudd.

O'Malley had forced me to leave Dodger publicity work and take a ticket director's post I had fought to avoid. Patterson would not have gotten my goat in the publicity department, for I understood his rough-hewn talents from our days together in newspaper work.

Everything Red became involved in was automatically the biggest and the greatest ever.

One spring, while he was writing baseball for the New York *Herald Tribune,* Red did a two-part series on a pitcher named Buck Tanner, who came out of a place named Rattlesnake, Florida. It was the first two-parter ever done on a raw rookie, whom Patterson said would be the new Dizzy Dean.

It was also the last two-parter on any rookie. Tanner never pitched an inning in the majors and was soon back in Rattlesnake.

There was a lot of Cecil B. De Mille, or maybe it was Barnum, in Patterson.

With the Yankees, Red started tape-measuring home runs, and this helped make Mickey Mantle famous. I think Patterson really believes he *invented* Mantle.

When Red joined the Dodgers, there were a lot of telegrams of congratulation that came in from friends he had made while with the Yanks. Hurriedly he shuffled through the stack, in which were wires from many big names.

Finally he threw up his hands in despair. "Can you imagine?" Red said to me. "Not a word from Mantle!"

I laughed, for ballplayers are notoriously short on sentiment, and spending money at Western Union ranked very low among their favored pastimes.

"But . . . but," Patterson stuttered, "I *made* Mantle!"

Red Patterson was a climber, more ambitious for a baseball title than for a big salary. The title he wanted with all his heart was "general manager." But there was no general manager on the Dodgers. Rickey was the last, and when O'Malley ditched Rickey the title went out with him. Instead, O'Malley had two vice-presidents running the club for him: Buzzie Bavasi and Fresco Thompson.

That did not stop Patterson, who listed himself as "assistant general manager" when he published the Dodger roster for spring training.

This little bit of gamesmanship did not escape Dan Parker, the sharp-eyed wit of the New York *Mirror.* Dan forever after referred to Patterson in his column as "Assistant to the nonexistent General Manager of the Dodgers."

As time passed, along with Bavasi and Thompson, O'Malley put two new vice-presidents in charge: Al Campanis, who handled all the deals, player salaries, and the manager, and Patterson, who handled publicity and promotions.

This did not satisfy the redhead; he had to be *first* vice-president. To accomplish this, Red got himself a personalized license plate, the kind that are in vogue everywhere now, particularly in California.

Someone driving behind him on the Freeway might not have deciphered that plate: "LAD VPI." But it satisfied Patterson, for it put Campanis down into "VP2."

Red Patterson will never make general manager rank now. He skipped it. Red went to breakfast one morning with Gene Autry to offer the Cowboy some advice and emerged as the new president of the Angels. In one of the strangest public announcements ever made, Red issued a bulletin with this quote: "I will refuse," he said, "to take a single dollar more than the salary [Angel general manager] Harry Dalton is making." Dalton, you see, had wanted the job, and this was Red's way of soothing Harry's hide with sandpaper.

I never thought Patterson would leave O'Malley and the Dodgers, particularly after Red got those license plates.

But O'Malley is not much for sentiment; people come and go, and he shows no emotion.

The Big Oom asked me to forget my ticket department duties for a couple of months after the 1956 season and organize the Dodgers' first trip to Japan. "You and Josephine will love the Orient," he predicted.

Back in harness as the traveling secretary for this special occasion, I got a call from Mrs. Harry Hickey saying that she and Harry wanted to join the party. Harry was on the Dodger board, a close pal of the Irishman. He had been very ill but now was well enough to take the trip. I told O'Malley that I had added the Hickeys to our travel roster.

"Take their names off the list," said the Big Oom.

"But . . . but . . ." was all I could get out. I knew how close the two had been at Room 40 and through the years.

"Have you stopped to think," said O'Malley sternly, "what it would cost to send a body home from Japan? We can't take that chance."

$$\times\!\circ\!\circ\!\times\!\circ\!\circ\!\times$$

3. Rickey Casts His Spell

It was easier to decipher Sanskrit in the dark than follow the workings of the devious O'Malley mind. He was the original intimidator, and he would call your parish priest or even your wife to maneuver you into something you didn't like.

Rickey was no easier to read, especially when he was on a selling spree. Owners like Wrigley of the Cubs and the Pirates' Galbreath were like children in his hands. He would hide the junk ballplayer he was trying to sell, pushing at them meanwhile a star that he had no intention of letting go. The gullibles, thinking to outwit him, would reach for the player he was holding back; and that was the one they would get, to their eventual discomfiture.

Pittsburgh's John Galbreath was probably Rickey's greatest patsy. This man's a giant in the field of finance; his skyscrapers dot our continent, steel and coal hold no mystery for him, and Derby winners are his toys.

But in the fishpond that is baseball—Branch Rickey's fishpond—Galbreath got hooked again and again.

The magnitude of these fancy ripoffs is even now hard to grasp. Rickey palmed off close to $2 million in players of minimum talent to Galbreath and his Pittsburgh bankroll in the forties alone. These were clucks Rickey knew in his heart could never make it with his own Dodgers; and to compound the heist, the Old Spieler lifted out of Pittsburgh, along with the cash, gems like master pitcher Preacher Roe and super third baseman Billy Cox.

One deal alone shipped five Dodger mediocrities to Galbreath for $300,000 plus a midget outfielder named Al Gionfriddo.

"What does Brooklyn want with a freak like Gionfriddo?" puzzled one critic.

"Rickey needed him," cracked Tom Meany, "to carry all that gold back to the Dodgers."

I sat enthralled through nine innings of a ballgame in Pittsburgh one day listening to Rickey cast a spell over Galbreath. The burden of the Mahatma's spiel was that no price, however inflated, is too high if it brings you the one key ballplayer you need to win a pennant. To "prove" his point, Rickey offered $300,000 in cash for a pitcher named Bill Werle, who he said could wrap up for the Dodgers a nip-and-tuck 1950 pennant race that was then in progress.

Werle was a left-hander who could not black your eye with his best fastball; I knew Rickey could not really want a second-rater like him, and certainly not for a pile of cash, which the Old Man gave away about as readily as his own blood. Yet there was the "offer" penciled on the back of Galbreath's scorecard in Rickey's elliptical scribbling: "Brooklyn club offers $300,000 for contract of pitcher William Werle. Branch Rickey."

Galbreath just blinked at this stunning offer and said he would talk to his manager about it. Up until that very moment the Pirate owner had no idea at all that any one of his raggedy has-been and never-was ballplayers was worth anything like a tenth of that amount, for this sorry team was dead last and would finish that way. But the notion of Rickey *buying*, instead of selling as usual, completely floored the tycoon.

Next morning the phone in my room in the charming old Schenley, right across from Forbes Field, got me out of bed at six. It was Rickey, and he had obviously been having $300,000 nightmares. "Get to Galbreath's office in his downtown tower by eight. Tell him that offer for Werle expired at midnight," said the Old Man, breathing hard. "One other thing—be sure to bring back with you that scorecard with my writing on it!"

Galbreath knew me as the traveling secretary of the Dodgers, and he willingly handed over the scorecard, although there was a puzzled smile on his face. I am sure he did not realize then that he had been set up for Rickey's next sales pitch.

What was the purpose of this silly game? Galbreath could not have been ripped off that way in real estate or steel, or horseflesh. But in baseball, where he most wanted to be a wizard, he was like putty in Rickey's hands, and the Mahatma had both the gall and the glibness to roll this financial giant for the last nickel in his pocket.

Galbreath's pocket? Rickey dipped in there again and again, which reminds me of the unusual bet the two had—a $200 suit of clothes, the winner to choose his own tailor.

Things got so bad, with Rickey pushing off second-rate ballplayers on the Pirates and Galbreath being ridiculed in the Pittsburgh press as a result of these one-sided deals, that the horseman finally declared, in my presence, "Branch, I have made my last deal with you. I like your charming company, but I just cannot buy another ballplayer from you—ever!"

"Oh, yes you will," said the old huckster, while Galbreath shook his head in a vigorous negative. "In fact," Rickey grinned, "I'll bet on it!"

That last got Galbreath's attention. Like all horsemen, he loved a wager.

They spelled it out in great detail. The bet would not hinge on any nickel-and-dime ballplayer, such as a waiver-price castoff. To win, Rickey would have to sell the Pirates an athlete of "more than $50,000 in value," and the deal would have to be made within the next twelve months or Galbreath would collect his suit.

The Pittsburgh millionaire lost his bet, and you can verify that in the National League archives. I read the official transfer papers myself; Rickey got exactly $50,001 out of the Pirates for a banjo-hitting infielder then playing on the Dodger farm at Forth Worth. Monty Basgall was his name, and Rickey had somehow convinced the Pittsburgh people that this was the fellow they desperately needed to plug up their porous infield. After a fairly brief flop with the Pirates, Monty came back like a homing pigeon to the fold and is now a Dodger coach.

Rickey boasted more about that suit he had won from Galbreath than about the dozens of one-sided deals he put over. Branch was notoriously sloppy about his clothes, and it had been written that he often looked like an unmade bed. As the Old Man talked, with gestures, he spilled a lot of food, which made Fresco Thompson observe, "Everything the boss eats looks well on him."

But the Galbreath suit was something else; Rickey was extremely careful of it and wore it everywhere so that he could bring up the yarn that went with it.

This story has a fitting conclusion. Galbreath eventually hired Rickey to run his entire Pittsburgh organization, even though he had accused the Old Man of goldbricking him! It proved expensive, for Branch ran up $2 million in losses at Pittsburgh in the fifties while he installed a youth movement.

That must have been painful for Galbreath.

Even more painful was Rickey's decision to sell down the river Ralph Kiner, the motionless outfielder who had been the darling of Pittsburgh's fans and newspapermen through the bleak years because he hit home runs.

Then Galbreath hit bingo.

When Bill Mazeroski stung the home run for the Pirates that won the 1960 World Series from the Yankees, the pains and debts that Rickey had caused were forgiven across the board.

Galbreath unashamedly ascended to Cloud Nine as Pittsburgh went stark, raving mad.

Forgotten were the Derby winners, the spires and towers and other exciting skyscrapers on his drawing board; erased were the regrets about the dozens of deals that had flivvered, the millions that had been squandered.

Galbreath, the man who had conquered the worlds of finance, steel, real estate, and horseflesh, dramatically announced:

"This is the greatest day of my entire life!"

That, in a nutshell, is what it takes to make a magnate, one of the Lords of Baseball.

Rickey went to Pittsburgh only because he was forced out of Brooklyn against his will after colliding head-on with O'Malley.

There had been peace of sorts between the two sharpshooters as long as each worked his own side of the street; but when the Irishman decided to make his move and take over the whole Dodger show, a terrific battle developed, pro and con. Rickey was the old pro, O'Malley the con.

The Mahatma's contract as Dodger president—it had been another embarrassing one-year renewal, grudgingly granted, of what had happily started out as a five-year covenant—was due to run out Saturday, October 28, 1950. His pay would stop.

Rickey was in a financial jam. He had taken a terrific loss in Air Reduction, a stock he held on margin, and had borrowed up to the limit on his life insurance. Worse, O'Malley knew these things.

The Old Man had talked Galbreath into giving him the job of rehabilitating the Pittsburgh team. But he couldn't move there, under league rules, until he sold his Brooklyn stock. O'Malley knew that, too.

Rickey's Dodger stock had cost him $346,667, exactly the same as O'Malley's 25 percent.

But everyone knew that Rickey's shares in what was now a prosperous ball club had at least tripled in value. The Dodger corporation, close to bankruptcy in 1943 when the Old Man took over, now had an earned surplus of $2,597,879 and had $900,000 in the bank.

O'Malley wasn't talking that way, however. He offered $346,667, exactly the price the Old Man had paid!

Appalled, Rickey offered $1 million for O'Malley's one-quarter share, the same chunk of stock O'Malley was trying to get for one-third that price.

Almost sneering, O'Malley turned that down. He refused to raise his offer to Rickey by even a nickel.

Moreover, the Dodger board of directors, stacked with O'Malley cronies from Room 40, refused even to entertain a new contract for Rickey.

The Mahatma was caught in a squeeze play. O'Malley thought it was a foolproof trap he had set, and he sat back for the kill, like the mortgage-holder dispossessing the widow.

Rickey's only chance was to find an outside buyer who would pay something close to the real value of one-quarter of a prosperous ball club that had just missed a second straight pennant in 1950 by the length of one of Cal Abrams's big feet. The Dodger outfielder failed to score from second on Duke Snider's single, and the Phillies went on to win that game—and the flag.

But whoever bought Rickey's share would have to buck O'Malley, who now had control of the widow Smith's 25 percent, as well as his own. John L. Smith, the original bankroller, had died unexpectedly during the summer. On top of that, the new buyer, even if O'Malley condescended to smile upon him, would be facing another unhappy stockholder, Jim Mulvey, who had been thrown off the board by the Big Oom. The whole deal seemed about as attractive as buying into a private war.

Stories in the newspapers didn't help. Tommy Holmes wrote in the *Eagle* that any buyer of Rickey's 25 percent would have "about as much authority in the ball club as the head usher at Ebbets Field."

Rickey seemed to be caught in a vise, and O'Malley was gleefully screwing it tighter.

But the Big Oom had underestimated his prey. Like Perry Mason, Rickey contrived to pull out a victory at the very last minute, and against tremendous odds.

The Mahatma liked to read melodramas in which a character named Ephraim Tutt would free the heroine just as the Limited raced within inches of grinding her to bits. Now he had pulled an Ephraim Tutt himself.

Rickey dug up a buyer who would pay more than a million bucks for the one-quarter of the Dodger ball club that the Old Man was trying to unload. The guy's name was Bill Zeckendorf.

Very few newspapersmen knew much about Zeckendorf, although he was to become famous later as owner of the Empire State Building and a real-estate plunger who would eventually swan-dive into a spectacular bankruptcy.

Curiously, Zeckendorf was a fraternity brother of Galbreath.

Now it was O'Malley's turn to sweat.

⚹⚹⚹

4. The Phony Press Release

Was this Zeckendorf for real? Did Rickey's mystery man really want into baseball? What kind of bedfellow would he make for Walter O'Malley if he did elbow his way in?

Or was the whole caper rigged by a sharpie who was just bluffing to jack up the price as a favor to Rickey?

O'Malley couldn't be sure.

This whole thing was a poker game, and Walter ordinarily reveled in that. He loved a bluff-and-bluster contest for nickels and dimes against the reporters during spring training at Vero Beach.

This was different. The stakes in the pot in front of him were big enough to make a man dizzy.

Besides, the positions were reversed now: All O'Malley's pasteboards were face-up on the table, and it was Rickey who held the hole card. Only the Old Man knew the real intentions of his ace in the hole, Bill Zeckendorf.

Finally, O'Malley paid to keep Zeckendorf out. It cost him and the widow Smith about $700,000, and what stung most was that it went into Rickey's pocket.

There was another sting, too. Under the terms of the three-way pooling agreement among Smith, O'Malley, and Rickey, any disappointed buyer whose bid was matched by one of the three would have to be paid a $50,000 balm. It was really "mad money," although its official name was "commitment money."

Rickey told me that O'Malley's $50,000 check was endorsed over to him by Zeckendorf. O'Malley denies this. Before you decide who's to be believed, read the press release O'Malley had mimeographed in his own office—not the Dodger offices—to hand to gullible newspapermen. The press conference, which was to be the final ploy in this game of shin-kicking and gutter-fighting for control of the Dodgers, was held on the O'Malley home court, the famous Room 40. It was a bunco classic, and here is the matchless malarkey in the press release, a copy of which I still treasure:

> I would like to say for the record that over the seven years that I have been associated with Mr. Rickey . . . I have developed the warmest possible feelings for him as a man. I have admired his intense devotion to his family. I do not know of anyone who can approach Mr. Rickey in the realm of executive ability in baseball. I am terribly sorry and hurt personally that we now have to face this resignation.
>
> WALTER F. O'MALLEY

Rickey filled me in on the shabby details of this whole squeeze play while we talked on the sidewalk in front of the Bossert. He was in tears, despite the million bucks in his pocket. He did not want to leave this baseball juggernaut he had built, with all its fine, upcoming young stars. The pain showed on his face in a front-page picture of Rickey, with the story of his abdication, that the *Herald Tribune* ran the day after the baloney in O'Malley's press release was handed to the reporters. I still have that clipping of October 27, 1950.

I got a personal taste of the devious O'Malley diplomacy the very first year he sat in Rickey's chair. But I was no Mahatma, so I was no match for the Big Oom's Machiavellian machinations.

In that first year, with its missed 1951 pennant in a disastrous playoff with the Giants, a large sum of money was missing from the Dodger ticket department. The Brooklyn District Attorney was called in, and a stench arose that embarrassed the Big Oom.

O'Malley decided that I was to be his new business manager to straighten things out; he offered me a $2,500 raise.

I broke all speed records in declining. The post Walter was offering was a thankless one. With the Dodgers winning consistently, all of Brooklyn and half of tourist America, it seemed, wanted to get into the shoe box they called Ebbets Field. We were drawing close to 2 million in a park that had only thirty-one thousand seats, and that meant we had to average close to twenty-five thousand per game, day and night—and sometimes morning. Yes, we did have morning games as the first part of double-admission doubleheaders.

There was another, more important, reason I wanted no part of that job. It would mean that I would have to give up traveling with the team; and give up, too, the $10,000 a year I was making by writing articles for the magazines, as well as putting together the script for Jackie Robinson's coast-to-coast radio program.

Also, I would lose my secretary's share of the World Series money, which was about $5,000 for the losing side (and we seemed to lose to the Yankees every year).

O'Malley offered to match my World Series money with a bonus. Again I declined.

The old schemer then called my wife, Josephine, who was bringing up our four sons while I raced around the country—and other countries as well—with the Dodgers.

The line of palaver he handed Josephine reminded me of Rex Harrison's song in *My Fair Lady*, when he was describing the leering Hungarian diplomat at the Ascot Ball who was making passes at Julie Andrews:

He oiled his way around the floor,
Oozing charm from ev'ry pore.

O'Malley came over the phone in unctuous tones, and my lady was flattered to hear from so great a man, even if he was the villain who had forced our dear Mr. Rickey to walk the plank.

"I know Harold is away from you a lot when he's on the road with that team of ours, dear," O'Malley began. "How you must miss him!"

There was a pause, and then the bait, with the hook in it: "Wouldn't you like him home with you all year round, dear? Perhaps the two of us—you and I—can do something about that. Why don't you speak to Harold? I've offered him a new position that would keep him in Brooklyn all the time, and at a nice big raise, too—"

I was beaten, and I knew it the moment I got home. There was no chance now to wiggle out of the job as business manager and ticket director he was trapping me into.

In my first year on the new job, we won the pennant. O'Malley was now at center stage. It was a new and dizzying experience, and he enjoyed bestowing World Series tickets on every hack politician and two-bit actor who sought him out; Yankee Stadium wouldn't have been large enough to hold the Irishman's new-found friends, most of whom hadn't been in any ballpark, much less Brooklyn's, all year. Despite my pleas and Bavasi's, a lot of the Dodger regulars were left out in the cold.

I caught all the backlash from this, and I could have used a hard hat and earplugs.

After the Series, O'Malley grudgingly matched what would have been my share, as traveling secretary, of the Dodgers' winning pot.

The next season, 1953, the Dodgers won again. O'Malley ignored the celebrities, and we took care of the hard-core Brooklyn bugs. He too had caught his share of the scorching mail and blistering phone calls from the fans he had shut out the year before.

But when I asked for the bonus we had agreed on, to match the winners' share again, he skewered me with a stony stare.

"How long," he growled, "did you think a giveaway like that was going to continue?"

I was shocked, but I shouldn't have been. I had seen firsthand how rough the Big Boys can be when they start kicking the help around. I had sat in on a lot of these murders and was in fact the unwilling executioner who axed Durocher in the middle of the 1948 season.

Rickey, the man who ordered this deed, was hiding behind a haystack on a farm a couple of hundred miles away, and I was the one who might have been killed.

As I approached Durocher to hand him the black spot, he was in the Dodger locker room, still seething about being thrown out of the first game of a doubleheader. I felt very much like the overmatched pug who was being shoved into the ring by his manager to battle a ferocious opponent.

"Go in there and punch, kid," said the manager. "This guy can't hurt *us!*"

5. Rickey's Picture in the Toilet

Durocher was shaving when I gingerly approached him with my bad news. He was raving about Larry Goetz, the umpire who had thrown him out of the game as he tried to rally a team he thought was lying down on him.

Right then we were eight runs behind the Giants, and you could hear the groans of the Flatbush Faithful even down there in the dressing-room dungeon far below the stands.

Durocher was raking his chin with the razor and cursing Goetz so hard he was blowing flecks of lather from his lips onto the mirror in front of him.

It was not a happy moment.

But the dirty deed had to be done right then, before actress Laraine Day, Leo's pretty wife, came down to his quarters as she always did between games. She had gussied up the rooms with some nice rugs, and there were pictures of her and her dashing hero on all the walls; shots of her with the Rickeys and the Lip in Santo Domingo, where the team trained, and a portrait of the Mahatma specially autographed to her in loving terms.

But she had a sharp tongue, and she had begun to resent the way Rickey was leaning on her man, blaming him for the team's seventh-place problems, and I was pretty sure she would explode like a string of firecrackers when she found out what was up. Frankly, I was afraid of this fiery femme.

I was also afraid that Leo might cut his throat as I gave him the news that he was through as Dodger manager. But he never missed a stroke with the razor when I delivered my grim message—nor a syllable either, as he screamed defiance at the missing Rickey, who he knew had given me the orders to fire him.

"The Old Man will have to fire me himself, face to face," snarled the Lip, "an' he hasn't got the guts!"

Just then Clyde Sukeforth, who was running the team because Leo had been kicked out of the game, stuck his head in the door. "Campanella just hit one in the upper deck," he said, "with a man on." He could tell from the look on my face that something bad was happening, so he backed out of there in a hurry and slammed the door.

There was a comic touch to this execution too, as I see it now. Rickey, who had writhed convincingly on what I believed was a bed of pain in nearby Peck Memorial Hospital when he gave me the orders at his bedside to uncouple Durocher, had made a miraculous recovery the moment I left. He had checked out of the hospital within minutes, as Leo and I learned when we tried to get him on the phone.

In fact, he ran all the way to Maryland, where he owned a small farm. In the next day's New York *Journal-American,* where Durocher leaked the story of his firing to columnist Bill Corum, a six-column cartoon by Burris Jenkins, Jr., showed Rickey hiding behind a haystack.

Now the door flew open again, and there was Sukeforth wearing a grin as wide as one of those apple pies mother used to bake. "Campy just hit another, longer than his first one," he blurted. "An' this time there were two on."

"I'll win every fuckin' game from here to the end of the season," barked Durocher, "an' then he *can't* fire me! What will the old doublecrossin' bastard do *then?*"

I hadn't thought of that. But I began to wonder if Leo could make this wild dream come true when we came on to win that game by something like 15–12. We took the second one, too.

The next day in Philadelphia, Durocher got a good game out of wild man Rex Barney, driving him on every pitch. It was close, but when we won it the Lip turned to where I was sitting in the club box and screamed across the top of the dugout, "There's another one the old bastard can't take away from me; he can't fire me today, can he?" The fans in the stands around us must have thought we were both nuts.

Eventually Rickey had to surface and face Leo's music, but not before he further postponed the fatal minute by sending his manager on a wild goose chase to Montreal and Toronto, supposedly to look over some rookie Dodgers.

Eventually Rickey pulled out of his black hat the most improbable deal in the history of the game; he "sold" Durocher to Horace Stoneham, who was sacking Mel Ott as manager. So the Lip, who had been thoroughly hated for years in the Polo Grounds, marched in there to replace an all-time Giant idol. The whole thing was insane!

When I got back to Ebbets Field with the Durocherless team, I walked into the manager's quarters. They were bare as a barn, the rugs ripped up, all the pictures gone from the walls. Laraine had been at work. Furiously.

She did leave just one picture behind, as I discovered when I opened the bathroom door. It was the autographed portrait of Rickey, and she had hung it right over the toilet!

Even more messy than Durocher's execution, if possible, was O'Malley's erasure of Charley Dressen as Dodger manager. I was with Charley at the bedside of his sick wife in a Brooklyn hospital when he had his head lopped off. He was the winningest manager any owner *ever* had: three first places (one of which he lost in a 1951 playoff) in three years (1951–53) of managing for O'Malley, who by now was the rookie member in the owners' lodge.

The Smiling Irishman might have been a rookie, but he quickly learned how to get tough with the help. Dressen, seeking the security his sick wife had begged him to get, wanted a two-year contract.

"One year or nothing, take it or leave it," O'Malley growled at the manager of his National League champions.

But the Big Oom had added, "Call me back if you decide to take the one-year deal." It was a ray of hope for Charley as he went out the door.

It was also a snare and a delusion.

I was with Charley as he tried to call O'Malley back. Again and again he tried. No answer. Then he finally got a secretary: Sorry, the boss couldn't be found; gone fishing or something.

Until that moment, he had been Jolly Charley Dressen. I roomed with him, and we had fun going on the air with disc jockey Ted Brown over station WMGM every morning we were on the road. We would talk about why Charley had jerked a pitcher the night before or why he had let Duke Snider hit with the count three balls and no strikes; we handed the telephone back and forth between our beds to do this gossipy program, which the Brooklyn fans ate up. The show was called "The Parrott Talks," and neither Charley nor I got a nickel for the promotional stunt. Nor did we expect anything.

Dressen was a fine gentleman and a finer manager, and it tore me up to see how he was murdered in the pages of the book *The Boys of Summer*. Roger Kahn, one of the new breed of sports journalists, who authored the book, was allowed a brief peek and thought he saw the whole Dodger picture. We'll get to the new breed in another chapter.

Dressen's guillotining by O'Malley wrung all the jollies out of Jolly Charley. He had to sink all the way to the minors to get his next job. From a pennant winner down to the Pacific Coast League—it was like going from caviar and champagne to beans and stale beer.

But there were no tears shed for Charley Dressen in the owners' halls. Whose turn was next on the chopping block?

As if to justify his sacking of a manager who had the gall to ask for a two-year contract, O'Malley has kept his successor, Automatic Alston, on twenty-four successive one-year contracts, often pointing out the "security" such dutiful servility brings.

What very few know is that Walter Alston narrowly escaped

being let out twice by the Irishman. He got that one reprieve in 1974, when Durocher was already in O'Malley's box. But Walter really had the gun loaded for him in 1962, after he blew a playoff to the Giants. The way O'Malley's blunderbuss failed to go off was a masterpiece of misfiring in itself.

The Dodgers had a two-run lead going into the ninth inning of the final 1962 playoff game with the Giants; had they held on, it would be the pennant.

Durocher was Alston's third base coach, but he had been running a revolt, as well as the team. Alston would flash the bunt sign, and the Lip would gamble with the hit and run. Alston would order "take," and Durocher would let the batter hit away.

This was open mutiny, but what could Alston do? Durocher was winning, and none of Alston's ideas seemed to work.

After pitching the eighth inning, Ed Roebuck told Leo his arm was dead from weariness, and he couldn't go another three outs. Alston insisted, "We'll go all the way with Roebuck." When Ed filled the bases in the top of the ninth, Durocher wanted to bring in Don Drysdale to relieve, but Alston, thinking of the World Series opener, insisted on Stan Williams, a wild young pitcher. At this point the Quiet Man and the Loud One did everything but swing at each other.

Alston had his way, brought in Williams, and blew the game. After the disaster, at what was supposed to have been a Dodger victory party at the Grenadier Restaurant on Sunset Boulevard, Durocher told everybody, including Vin Scully and a lot of Dodger officials, how *he* would have won the game and put the Dodgers into the World Series.

This got back to Bavasi, who was loyal to his longtime pal, Alston. So when O'Malley, smarting from the fiasco that was going to cost him a bundle of World Series dollars, proposed firing the Quiet Man, Bavasi revolted. Buzzie said he'd quit too, unless another major league managing berth could be found for Alston.

Bavasi and O'Malley thought they had the soft spot picked out for Alston to land—Milwaukee, where Lou Perini was ditching Birdie Tebbetts. In a plot that lacked the credibility of a Grade B Hollywood potboiler, Branch Rickey, who was still seething at O'Malley, got wind of this plan. The Mahatma killed it by squeezing his own candidate, Bobby Bragan, in at Milwaukee!

They were all acting like little boys, playing with men's careers and million-dollar ball clubs as if they were tin soldiers in a pasteboard war game.

Cut off at the pass, a reluctant O'Malley was forced to keep Alston.

The most bewildered one in the whole affair, which read like a bungled CIA plot, was Bragan. He had received mysterious orders from Rickey to fly into Milwaukee, see Perini, and take the job as Braves' manager.

Two years later Bobby still didn't know what had really happened.

I sat next to him at Rickey's funeral in St. Louis in December of 1965; I asked if he felt there was anything fishy about the way he had moved into the Milwaukee job.

"Strangest thing that ever happened to me," drawled Bobby. "Rickey got me on the phone, told me to take the first plane I could get, and rush to meet Perini at Milwaukee. He cautioned me to take the first contract the Braves' owner offered. 'Don't haggle over salary,' the Old Man said, promising to explain later. He never got around to it."

I filled in the whole silly scenario for Bragan.

A few months after that Bobby got the ax in the middle of the season at Milwaukee.

I was getting a cram course in the Dirty Tricks Department; I couldn't figure out why the owners acted this way inside the medieval cell block that is Organized Baseball.

Then old friend Walter Kennedy explained it one day. He said he had had to sit on top of his basketball league of squalling owners—the NBA—for twelve years, and it had taught him a few things.

"The publicity that owners of teams get knocks them off balance," he said. "They get hooked on headlines, and it's a narcotic they must have in larger and larger doses."

Kennedy, a friend of thirty-five years, looked at the bright sunlight flooding our hotel room as we chatted. "If I had our eighteen basketball owners and their lawyers here right now," he said, "and I asked for a vote on whether or not the sun was shining, I can tell you exactly how it would come out.

"Eight yes votes, eight no, with two abstentions," he laughed.

"And they wouldn't even look outside to make up their minds. They would be trading votes, bickering to see how they could get together to round up enough to beat the faction they didn't like.

"A successful businessman buys a basketball team," Kennedy explained. "And the rush of attention he gets seems to tilt him off balance. It develops into a mania for headlines and publicity. They can't handle it at all—"

"Sounds like the case of Charley Finley," I chuckled.

"Exactly," he said. "Men who have been successful on their own simply cannot cope with the word 'no' when you say it. That is why Finley resents the commissioner, and the president of his league; they are saying 'no' to his wild ideas a lot of the time, and he rebels."

The man who made basketball as big as it is today paused a bit before his face lit up and the words started to tumble out of him again. "I was absolutely stunned," he said, "at the way Jack Kent Cooke went bananas the very first time I had to say 'no' to him on a league matter. Jack started to choke and gurgle on the other end of the phone, and I really thought he was having a heart attack."

Cooke is the multimillionaire owner of basketball's Los Angeles Lakers and the L.A. Kings in hockey's big league, and he is a czar who fires as many people as Finley. He is an intellectual, a one-man whirlwind, and such a supreme egotist that author Bud Tucker once wrote that Jack's number-one ambition is "to die in his own arms."

"After I finished that phone conversation with Cooke," Kennedy went on, "it started to dawn on me that very probably nobody had said 'no' to this man since his mother had told him to stop sucking his thumb."

We chatted a bit about how Cooke compares with the Big Boys of baseball in going haywire over headlines and power, and suddenly Kennedy said, "When Marvin Kratter got bitten by the publicity bug, he had the worst case I've ever seen."

"*Marvin Kratter? Not the same Marvin Kratter who bought Ebbets Field from O'Malley, and made an apartment house out of it?*" I asked.

"The same," laughed Kennedy. "When Kratter bought the Boston Celtics and sat on the bench with Red Auerbach that first night, he just came apart.

"Kratter was a millionaire many times over," Walter explained, "but he was still a nobody. Oh, he got a paragraph here or there in *Forbes* magazine for one of his big deals, but really very few people knew who he was.

"At the very first Celtic game after the deal was made, there was Kratter down on the bench, being introduced around by Auerbach. The game was on national TV in Boston, and I was home in New York watching it. When the game started, Marvin plunked himself down right next to the coach."

Here Kennedy got into the narrative with obvious relish.

"You know how Auerbach is," he laughed. "Every time there was a big play or a tough call by the referee, Red reacted as he always does. The TV cameramen are always ready for Red's explosions, and they picked him up every time. Only now it was different, because Marvin Kratter was on camera every time Auerbach was. All night, in fact. I remember my wife saying, 'What is that fat little bald-headed man doing on the Celtics' bench, anyway?'

"I told her that he was Mr. Marvin Kratter, and that he had just bought the Boston Celtics."

Kennedy chuckled at the thought. "At first she didn't believe me, but then she kind of let out a little gasp, and then a little later she said, 'I just can't believe it, Walter.' She said it as if some dear friend had just passed on.

"Kratter couldn't believe what happened either," said Kennedy. "He called me in the NBA office about noon, and he was stuttering, he was so excited. Said his phone had been ringing off the hook all morning. 'Would you believe it, Kennedy, I am a celebrity?' he shouted to me. 'Four big deals I had hanging, and the people would not even return my calls. This morning, Kennedy, would you believe three of them called *me*, and it went like this: "I seen you on television last night, Marvin, how about taking me to a Celtics game some time, so I could meet the players? And by the way, Marvin, that deal we got on the fire, it's been cooking too long now; how about lunch tomorrow, and we'll wrap it up?"'

"From the tone Kratter used," Kennedy said, "I got the idea he was saying to me 'Why didn't somebody tell me about this sooner?'"

I felt sure I knew what my old friend's punch line would be on

Mr. Kratter. It came out this way: "Three months later," Kennedy said with a wry smile, "Marvin was telling *me* how to run the league."

You might cross out the name "Kratter" in that story and write in "Finley," and you'd have about the same general idea. Or you could write in "O'Malley," and he'd fit Kratter's part without changing more than a word or two.

✕✕✕

6. Red Barber — the Pea in the Pipe

The urge to jump onto center stage sometimes becomes uncontrollable in owners like the Big Oom and Far-out Finley. Both have paid dearly for it at times.

O'Malley had been a plodding nobody of a lawyer in New York. Stuck backstage while the theatrical Rickey took all the bows out front for the Dodgers, Walter had the ego itch for recognition. He longed to show them all that he could steer a press conference, sparring with the syndicated columnists and big by-liners while the flashbulbs popped, even better than that hick Rickey.

The moment he bought Branch out of the picture, the Big Oom jumped into the limelight with both feet. Not exactly *both* feet, for Walter frequently found himself with one brogan in his mouth during his rookie years.

His first embarrassment arose out of an operation on Roy Campanella. The catcher's left hand had begun clenching into a claw-like fist, and Roy couldn't straighten it. It was diagnosed as a rare ailment of the tendons and ligaments under the palm, caused by the shocks from thousands of fastballs.

Campy had his own favorite surgeon, a black, who was commissioned to do the job. The operation went well, and the bulky catcher's hand was put in a cast.

I was in O'Malley's office chatting with Fresco Thompson the day the doctor's bill arrived in the mail. The Irishman rose a foot off his swivel chair when he opened it; the charge was $8,000!

Without cracking a smile, Thompson asked whether the invoice stated the nature of the surgery. "Maybe the Doc got mixed up," cracked Fresco, "and thought he was operating on our bank account instead of the hand." Thompson had been the court jester in the Rickey regime; now he entertained O'Malley.

Two or three days later the Big Oom was performing as ringmaster at one of his first press conferences. He was reveling in the TV kliegs and trading chaff and banter with Frankie Graham of the *Journal-American*, Milton Gross of the *Post*, Dick Young, and all the rest. Cosell was there too, as I recall; Howard used to tape interviews and peddle them to radio stations.

Of course, the subject of Campanella's operation came up.

As shamelessly as Milton Berle, the Big Oom stole Fresco's wisecrack about the doctor. "Dr. So-and-So," he blandly chuckled, "must have thought he was operating on the Dodger bank account, instead of Campy's hand!"

The doctor could read, too. He slapped O'Malley with a defamation suit before the week was out, and he had plenty of evidence at his fingertips. Every paper in the city had printed Walter's funny.

As a lawyer, Walter should have known better; to save face he settled that one quietly, out of court. Around the office we heard it cost him $11,000 more. Anyway, it set a record at the time for a hand operation.

Before Finley elbowed his way into baseball, he was as anonymous as a ransom note. He wrote million-dollar contracts for disability insurance with the American Medical Association, but who ever heard of him?

Then he fired jut-chinned Hank Bauer, the popular ex-Marine who was managing his rag-tag Kansas City team.

The furor that arose—headlines, quotes from the man in the street, even editorials—set bells ringing in Finley's head. He ate up the vituperation, the bitterness, the push-and-shove of it all.

Perhaps Charley has overdone it, like a kid let loose in a toy store. Since 1961 he has chopped off thirteen managers (Bauer and Alvin Dark twice each), twenty-seven coaches, five general managers, eight publicity directors, five scouting directors, seven traveling secretaries, and his wife of thirty years. Each execution

brought big stories that mentioned the Finley name again and
again.

Charley's broadcasters come and go as if by a revolving door;
he has had fifteen of them since buying into baseball. Al Helfer—
the "Brother Al" who was Red Barber's partner in the early radio
days in Brooklyn—was a solid man on the mike. He had been the
original broadcaster for "Game of the Day" in 1950. Al told me
plenty about how it was to work for a wild man when I visited
him in Sacramento a few weeks before his death in May 1975.

"Charley called me in the seventh inning of Catfish Hunter's
first no-hitter," Helfer chuckled. "He was half a continent away,
but he had a secretary prop an open phone in front of a loud
speaker in his Oakland office so he could listen to me by long distance. I had learned my homework under Red Barber, whom I
thought was the best, and I never fooled the listeners about a no-
hitter that was building. Some announcers do, you know, claim-
ing they don't want to jinx the pitcher. Anyway, I was 'setting the
table,' as we used to say in the business, building up to the real
drama I hoped was ahead, but not overplaying things in the sixth
and seventh innings.

"Finley got through to me on the phone we had right in the
booth, and he screamed, 'Pump it up more, Helfer. You're not excited enough. Raise your voice.' I hung up on the man.

"Another time I answered the phone in our booth while the
game was on," Helfer chuckled, "and he commanded me to put
my broadcasting partner, Monty Moore, on the line. I tried to explain that it was impossible, that Moore was on the air right then.
'I don't care what he's doing,' Finley barked back at me. 'I want
him right now. I want to fire him.' I hung up that time, too. And
I might have saved Monty's job, too, because the last time I listened he was still there, although a lot of his partners have been
shot down since I left. Frankly, I don't know how Moore stands
the heat from Finley."

Charley puts pressure on the writers who follow his team to
keep them in line—his line. If he does not like their stories, they
may find themselves barred from the plane the A's are flying on,
or their hotel reservations may be canceled. This is a serious matter for reporters, who must cover a championship team on which

a fight may break out as quickly as an anti-Finley quote by one of his players.

Of course, some of this may be caused by the new breed of baseball writer. Nowadays, a visting reporter's first questions to a manager no longer concern his hottest hitter or his pitching rotation. More likely they will pry into how much so-and-so was fined for coming in·late, or who won the fistfight in the dugout during the last series. A lot of the new breed in the newspapers, radio, and TV go in for the Winchell peep-and-tell stuff. This can approach porno, as it did when the wife-swapping by Mike Kekich and Fritz Peterson hit the sports pages. Such details would never have made those columns in the thirties, when the writers built up every ballplayer as a hero for the youngsters.

David Shaw, in a recent story six columns long that started on the front page of the L.A. *Times*, sharply puts down the writers of that era. He tells us that the public now demands this Winchell-type tattling, this lurid approach to games that once were played entirely outside the covers. "Today's readers," he asserts, "want to know more than just what happened on the field. . . . They demand to be told what may have happened before or after the event, in the locker room, the courtroom, the board room—or the bedroom."

Self-appointed analyst Shaw concludes that it was *Sports Illustrated* that had a heavy influence in "making over" the nation's sports pages, and that it started in 1953. That was when, he says, the reporters started dipping into the "slime of sports"—his words, not mine.

Tim Cohane, a fine writer for the New York *World Telegram* during Larry MacPhail's glory days with the Dodgers, calls these new muckrakers "stylists in stench." Tim deplores cheap-shot guys like Jim (*Ball Four*) Bouton, who tattle on their teammates for a buck; even worse, he says, are the writers who ghost books— "more ghastly than ghostly," Tim says—for these wretches.

Charley Finley uses a kind of polite blackmail to pressure the writers who follow his Athletics into writing things the way he wants them, knocking the people he wants knocked, and giving credit, plenty of credit, please, to Charley O. Hearing that Herb Michelson, a Bay Area reporter, was putting together a biography on him, Finley called the culprit on the phone. "I have secured an injunction against you," he snapped. "You must have my authorization for any book about me, and I have a court order to prove it. You will be served with papers tomorrow!" The call was loaded with the usual Finley obscenities.

It was sheer bluff, of course. Michelson didn't scare, and the book, a very irreverent treatment of Charlie O., was published by Bobbs-Merrill in 1975.

Much, much farther down the scale in baseball—below the belt, you might say—even worse things go on.

When you are the very worst team in the major leagues, which the Padres of San Diego have been for five of their first seven years, it is to be expected that some harsh things will be written about you. One critic on the San Diego *Tribune* was squelched by a tattling phone call to the paper's editor from the Padre front office; the call snitched about the married writer's romantic didos during Padre road trips.

Such blue behavior by its staff writers is not countenanced by the quite proper Copley newspaper chain, and after the tattling the undercover romancing came to an end. So did the writer. He was canned.

Buzzie Bavasi, a square baseball man with a long and honorable record, would never have tolerated such keyhole-peeping in the days before he was entrapped by Banker Smith.

Amazingly, this tattling stirred hardly a ripple inside the newspaper fraternity in San Diego, or even outside of it. The writer sank without a trace.

When you're losing a hundred games a year, who's watching?

O'Malley was every bit as brutal with Red Barber as Finley has been with his broadcasters.

I remember the Big Oom grinning as he described the Ol' Redhead as "just another pea in a pipe" to Bavasi, Fresco Thompson, and me in his office one day. He was about to sack the "Voice of Brooklyn," who had been just a shade below a deity to the Flatbush fans for almost twenty years, all the while promoting the team from near-bankruptcy to a big winner at the boxoffice and with radio and TV sponsors.

Barber had sold the game to the housewives of Brooklyn as nobody had anywhere, at any time. He had become a legend, a key part of the Bums of Brooklyn mystique, which was a rags-to-riches theme that had people rooting all over the country and struggling to include Ebbets Field on their visiting list whenever they were within miles of New York.

Bavasi, Thompson, and I thought ditching Barber was sheer heresy, and O'Malley read it on our faces as he explained what he planned to do. Connie Desmond had been Barber's partner, but there was also a third face in the booth, someone who had been little more than a spear-carrier. In fact, he did lug from city to city the broadcasters' record books and statistics and a reading lamp they used at night games. He was a red-haired kid just out of Fordham, and his name was Vince Scully.

Barber was getting $50,000, and after one particularly big year he asked for a $5,000 raise.

O'Malley described an imaginary six-inch length of pipe he was holding aloft as he explained what he was going to do. The pipe, he said, contained a row of peas, lying there as if in a pea pod; it was full, so that if you squeezed another pea in the near end, a pea rolled out of the other end.

"You put in Vin Scully at $7,500 here," said the Big Oom, grinning with delight at his own little show, "and out there, at the other end, drops Barber at $50,000. That, gentlemen, is how you make money!"

O'Malley got away with it, of course, because Scully has turned out to be as good as Barber over the years. O'Malley was lucky that he came up with a play-by-play man who was almost an instantaneous success, although he had no clue that it would happen. Scully once televised a Dodger World Series around the world for NBC with exactly one inning of TV play-by-play experience, and brought it off successfully. He was phenomenal, and the Big Oom was phenomenally lucky to have him.

Barber, of course, was crushed. I believe he never got over this bout with O'Malley, although he went on to other big things with the Yankees and Mel Allen. Incidentally, Barber was bumped off again there by Mike Burke, a pseudo-poobah in baseball, a Johnny-come-lately expert CBS had snatched from the Barnum & Bailey circus to run the failing Yankees for them.

But the Barber firing was educational for Bavasi, Thompson, and me. O'Malley had given us the working blueprint the Dodgers were being run by, in a nutshell. Or in a six-inch piece of pipe.

After that demonstration, I never thought Bavasi would rough up anybody the way O'Malley had brutalized Red Barber.

But Buzzie did push Jackie Robinson around, as you shall see, in a vendetta in which Robbie very definitely had the last word, or perhaps five hundred of them. Thus arrived Buzzie's turn to go through the wringer.

XoXooX

7. The Mind Readers in San Diego

The lights were dimmed in the corner of the posh restaurant where the three of us were sitting in Long Beach, California, but Bavasi's words were clear enough: "Arnholt Smith in San Diego is trying to make a rich man out of me," Buzzie was saying, "and I can't put him off any longer—"

This was late in 1968, and I was the intermediary in a hush-hush deal to bring Bavasi in as general manager of the American League Angels, who had decided to nudge seventy-three-year-old Fred Haney into retirement. When the story leaked in Eddie West's column in the Santa Ana *Register*, Haney blew a fuse—not about being pushed into drydock, but about his published age.

He screamed that he was only seventy-two. It was just another little Harpo Marx touch to a caper that plays back now like a series of corny sight gags.

Angel owner Gene Autry had promised Buzzie stock in the Angel organization if he would pump some life into the dawdling team that had a sparkling new stadium next to Disneyland and not much else. There were times when Snow White and her seven pals might have fielded baseballs better than the motley nine Autry had.

The third plotter in our group was the late George Brower, owner of the Continentale restaurant, a longtime friend of Bavasi's and mine. He had been a councilman in Long Beach and had many high-placed friends. Brower and I were trying to talk

Bavasi out of making any deal with Smith, who had apparently conned and doublecrossed some shipbuilding friends of the restaurant man.

Buzzie, being nudged overboard by O'Malley after thirty years with the Dodgers, definitely had to swim for his life. Both Brower and I wanted him to catch on with the Angels, where I was promotion director at the time.

But every once in a while the millions that Smith was promising would rise up in front of Buzzie like a mirage, luring him on.

Smith, who even then was playing tag with the bank examiners, had promised Bavasi 32 percent of the franchise they were to pay an overpriced $10 million for. Buzzie figured it would be 8 percent for each of his four sons, when he paid for it "out of profits."

It seemed for a while in the restaurant that day that good sense would prevail. "You know, I'd rather go with Autry and the Angels," Buzzie mused. "They have scouts, a farm system, and they're already in business. In San Diego we'd have to start everything from scratch. Still, Smith is offering me more."

In the end, Autry settled it. Acting as erratically as owners usually do, the Cowboy disappeared, and not into the sunset he used to ride into at the end of his film potboilers. This time he went on a toot, and even his lovely wife, Ina, couldn't track him down for a week by long-distance or even dog-sled.

So when Bavasi walked out of Brower's that day he made the biggest wrong turn of his life—toward San Diego, where Svengali Smith waited at the airport with his deal.

Nobody could prove to Buzzie then that 32 percent of nothing was still zero.

He was to learn that shortly, when Smith's "millions" turned to ashes in his hands and he had to start raffling off important Padre players to keep from going under.

Smith lured Bavasi into a mistake he will rue to his grave; a disaster that set off a chain of bombs that were still shaking baseball years later.

The first explosion occurred in Anaheim, where owner Autry, having lost the baseball mechanic he wanted in Bavasi, reappeared from the mists and fell for a get-rich-quick fast talker named Dick Walsh. Walsh, who had also studied in the O'Malley school, was known among the ballplayers as the Smiling Shark.

Clyde Wright, the Angel pitcher, had told his mates that he had been charmed to death by Walsh's tap-dancer smile and apparent friendliness when they sat down to talk contract. "But then," Wright went on, "you look down and your leg is off at the knee!"

Walsh planned what he thought would be an instant pennant for the Angels; he traded off most of Autry's good young players for the worst collection of problem veterans ever assembled outside a nursing home. One, Alex Johnson, even brought his own gun into a nervous Angel clubhouse "to protect himself." Walsh fired the popular Bill Rigney and installed his own best friend, Lefty Phillips, as manager. Then he fired Phillips.

Autry had to get out his own six-shooter to gun down Walsh by buying up his contract before he did any more damage. But the Angels had been set back five years, and Anaheim attendance dwindled, costing the Cowboy millions. Fortunately, Gene could afford it.

Anaheim might have been awful, but in San Diego the Padres, who wouldn't even have been in existence had Bavasi opted to go with Autry, were positively putrid. Buzzie and all the National League owners had been swindled.

Even then, as it developed, Banker Smith was juggling millions, switching a fortune to his airline, getting it back in time to cover his taxi fleet and his Alice-in-Wonderland luxury hotel fiasco that his wife had decorated at a fantastic fee, then getting it over to the U.S. National Bank vaults to keep up appearances there, so the marshal wouldn't slap a lien on his tuna fleet. He was trying to keep one scant step ahead of the Internal Revenue bloodhounds, the Securities and Exchange Commission, and the FBI, but it was a losing race even then.

This old conniver put the Padres on a poverty budget so piddling that the team couldn't even pick up waiver-price ballplayers. Before long Buzzie, still seeing the mirage of ownership through his nightmares, was signing his and his wife's name to million-dollar loans he never could pay off.

Meanwhile the gullibles of the National League—the owners who had let a glib O'Malley shove Arnholt Smith down their throats—went through five starvation years visiting San Diego, where they got thin visiting-club checks from a cellar-locked team that staggered through five years of sub-700,000 attendances.

I was there working in the Padre boiler room when the whole charade blew apart, and Smith's bank went belly-up in one of the largest ($200 million) bank failures in U.S. history. And O'Malley and his cronies had to be even more embarrassed by the con man they had let into their parlor when Smith at first escaped jail. Although he had ruined thousands upon thousands of honest people who had trusted him and dragged other reputations through the mud with his own, the man still pulled enough political strings to avoid a prison sentence. He suffered only a wrist-slap fine of $30,000, which he started paying off—as he neared eighty—at $100 a month!

Even though Smith lost his gold owner's pass, his Padres went on hatching more mischief. Pinched by Banker Smith's poverty budget and perverted by younger Peter Bavasi's kinky ideas about baseball, the San Diego team was simply not believable, it was so very, very bad.

Sound baseball men like Sparky Anderson fled the organization after a one-year taste to save face, and perhaps sanity. Broadcasters like Frank Sims, Gerry Gross, and Duke Snider were demoted or sacked. Publicity men like Bud Tucker and Irv Grossman came and went; stadium managers, promotion and sales directors, and ticket managers had a higher mortality rate than Finley's staff. Eddie Leishman, the kindly man who had been general manager of the team even back in its minor league days, was hastened to his death by the intrigue around him.

The Padre ball club was being run like the back room of a political convention. In fact, it became for a time baseball's own Little Watergate. There was a department of Dirty Tricks, even lie-detector tests. The Padre player representative told me that his phone conversations were taped without his knowledge.

Young Bavasi seemed intent on discrediting, disparaging, and discouraging his father's old baseball associates and installing his own cronies.

At one game late in 1972 I was working on one of our promotions, handing out bats or baseball caps to the youngsters, when Peter Bavasi sidled up to me. There was an odd look on his face, as if he were enjoying something I didn't know.

"Jack Murphy had you in his column this morning," he said, watching me sharply. "Did you see it?"

Murphy was a columnist on the San Diego *Union*, and its sports editor. I had perused his column that morning, but had noted nothing unusual. I was sure my name hadn't been mentioned.

At the first chance, I got a copy of the paper and reread Murphy more carefully. I found then that Peter had planted there the idea for a Padre house-cleaning. Older baseball men became discouraged too easily, he had indicated, and he was going to import a more aggressive flock of young lions.

It was a bit of in-house intrigue that wouldn't be understood unless the connection were established by somebody who wanted it to hurt. The fact that Peter Bavasi was so obviously enjoying his private little stab made a deep impression on me.

The same sort of thing was going on at all levels of the organization, even down in the clubhouse. The unrest spread onto the field, and the players began to perform so badly that few wanted to admit being part of such a sorry organization.

One of a line of Padre publicity men was called Smiley Grossman, because he so seldom did. After all, what was there to grin about with a bunch of losers like this? Smiley wore the team's prescribed brown blazer—it had to be brown, because owner Arnholt Smith wore only brown suits, hats, and shoes, rode in brown Cadillacs, and wrote on brown paper—but only after he had carefully removed from the breast pocket the Padre emblem, which was a swinging monk. Grossman had no desire to be identified on the streets of San Diego as a member of this troupe of clowns.

Even Smith, preoccupied as he must have been with the bloodhounds who were pursuing him, was worried about the shabby image the Padres were giving the City of San Diego, and him.

One night I got a startling phone call from an old friend, Clark Graves, a crack advertising man I had known for years. Graves said he must see me that night. Tomorrow morning wouldn't do.

We met in the bar of Lubach's, a German restaurant on the waterfront, while my dinner guests in the restaurant wondered where I had disappeared to.

This was the strange story Graves told: Smith had brought

Bill Sang in the Wrong Key for Moguls Bill Veeck (right) was locked out of baseball for years by the stuffed shirts of the game—but here he accepts the key to Chicago's White Sox Park from ex-owner John Allyn. The owners kept switching keys on Bill; the ex-marine scaled the walls anyway. *Wide World Photos*

"Charlie O" Makes a Statement Charley Finley's pet mule, who, like his owner, usually has his mouth open, mouths off at a 1972 World Series game between the Athletics and Reds. Reds manager Sparky Anderson is at left. Other baseball owners usually link Finley with the animal's other end (not shown in picture). *Wide World Photos*

Three Strikes in Seattle   Charley Finley (left), who took a long look at the Washington city, decided to walk to Oakland, after quitting Kansas City. Bill Daley (center) and Dewey Soriano (right) went for a bad pitch and both struck out. Daley lost millions, Soriano turned bankruptcy into a profit, and they're still arguing about how he hustled the franchise to Milwaukee.

United Press International Photo

A Kroc That Cracked   Hamburger wizard Ray Kroc, pictured as he prepared to don a Padre straitjacket (shirt, right) before the opening game in San Diego in 1974. Kroc had just put up millions to save the San Diego club from deportation to Washington, D.C. An hour later, he grabbed a pressbox mike and denounced the team as "stupid" to a stunned crowd. That put fat in the fire for fair, and another Big Mac (Willie McCovey, Padre player rep) demanded (and got) an apology from Kroc to soothe the players' wounded feelings.   *Wide World Photos*

"My Horse for a Kingdom" Singing cowboy Gene Autry rode a palomino named Champion to riches greater, some say, than those amassed by other lords of baseball. Champion, every fetlock as famous as the Lone Ranger's Silver, was at the bottom of it all. When Autry acquired the California Angels, he was introduced to other league moguls as "the cowboy who used to ride into the sunset at the close of all his movies. Now he owns it." Autry once dabbled in hotels, and owned the famous Mark Hopkins in San Francisco. He picked up plush Ocotillo Lodge in Palm Springs as lodgings for his bedraggled Angel team. "When you order a steak here," cautioned Autry disc jockey Johnny Grant, "always check the barn out back while the steak is cooking to make sure Champion is still in his stall." *Wide World Photos*

"This'll Get My Team Out of Hock in Yuma" The poverty stricken San Diego Padres were put on such a miserly budget by bankrupt banker Arnhold Smith that Buzzy Bavasi had to sell livestock to keep ahead of the sheriff. Buzzy is seen here at the start of the 1973 season, just after he sold southpaw pitcher Fred Norman to the Reds. He is showing the check in payment for Norman to Roy Hamey, former general manager of the Pittsburgh Pirates, to whom Bavasi had sold many Dodger players. The money paid the team's spring training expenses in Yuma, Arizona. For all his baseball life until then, Bavasi had been buying what he needed, not selling; but that was when he had a fat Dodger bankroll behind him. Norman hurled 240 innings for the first-place Reds that year. *Wide World Photos*

The Man with the "Pocket-Full of Schemes" Larry MacPhail
gets the bad word from Branch Rickey. "People are watching, so
I must be civil," said the Mahatma, "but you know what I really
think of you. Never speak to me again!" The figure behind
MacPhail's elbow is his son Lee, now American League president.

The Sporting News

(*Left*) The ranting Redhead holds
the note he scribbled to fire
Durocher (again) in the middle
of a 1942 ballgame at Ebbets Field.
The Dodgers blew the pennant,
MacPhail blew town.

United Press International Photo

(*Right*) MacPhail seems to be
drawing images out of a whisky
glass as he orates on radio play-by-
play, night baseball, satin uniforms,
and yellow baseballs. Fumes from
MacPhail's dream factory appear
to have stupefied New York *Mirror*
writer Eddie Zeltner. It was Zeltner
who hired a plane, got Dodger
pitcher Van Lingle Mungo drunk,
and convinced Mungo he should
jump the team to give Zeltner a
scoop. *United Press International Photo*

MacPhail mugging with DiMaggio and Joe Page in
Yankee World Series victory. Moments later, the
unpredictable Yankee owner stole the whole scene by
quitting baseball—for good. *The Sporting News*

him into San Diego two months earlier and kept him hidden in an office directly under his own. The Barnes-Champ advertising agency, later Barnes-Chase, which Smith also owned, was the "cover" Graves was using. The Banker was grooming him to take over the Padres. He was to have complete control of every contact the front office and team had with the public. Some of Peter Bavasi's imports, particularly a dictatorial type named Schiller, had been pretty gauche with the few customers there were.

I gasped as my old friend poured out his bizarre story. He was to move in and take charge of the club's public relations, as well as the Padres' radio broadcasts. And he was to answer only to owner Arnholt Smith himself. Graves wanted my help, and he had plans for me in the new setup.

Bluntly, I advised my friend to back off. He did not know enough baseball to run the whole show, and he would soon be outmuscled and mauled by Buzzie's son, even though the elder Bavasi would play fair with him.

Clark Graves took my advice and wrote off the two months he had wasted as Smith's "undercover man."

When I met him around Christmas time in 1975, he said with a grin, "Just think: If I'd plunged ahead as Smith's agent with the Padres, I might be in jail today!"

Wheels turned within wheels in this kinky organization, and Peter Bavasi, who had never picked up a baseball in his life, much less thrown or batted one, inched into power as his father despaired. Upon Leishman's death, Peter had seized the office of the general manager, including his personal furniture, before the chair was cold.

Young Bavasi decided to pour this sad sack of a team into a kind of computerized question-and-answer machine that was supposed to massage the minds of managers, coaches, and ballplayers, extracting what was needed to compile ratings on which the front office acted.

Pulling the levers with Peter on this brain boggler was a Professor Bruce Ogilvie of San Jose State University in California. It should be noted that this is the same Professor Ogilvie who surfaced late in 1975 with an analysis of the "scientific" reasons behind the four straight shocking defeats of the muscular University of Southern California Trojans, a team supposedly bound for the

Rose Bowl. Just before the defeats, the ringmaster of these mastodons, long-time USC coach John McKay, had announced that he might leave the campus to accept a few million bucks as head brain of the new Tampa Bay team in the National Football League.

Professor Ogilvie sensed all this was a dandy springboard into more publicity than he had ever milked out of the Padres, and he came out with a comprehensive diagnosis of the malaise that was afflicting the fallen USC behemoths.

"This is an extension of the rejected child syndrome," boomed the professor in impressive tones. "The players feel bewildered and lost now that their coach is abandoning them."

This was a pretty funny handout, particularly in view of the fact that Coach McKay hadn't even deserted his troops yet but was just talking about leaving. Sports editors ate it up, and the Los Angeles *Times* ran the yarn on page one under a head that screamed, "They Miss Daddy." The very notion of 260-pound linemen suffering wounded feelings delighted the readers, and there was a flood of mail. This got a lot of laughs and a bundle of publicity for Professor Ogilvie.

All the "personality testing" program had earned the professor and Peter Bavasi in San Diego was ridicule. These mind-readers had begun to pick their playing talent—and indeed their present manager, John (who's he?) McNamara—from the percentages that came out of the personality tests they laid on everybody but Ol' Buzzie himself.

In their daffy charts, charisma, charm, and even grammar were computed along with glove skills, running speed, and throwing ability.

They were soon to discover that there was no syntax in the swing of a bat, and that a knowledge of geometry didn't help a kid control a curve ball.

The first few results out of the Mind Machine were weird. But then things got much worse.

Looking for a brainy manager, Peter and the Professor somehow let Sparky Anderson escape from their booby hatch. Sparky might not have produced personality ratings to satisfy the mind-readers, but he went on to put together all kinds of winners at Cincinnati.

The Brain Boys' first draft pick was Eli Borunda, who the formula insisted would develop into a strikeout pitcher. Something slipped here, and Borunda turned out to be a door-to-door evangelist.

He got shut out a lot doing that, too.

Another costly pick by the Ogilvie-Bavasi Ouija board was a big, strapping boy from Georgia; the gizmo indicated this indeed was the young catcher the Padre team needed so desperately.

Peter Bavasi paid young Mike Ivie close to $100,000 to catch before they discovered the machine had overlooked something; the kid couldn't throw the ball back to his pitcher. Oh, he could throw fine to second, third, or first, but when he aimed at the pitcher's mound, the ball hit the pitcher on the shins or sailed over his head. The shrinks have a word for this, but it is too long to spell.

There was no cure for Ivie's strange quirk, and Mike decided he would never catch, never mind what the Mind Machine had said. Not only that, but he went crying home to mother when they wouldn't let him play first base. He came back when the Brains relented and let him play first, and he now looks as if he might turn out to be a hitter.

Peter Bavasi often quit his job and went home in frustration, too, but his mother would get him on the phone, talk sense, and get him back to his charts and tests. The whole outfit seemed ready for the psychiatrist's couch.

Not long after that Rocky Perrone arrived.

The Ogilvie-Bavasi mind-reader must have given Rocky a fine personality rating; that, along with creams and facials to take out his age lines and a hair piece to cover his bald head, fooled all the Padre experts. They rated Rocky as a hot prospect at shortstop, and he actually got to play in one game to win a bet he had with the bartender. Then he confessed he was a thirty-eight-year-old busher who had been knocking around semipro sandlots since the Dodgers fled Brooklyn.

Everybody had a good laugh, or nearly everybody. Poor Buzzie couldn't even crack a smile. Young Bavasi had gone wild when his father let him play with the matches.

Things went from bad to abysmal on the Padres, and one day Buzzie called me into his office.

"Call your friend in Kentucky," he said wearily, "and see if he will come and take over this team for us."

The code was necessary to defeat eavesdroppers. Preston Gomez, the patient manager of this blundering bunch, had no idea he was being undermined by Peter Bavasi. Peter had his own pet manager behind the draperies.

By "friend in Kentucky" Buzzie meant Pee Wee Reese, who had retired to the quiet of Louisville, where the dropping of a putt was the loudest sound to be heard for days. Buzzie figured the smart old shortstop might by now be itching for a return to the limelight.

If I call Reese, the story may leak. And then Preston Gomez would be hurt, and you would wind up in the middle.

"Not me," said Buzzie quickly. "If that happens, I'll deny the whole thing and say you had no right to make the call."

I got Pee Wee off the golf course to make the offer.

"Not for a million bucks, Paw-row-tee," he laughed, using the pet name he had for me. "What are you trying to do, break up the nice life I have here in Louisville? Who needs a headache like the Padres?"

Pee Wee sounded as if I had asked him to contract a disease!

Two days later, Peter Bavasi boasted to me of how he was torturing Gomez, trying to get him to quit as manager. That afternoon he had taken coach Don Zimmer into the stands behind first base. It was three hours before game time, and the ballpark was almost empty.

The way young Bavasi proudly reported it to me, he had interrupted his chat with Zimmer to say: "Gomez can see us from where he's sitting in the dugout, Don. What do you suppose he thinks we're discussing?"

"Probably he knows exactly what we've been talking about," said Zimmer, who was honest through and through. "What pitching we have in Hawaii that can help us, or who we could bring up from the Alexandria club—"

"No, no," said young Bavasi. "I know that, but what does Gomez *think* we're saying as we sit here? He knows you're my bobo, and he's got to be worried about losing his job when he sees us together."

Peter was proud of that bit of psychological warfare he let me in on. "But don't you dare tell my father about it," he cautioned.

Young Bavasi was piling up a lot of tiny, niggling complaints and annoyances to erode the peace of mind of Gomez, who was a Cuban gentleman of real class. Peter hoped his psychological nitpicking would build into a mountain of frustration that would make Gomez quit.

This is known in the trade as the Chinese water torture method of eliminating a manager. There are other devices used by the front office, such as walk-the-plank-blindfolded ("He'll assume another position in the organization"), pull-the-rug ("Believe me, this is the hardest task I've ever had to face"), optional hara-kiri ("For the good of the team"), and that particularly lethal ploy, the vote of confidence, which is baseball's surest kiss of death.

Within a month Gomez was gone, and Zimmer got the job. A year later Don was to learn that the friendly arm around his shoulder could also hold a knife: Peter Bavasi cut him down, too.

So Zimmer, who was not good enough to please young Bavasi, escaped into the 1975 World Series, where he was the much-praised third base coach of the Red Sox. There with him atop the baseball world was Sparky Anderson, managing Cincinnati's world champions. How lucky they were to have escaped from the San Diego booby hatch!

Before Peter Bavasi's weird ideas could do much more harm, the mixed-up revolving-door muddle of a team was bought by Ray Kroc, the McDonald's hamburger wizard. Kroc's area of expertise was solid stuff like fries, shakes, and Big Macs. He definitely was not into mind-reading and character analysis; the ballplayers he had admired for years in Chicago were often dem-and-dose guys who happened to be able to run the fastest and hit the ball farthest.

Kroc started asking questions. How, he asked the Bavasis, would Babe Ruth and Dizzy Dean and Willie Mays have scored on the Brain Machine? Would John McGraw, out of whose mouth came little else but cusswords and tobacco juice, have passed the test as well as the present brainy Padre manager? Would Casey Stengel and his scrambled syntax ever have had the chance to win all those Yankee pennants if he had to get by the Bavasi rating system?

Owner Kroc found that baseball's insides had changed a lot

since his younger days in Chicago, when he followed the day-to-day deeds of Cub heroes like Kiki Cuyler, Pat Malone, Guy Bush, and Swish Nicholson.

And Kroc was far from sure the changes were for the better.

Although the Padres that Bankrupt Smith put across on the National League were laughable, the damage that Charley Finley caused has been much, much worse.

While mucking up baseball's map and dragging the game through the law courts, Finley has been giving the brothers the shiv in another embarrassing way. He put together three straight world champion teams, plus a 1975 division winner, while the rest of the millionaire geniuses have been fumbling year after year with pitiable results. And our bully boy has done it with fewer bucks, from an anemic Oakland gate, than they have to play with, less front-office staff than you'd find with a one-night carnival, and no tact at all.

The man keeps building skyscrapers out of some do-it-yourself manual he seems to have picked up at the five-and-dime, while the great architects of the game, self-styled, are still stumbling around in their cellars. He has fired dozens of good people on a whim and hatched a festering team of unhappy, cursing, brawling players who punch each other out of playing condition and give the Grand Old Game a mean and nasty face the Lords of Baseball shudder to have Little Leaguers look up to.

Finley has changed the face of baseball, and its rear end as well, for that has been dragging through the law courts since he got in the back door.

First, he threatened his new partners with a lawsuit if they wouldn't let him move out of Kansas City, where he had held down attendance to strengthen his case and publicly ridiculed the local press, making his plight insoluble.

As soon as he landed in Oakland, Charley began to strangle Stoneham and the Giants.

Now Kansas City fired back at the American League, suing because Finley had jilted them and broke contracts. To keep them quiet, the nervous brothers had to install a new franchise in K.C. They managed to dig up another eccentric sportsman to sell it to: Ewing Kaufman, a wizard at making pills. Right off, Kaufman blew a million bucks financing a baseball academy in Florida, where young bodies who had absolutely no baseball background would be force-fed the game from the ground up. It just didn't work.

But trouble begets trouble. When the Lords of the American League created a new Kansas City team, they had to balance it with a matching expansion headache somewhere else. Here they outdid themselves in orchestrating disaster.

Would lumber baron Tom Yawkey, whose play-toys are the Red Sox, have built a sawmill where there are no trees?

Would CBS, which then owned the Yankees, have televised New Year's Eve from Bridgeport or Peoria, instead of Times Square?

Yet that's just about what Yawkey and CBS and their partners in the American League lodge agreed to when they booked their million-dollar show, with Mantle and Yastrzemski and Brooks Robinson and the rest of their stars, into a two-bit, sub-minor league ballyard in Seattle.

The name of the ballpark didn't help, either: Sicks Stadium.

This was worse than staging Grand Opera in a bar and grill.

⚓✕✕✕

8. A One-Man Ripoff in Seattle

When I arrived in Seattle to take the job as promotion director of the soon-to-be-born Pilots at a salary twice as good as I had ever earned in twenty years with the Dodgers, I felt an immediate chill run up my spine.

It should have told me plenty that the man who was trying to sell the Pilots to a skeptical public named the team after himself. He was a ship pilot, although the U.S. Coast Guard had beached him for steering the wrong course.

The American League was slower to learn than the Coast Guard.

The brothers had conferred this expansion franchise on a man who was not glib or dapper as most quick-buck operators are. He was a walking mountain of flesh, who operated out of a trailer drawn up alongside the shell of an old rundown minor league park where he was pushing six-buck tickets, more costly than Yankee Stadium prices.

I had the feeling that the whole franchise was flimsy as a carnival tent. Dewey Soriano talked like a barker, and he seemed the type who kept a furtive eye peeled for the cops, and who might fold his suitcase full of neckties and run at any moment, like those sidewalk peddlers in the big cities when they spot a bluecoat.

Seattle saw through the sham from the start and simply ignored the Pilots.

When we had moved the Dodgers into Los Angeles, a blizzard of ticket orders had descended, and we soon sold eight thousand season box seats at $250 each.

In Seattle, practically nothing happened.

I tried everything that had worked so well in Brooklyn, Los Angeles, and Anaheim.

Seeking to stimulate a youth program, I had literature printed offering youngsters a two-dollar package that included a Pilots' baseball cap—which I hoped they'd wear around town—and tickets to nine ball games. It was planned, of course, that Mom and Pop, and maybe Sis, would have to come when they brought Junior with his free ticket.

We had sold eight thousand of these kid memberships for a dollar apiece with the Dodgers, where the thing started. Moving to the Angels, I had enticed five thousand "Junior Angels" at two bucks. In Seattle, I thought we had a good name for the kid members—"Co-Pilots"—along with our high hopes.

Soriano took care of that. He got wind of what I was doing and commanded me to raise the price to five bucks!

I pleaded that kids who ran paper routes and did yard work for weekly allowances didn't have that kind of cash.

"Things have passed you by, Parrott," he answered, with a pitying look. "All kids have money today. Get five bucks out of them."

Sensing I was beaten, I made one last stand, hoping to hold

the fee down to three dollars, so I could promote a large membership.

Soriano growled a negative. "It's much easier for the old man to peel off a five," he said, "than to go hunting for three singles."

This was the big thinker, the economic giant to whom President Joe Cronin and his American League owners had entrusted their branch store in the Great Northwest. This was the guy they had invited into their parlor to sit down at their councils beside Columbia Broadcasting's best brains and to rub elbows with such as Arthur Allyn, the trucking magnate, and Jerry Hoffberger, the brewing nabob from Baltimore, and Yawkey, the lumber baron. I began to wonder whether they had even bothered to meet Soriano, much less research his ballpark and his rating in Seattle.

A gimmick Marvin Milkes and I used trying to stir up Seattle interest that spring of 1969 was to invite big businessmen into the Soriano trailer for lunch; while we were making our season-ticket pitch, we entertained them with a telephone hookup with Mesa, Arizona, so they could chat with the Pilot players, manager Joe Schultz, and the coaches. We might have advertised the Pilots' Jim Bouton more, had we known then that he was going to turn into a better peep-and-prattle writer than a pitcher.

One day one of our guests, a very impressive man named Jim Douglas, read me the riot act. "This thing is going to fall flat on its face," he said, "and we just can't afford to have a major league franchise flop here in Seattle; it would hurt the whole city. I have an associate, Eddie Carlson, and we have talked the problem over. We want to do something big to help. Mind you, we don't give a damn about Soriano. It's the city we're worried about."

Douglas proposed a breakfast meeting of the city's business leaders. It would be in Carlson's suite at the Olympic Hotel, and they would host it. They would try to persuade all these men, whom they knew well, to get behind a ticket drive. Could we have a few players there, perhaps the manager? Soriano? He didn't really matter, but I could bring him if I chose.

Carlson was the head of International Hotels, and soon afterward he was named board chairman of United Air Lines. Douglas, the outspoken one, was president of the prestigious Northgate Centers, a Seattle showplace, and had other interests.

Racing back to my typewriter after they'd gone, I dashed off a memorandum to Soriano, including every detail of Douglas's forthright talk and his offer to help. This was a ray of hope, I felt. I practically knocked down Soriano's door to put my burning news in his hand.

The rookie member of the Lords of Baseball read the whole thing and scaled it into his wastebasket with a disdainful flourish.

"We don't need help from outsiders," he grunted.

I kept busy, organizing a fifty-one-station radio network that had as a flagship station Gene Autry's Golden West Network outlet in Seattle. It stretched through five states and Canada. I put out a combination program and scorebook that was filled with ads, wrote copy for the broadcasters, and sold what tickets I could.

On opening day Soriano asked me to meet Senator Henry Jackson and escort him to the reception and ceremonies.

On the second day of the season the Pilot owner called me in and said he couldn't afford me, and I was out of a job. All the handshake agreements, all the promises he used to lure me from Autry and Anaheim were worthless.

Commissioner Bowie Kuhn couldn't muster the nerve to answer his phone when I called him in New York to tell him what was happening to the baby franchise. Nor would he answer my letters. I was stranded in the Northwest with my family, my furniture, and a lease on a Mercer Island house.

There was no doubt in my mind by then that Soriano had planned from the very start a quick ripoff of the city of Seattle and the nice little old man who had bankrolled him, a Cleveland financier named Bill Daly. I think he planned to resell the franchise, possibly to another promoter or a city like Milwaukee, and get out fast with his bundle.

He fitted nicely into the Rogues' Gallery of baseball, right beside Arnholt Smith, the San Diego super-swindler, and a few rows behind Charley Outrageous Finley.

How do the good people of baseball—and there are many, like Horace Stoneham and Gene Autry—keep coming up with outlandish lodge brothers like these?

Stoneham is on his way out, and the Big Boys have let him go down the tube; they may not have the Cowboy to kick around much longer either, if they keep picking him clean as Finley did when he charged the Angels' owner a cool $100,000 for an ex-manager (Dick Williams) he was no longer paying, or even talking to!

Here is a letter Jim Douglas wrote me a year after I had left Seattle. It has never been published, but it could turn out to be an important bit of evidence in the ongoing and upcoming $30 million suit Seattle, King County, and the rest of the Domed Stadium planners have against the American League.

> Dear Harold:
>
> I well remember the visit I had with you on the subject of the Seattle Pilots. I'm not sure the plan Eddie Carlson and I came up with would have worked, but certainly the plan that was carried out by Soriano didn't work. I was surprised that they would hire a pro like you and not listen to what you had to say!
>
> You may not know the sequel to the chapter you and I were involved in. When the Owners ran out of money they began negotiations for the sale of the franchise elsewhere than in Seattle. Since we were anxious that the team stay in Seattle, particularly since the proposed Domed Stadium was resting on this franchise, a group of us negotiated to buy the franchise. It's a long story but Eddie Carlson ended up as Chairman of the Board and I as President of the group that raised $11,500,000 to buy the team. But our group was not acceptable to the American League, so our short term in the baseball business came to an end when the Seattle Pilots moved to Milwaukee.
>
> Eddie Carlson and I have thanked our lucky stars ever since that we were not acceptable partners to the other owners in the American League. I have other things I would rather do with my time and I'm not looking for a quick way to lose money.
>
> I hope our paths will cross soon.
>
> Yours Very Truly,
>
> JAMES B. DOUGLAS

9. Finley: Only Cancer Has a Worse Press

Soriano's sad-sack Pilots did not stay around Seattle long, but in the one season they were there writers like the veteran Hy Zimmerman treated the team as you would a sick child, petting and pampering it and hoping it would look better on the morrow.

It is the same in San Diego, where Phil Collier, a knowledgeable pressbox old-timer who knows better, is sometimes hard pressed to invent new excuses in his San Diego *Union* for a team that seems each day to find a new way to lose. In one burst of candor late last summer, which perhaps was designed to attract absentee owner Kroc's attention, Collier wrote, "Despite Mr. Kroc's assertion that his team would go first class, the Padres are the only one of 24 major league teams that is not operated first class; and what is worse, the San Diego players know this."

Even the failing Mets are treated kindly by the somewhat more cynical New York reporters, who lose their tempers only when a favorite like Yogi Berra is mistreated, or when M. Donald Grant, the high-toned chairman of the board, pulls something only a pompous member of the owners' fraternity would attempt. Grant last summer staged what amounted to a public humiliation of ballplayer Cleon Jones, who had sinned off the field. Subway straphanging fans of the Mets, who cannot forgive a man's strike-out with the winning run aboard, were much more understanding of Cleon's other transgressions than was the stern Grant. Jones had been observed in Florida sleeping in the nude in a truck with a woman other than his wife.

One angered Met rooter was quoted: "If they didden wanna see it, they shoulda looked d'udder way."

In Atlanta, grave things hamper a franchise that has lost a cool million in attendance since 1966, when the Braves first operated there, finished fifth, and attracted 1.5 million fans. In 1975 Atlanta drew little more than five hundred thousand, and "what's wrong with the Braves?" polls have appeared. The consensus seems to be that management is snooty and indifferent. There was cautious editorializing when the Black Babe Ruth, Henry Aaron, fled the organization after rapping it, but even so, the hatchet has not been swung cruelly in the pressbox.

Probing reporters are blamed in Los Angeles for the feuds that have apparently hurt Dodger morale, but writers like Bob Hunter and columnist Mel Durslag keep picking the club to win even in the years it finishes almost twenty games out of first place, like 1975. On the morning *Times,* John Hall and Ross Newhan are less enthusiastic than Hunter, but they are never harsh on the O'Malleys, who do run the biggest show in town. Incidentally, it was a girl reporter, quoting Davey Lopes and unnamed other teammates as being critical of Steve Garvey and his All-American image, who started a schism that hurt the 1975 team badly.

In Detroit a reporter was punched by manager Ralph Houk and sued in retaliation. In Pittsburgh the populace staged parades and protest meetings because the Pirates canned Bob Prince, a flaky broadcaster with twenty-eight years' tenure. But those things are patched up, and life goes on everywhere except in Oakland.

Nobody else catches hell in the media like Charley Finley, whose teams win almost all the time. He has a worse press than cancer.

Charley seems to enjoy it that way.

He went out of his way after the 1975 World Series to bounce Alvin Dark (for the second time) because of something the Bible-spouting manager said at a prayer meeting. Most of the words Charley says to reporters couldn't be used in front of longshoremen.

When star Oakland third baseman Sal Bando sympathized with Dark, Finley reacted again. "I don't care a goddam whether my manager pleases his players or the fans," barked Mr. Bad. "I am the one he must please. I pay his salary!" At least he leaves no doubt where he stands.

It would appear that Finley has taken as his model a wild man who terrorized his players, his managers, and the media in the thirties and forties, which he lit up very brightly in more ways than one. His name was Leland Stanford MacPhail—father of the present president of the American League—and he fought them all, including the Grim Reaper, whom he held off until late 1975, when he was eighty-five. All despite a roistering life, the rigors of cop-fighting and punching the press, two bouts with cancer, and, just before he stormed the Great Pressbox in the Sky, a bad heart.

There are startling similarities between the two mavericks, although the sometimes ferocious Finley comes off at best as a pale carbon copy of the mad genius, MacPhail. Durocher is in print with an apt line about that: "They say there is a thin line between genius and insanity," Leo the Lip philosophized, "and MacPhail was constantly wandering over the line."

Finley has indeed built a winner in Oakland; but MacPhail built winners in both leagues, and in three cities, not one: Cincinnati, Brooklyn, and the Bronx.

Finley sasses a baseball commissioner now and then; MacPhail installed one (Unhappy Chandler) and then broke him in half.

Both talked endlessly about yellow baseballs, which they never managed to put through. But in the area of innovation, to compare Finley with the greatest promoter in the history of the game is like putting a little boy with a candle alongside Thomas Edison.

Finley's best contributions were night World Series games, which he pushed strongly for, and bilious-looking baseball uniforms in outlandish colors, with sissy-white spiked shoes.

All MacPhail did was bring into the majors radio play-by-play broadcasts (over the screamed objections of owners who charged he was giving the game away). And of course he fought them all to install night baseball, which eventually saved all their hides.

And there are other striking differences.

MacPhail was always popular with the fans. Partners and stockholders asked him to leave, but never the man in the grandstand, for the Redhead built winners.

Even with his winning teams, Finley has never made it with his public. They seem to resent his antics, the way he belittles his own players, and the silly donkey image, which he tries to push onto Oakland with the mule he named after himself. During the 1973 World Series a bedsheet banner fluttered out of the upper deck in the Oakland ballpark which said it all: *"Finley: Get your ass out of town!"*

Even in firing people, MacPhail outdid Finley, again with a difference: Larry's firings never stuck. Durocher claims he was sacked forty times in his five years as Dodger manager; but I was there, and I can verify only twenty-seven.

Under the bluster, MacPhail was a compassionate man, and most of his harsh deeds came right out of a bottle. When Larry emerged the morning after from what the British like to call "the vapours," he would blithely ignore the whole episode. If pushed, he would deny, with great vigor and perhaps a few threats, that it ever *did* happen.

If it seemed MacPhail sometimes had a worse press than Finley, that was because there were three times as many newspapers in his day. And in each of them Larry gathered more ink than Finley gets today. Even conservative editors who cursed his antics had to assign a man to cover MacPhail almost twenty-four hours a day, lest they be scooped.

Here again is a striking difference between the two.

If Finley reads a story he does not like or hears a TV or radio man he does not agree with, he will often call the reporter's boss and try to get him fired. Ron Bergman of the Oakland *Tribune* told me he has often been on thin ice at his paper because of Charley's criticisms. "He's called my editor many times and tried to get me removed," Ron says, "and I really have not been that critical, certainly not in a personal way."

MacPhail never went over the heads of the working stiffs in the pressbox, as Pegler used to call us. Larry was more direct. He would take matters into his own hands. Or fists.

The Redhead has wrestled with and punched and mauled everybody, from important owners who were giants of the game down to mere newspapermen like me.

Oh, the next day, when he cooled off, he would send a plastic surgeon to remake your waffled face, if you needed it, and a case of booze to ease the pain. An ambulance with a nurse, too, if you wanted it.

If Finley is trying to imitate this man, I've news for him: He'll never make it!

Part II

✕✕✕

The Old Days, When Brooklyn Had a Newspaper and a Ball Team

10. The Brooklyn Eagle
Flaps Its Wings

One day Lucifer Sulphurious MacPhail, head man of the Dodgers, punched my nose at Ebbets Field.

The rhubarb—that was Red Barber Brooklynese for "ruckus" or "flap"—which this started at my newspaper was a very large one indeed.

The highly esteemed Brooklyn *Eagle*, which was then almost a hundred years old, had never before suffered a bloodied reporter, even during the Civil War. *Eagle* editors quivered with outrage; freedom of the press was at issue, along with my nose, they assured each other in serious tones. For MacPhail had delivered with his roundhouse the edict that I was to be barred from the Dodger ballpark.

"And that means for life!" the Redhead had roared as a parting shot.

This was war, and there in the front lines with me was Harris Crist, the managing editor with the piercing steel-blue eyes who ran the *Eagle* pages like a Napoleon. Crist was the blood, guts, and gristle of the paper, and had been since the turn of the century. He was not about to have any of his troops shoved around, least of all me. I am ashamed to say it even at this distance, but I was Crist's pet.

The old tyrant sent me everywhere, trying to dig up fresh viewpoints on sports events whose constant coverage had become stereotyped and old hat. He would yank experienced reporters off their regular beats for a day or two and tell me to write whatever I saw, anything I felt needed telling. Naturally this did not make the staff men too happy with a green pea like me.

One day Crist sent me to Belmont Park with fifty bucks of the *Eagle*'s money and told me to make a few bets and write it like it

was at the famous horse track. I had never seen a horse race, and
I was amazed to find the legalized bookmakers of that day alongside easels that held blackboards, on which they chalked the odds
on the various horses. The odds they set varied as you walked
down the line.

When I questioned the old geezer I selected about whether he
would be there with my money when I returned, I got a gruff
comeback: "Lissen, sonny," he growled, "forty-one years I bin
right on this here spot!"

For the next day's paper I wrote about this and a great deal
more that I discovered during my wide-eyed exploration of this
gambling hell, as my mother called it. She was sure that an evil
assignment like this was just another of the many pitfalls that lay
ahead for her little boy Harold—in her eyes, I never did grow
up!—doing the newspaper work I found so exciting.

When my story appeared, Crist was so pleased he let me keep
the fifty, along with the twelve bucks my beginner's luck had
won for me.

It should be stated early that the *Eagle* was no small-town
bladder. It put out five lively editions a day—more, if a big story
broke—and it had as much muscle in its own backyard—the
boroughs of Brooklyn and Queens—as the eleven giants publish-
ing across the river every day in Manhattan had in theirs. The
Eagle beat them all from time to time on big stories in crime or
politics, and severely ignored them otherwise. It pushed hard for
its own projects, like the Brooklyn Bridge, which it was anxious
to get because so many of its subscribers were being trapped on
ferryboats amid the ice floes in the East River on the way to and
from work in Manhattan. Getting the bridge built was sticky
business. It even involved the use of an *Eagle* editor as a bag
man, carrying a $45,000 bribe to a Tammany backroom across
the river. But the paper got the job done no matter what.
It liked to boast that its town had lower taxes, better schools, and
that its citizens lived longer among the churches and parks and
general peace and quiet, and dined in better style, particularly
in the great sea food restaurants on Sheepshead Bay.

The *Eagle* prospered and grew so that in the paper's richest
years, which were probably the twenties and early thirties, it had
a Washington bureau, and one in Rome and another in Paris. Its

man in Albany, the state capital, was Clint Mosher, a live-wire reporter who might have walked right out of the pages of *Five-Star Final* or *The Front Page,* and who knew where all the political bodies were buried.

The *Eagle* editorials were written by Cleveland Rodgers, who was to become a silver-maned giant among the city fathers, with suggestions from Crist; and by H. V. Kaltenborn, whose short-clipped, machine-gun style of talking made him one of the early stars of radio news, along with lugubrious Gabriel Heatter. Nelson Harding drew the editorial cartoons, which were reprinted all over the world. You were a nobody on Crown Heights or Park Slope or Shore Road if your name didn't pop up in the *Eagle* society columns conducted by Nella Brown, and later by Helen Brown. It was a very vital paper, often up to its masthead in controversy, as it had been in its very earliest days under editor Walt Whitman, whose book of poetry *Leaves of Grass* was burned and banned in all Brooklyn libraries. Whitman was a member of the Barnburners party, a radical segment of the Democrats.

When I landed on the *Eagle* in 1927, I found Harris Crist running the whole show, particularly the newsroom, like a ringmaster. He was using everything but a whip to prod any laggards into action. He sat there right in the vortex of this word foundry, fairly close to the slot, which was the perch where the city editor barked his commands to rewrite men and copyreaders and weighed the value of each story. Around the slot was the rim, where the copyreaders sat, jabbering like jays, their green visors bobbing up and down. They cut and slashed until there was blood on every page as well as in the eye of the rewrite slave, who was seeing his clever lines die. Then a headline was shaped and the whole package was crammed into a pneumatic tube that took it down to the composing room with an ominous gulp of air.

Crist's desk was unprotected by wall, partition, or secretary—she sat behind this stern character, not up front as a buffer—so that he could better overhear and oversee what was going on around him. And, believe me, he kept it going around and around, edition after edition, including three on Sunday morning, like some journalistic Marquis de Sade.

Copyboys gave Crist a wide berth, preferring to run an ob-

stacle race through the maze of desks rather than risk a stare
from the managing editor by using the aisle past where he sat;
he could stab you at thirty paces with those gimlet eyes through
the pince-nez. Only two men on the *Eagle* dared talk back to this
ogre: Mosher, the brassy, loud-talking high-roller from Albany;
and Horace Posey, the lean, Lincoln-like city editor from Ashe-
ville, Nawth Cahlina, suh.

All heads would turn in this madhouse whenever some poor
wretch was summoned to Crist's throne to explain away a sin.
The guilty party would find himself staring straight into a bright
light while the boss editor would skewer him from the side with
those piercing eyes, much as an entomologist might inspect an
insect under a microscope. Squirming to move himself so that his
eyes would be shielded from the glare and he could make it a
more even battle, the sinner would inevitably struggle to shift his
chair, only to find that Crist had bolted it to the floor!

Jimmy Murphy, whose unending—and totally unrewarded—
efforts had put the *Eagle* sports pages together day in and day
out for thirty years, shook visibly whenever Crist stared in his
direction. The old tyrant fired his workhorse sports editor regularly—every two or three months, or so it seemed. It usually happened because of some Alice-in-Wonderland story Murphy would
write under his own name, or because he let some similar drivel
get into the paper. Crist would then finger some hack from the
obituary desk or the financial page and invest him with the sports
editor title. Of course, Murphy would stay on the payroll and do
all the work as usual, while the imported hero basked in his new
glory. This would go on until something went wrong; the trans-
plant would be sent back to his normal habitat, and Murphy
would ease back in again as sports editor.

Murphy was a top copyreader, assignment editor, and makeup
man, but his typewriter, which lured him as a flame attracts the
moth, invariably got him into trouble. Jimmy viewed all sports
heroes through the eyes of an awe-struck child, and there were
times when he wrote like one. Apparently mesmerized by the
keyboard in front of him, he would take off on outrageous flights
of simile. To him, a home run was never that simple; rather it was
a Ruthian swat, a four-master or rousing round-tripper during
which a player propelled the horsehide (never the ball) out of

the ol' orchard, allowing him to touch the initial hassock, the key-stone sack, and the hot corner, and eventually dent the dish. This was the era when the Sultan of Swat, the Manassa Mauler, and the Galloping Ghost were running across the sports pages of the country, and that helped intoxicate Jimmy, too.

David Shaw, who analyzes trends and such in the *Los Angeles Times*, recently undertook to put the sportswriters of the thirties in their place as a group "of sophomoric, superficial and even sycophantic idiots [who] played on their typewriters and barely approached literacy . . . in what had to be the sandbox of the newspaper world." Obviously Shaw can put words together, but can he read? It would not have taken too much research for him to discover the writings of Damon Runyon or Ring Lardner or Westbrook Pegler, or a dozen more I will name later. Even today I would shudder to see the young man have to go one-on-one, on any topic, with a brain like John Kieran, who was then writing the sports pillar in the *New York Times* and was the resident genius of the radio program "Information, Please."

Even among the flowery writers Shaw puts down so badly, Murphy was definitely one of a kind. He was the motorman of a daily column full of hyperbole and heroics called "Scholastic Highlights." In it he conferred sainthood on high school boys in the form of "All-Scholastic" rankings. Despite the term, the honors had nothing to do with studies or mental achievement. Rather it was the "All-American" gimmick, but at the high school level. A youngster could often vault into a scholarship at Penn or Princeton or even at Notre Dame on the strength of being named to Murphy's sacred All-Scholastic First Team. Second-team honors might get him into Colby or Bowdoin or Lehigh on a free ride.

Athletic directors in the Big Ten and elsewhere in the nation read Murphy regularly for tips on good athletes, and Jimmy launched Sid Luckman of Erasmus Hall High in Brooklyn to fame at Columbia and fortune with the Chicago Bears. The Dodgers' very first tip on Sandy Koufax even came from Murphy, although the editor touted the muscular Jewish boy he first spotted on the Parade Grounds in Brooklyn as a first baseman (which Sandy was, originally) and spelled the name wrong.

It was Murphy who first called another Erasmus product,

Waite Hoyt, the "Merry Mortician of Flatbush" in the paper. Hoyt was one of those schoolboy wonders in Brooklyn, and his first wife happened to be an undertaker's daughter; by the time he had made it big with the Yankees of the Ruth era, Hoyt was quite a high roller and missed a lot of curfews, hence the "Merry." Murphy loved to roll little-known, unrelated trivia like this into a sports page soufflé that a great many people, Crist included, could not stomach.

Jimmy often made the sports pages up at eight in the morning, and he worked all afternoon getting out the makeover editions, one every hour from noon until five. These were marked MX1, MX2, and so on, and they contained the latest inning-by-inning scores on the Dodgers, golf's National Open, Wimbledon and Forest Hills tennis, and of course the race results; these were taken off the AP wire by Johnny Murray, a moon-faced man who had an endless supply of French postcards and filthy stories and who openly made book on the horses for all four floors of the *Eagle*. Radio had not yet started to compete in sports, and people waited for these late editions outside our building and at key points in Park Slope and Bay Ridge and Flatbush, where they would be rushed by delivery trucks that broke all the laws but paid off each traffic cop with free papers.

It took a couple of years of working after my college classes for me to become Murphy's assistant on the MX editions, and this was the most exciting part of all, because I had the authority to stop the presses. One moment I would be writing a new one-paragraph lead on Tommy Armour taking the lead in the Open, with a three-line No. 5 head; the next I'd be checking the Western Union operator right in our office for how the Dodgers were scoring in St. Louis, or wherever. If we went to press with seven innings of the Dodger game—all games were in the afternoon then!—in MX3, the rest of the spaces in the two-column line score, where the last two innings and the run-hit-error totals would appear in the Final, appeared as little black squares on the still-hot, half-round lead plate they slapped on the big press cylinder.

Now, if the Western Union man got the clack-clack news over his instrument that Herman had hit a homer with a man on in the top of the eighth to give our guys the lead, I went into action.

I would dash down three flights of stairs to where the big presses were throbbing the whole structure, and hold up my hand. While the foreman was winding the great cylinders down to a full stop, I would take from a special rack a hammer and a punch with a "2" on it, and imprint it on the black square that corresponded to the top of the eighth inning. In no time at all the presses would be spinning again, and I would grab one of the very first newspapers to come off, to exult over the "2" I had contributed and think how it would delight so many people in no time at all. Even by then the newsboys would be hawking the papers that still smelled of ink as they yelled "Hoiman hits anudder, gitcha papee here."

About this time Forbes, the bulldog of the night sports desk, got wise to the fact that I liked to write catchy heads, had a wide knowledge of all the sports, and could even spell, something very few of those who shoved their stories at him could manage. Ralph Trost, the golf writer who knocked off his stories with both feet propped up on his desk, was the worst. Trost had once spelled the winner's name in a golf tournament three different ways in one story. Forbes screamed, but Trost just twirled his mustache and went on typing. "If I didn't make a mistake now and then, Eddie, guys like you would be out of a job," he remarked, which increased the screams.

Forbes was a big-time referee, not only in boxing but for wrestling as well, which was filling Madison Square Garden regularly. Eddie made me his number-one stand-in on the night desk, which meant that any time he came in wearing the familiar gray flannel shirt with the little black bow tie that was the badge of all referees, I would be working in his place.

Forbes was quick pay, too. He slipped me a tenner before each shift I worked for him. But I would have done it for nothing, I got such a kick out of this kind of newspaper work. I felt like a Toscanini orchestrating the whole sports section, encouraging one writer to produce more copy if he had got onto a good story, or muting another if I thought he had padded his piece to collect another dollar or two on space rates.

I was still getting paid by the inch for the features I wrote. Murphy had showed me how to make up my bill, pasting the clippings of the stories I'd had published end to end on calibrated strips of paper furnished by the *Eagle* that were exactly one column long. "Don't paste up the heads on your stories," Murphy had warned. "You don't get paid for those."

I had been pasting up two weeks' work late one night when Nunnaly Johnson became intrigued with what I was doing. Johnson, who was to become one of Hollywood's most celebrated screenwriters and producers, was quartered at a desk one row in front of me, and I had heard in the washroom that he was making all of sixty bucks a week, so I was nervous with him watching me. By now my space bill stretched clear across the nearly empty city room, like the tail of a gigantic kite. When Kaltenborn came in a little later, Johnson called him over to see my bill. They couldn't believe how much I had succeeded in getting into the *Eagle*. "Kid, you've gained more yardage here," Johnson chuckled, "than Bronko Nagurski did last Sunday against the Football Giants!" They both had a good laugh.

There was no laugh from Murphy, however, when he observed my paste-up. Not even a smile. I was concerned because Jimmy had been a kind of sponsor and guardian angel for me at the *Eagle;* above all, I didn't want to displease him.

"Please don't put any more stories in for payment this week," Murphy said, "I'm already over my budget for space writers, and Crist will raise hell with me. Save some of your clippings for next week."

I was gaining on Murphy every week, for I kept pouring it on. Before long I had a drawer full of stories I hadn't been paid for, and some of them were still in the drawer when the paper decided to save dough by putting me on salary at $40 a week.

I was rolling in money, for the cash that Forbes paid me was extra. The fact that I always had a bankroll, plus mother's discovery of me tiptoeing into the house at three in the morning after pinch-hitting for Forbes on the night desk, convinced her that I was well on my way down the road to perdition.

After some of the Dempsey bouts that Forbes refereed, and when he handled the Tunney-Heeney fight, he drifted back to the office afterward just to tell the *Eagle* fight expert and cartoonist, Ed Hughes, how wrong he was in the way he had written about the fights. Eddie usually had a good load aboard by then. Sometimes he would come in and ask me to work for him even when he didn't have a refereeing assignment. That happened more and more often after he found he could rely on his pinch hitter. Forbes blamed Murphy for his drinking, saying Jimmy's scholastic gibberish was driving him crazy.

Murphy had Long Island covered like a blanket with schoolboy correspondents at every high school. They would call the *Eagle* collect with the lineups and scoring details as soon as their games were over. Jimmy had a squad of rewrite men drilled to take these results: Ben and Paul Goldberg, who brought sacks of food in with them and could take football or basketball lineups on the phone one after another without missing a bite; an inseparable pair named Baker and Jones; Thomas J. Deegan, later a public relations consultant to clients like the Pennsylvania Railroad; and Harold Conrad, younger but wiser than a lot of us, who was living with a beautiful Chinese girl in Brooklyn Heights. One day I got a panic plea from Conrad: Would I temporarily pile all his girl's belongings in my car? His mother and father were coming to visit his apartment for the first time.

Murphy drilled his rewrite team like a Marine sergeant, and he had a code that he rasped at his rookies two or three times a night: "Keep your mouth shut, your ears open, your pants buttoned, your feet on the ground," he would say, "and keep one eye on the clock." Notice the "one eye" on the clock; presumably your other eye should be occupied with a score on the Huntington-Hempstead game. Murphy's squad took as many as seventy games on a Friday or Saturday night from outposts as far removed as East Hampton and Northport, on Long Island. He would tolerate no horseplay, and he was always riding Harold Conrad, who was usually saying or doing something funny.

Conrad got his revenge by writing mythical stories about Murphy, whom he compared to Attila the Hun. Harold would sit there right in front of Jimmy, who thought he was typing something vital, and compose leads like: "The bruised and bleeding body of Sports Editor James J. Murphy, battered beyond recognition, was found stuffed into a fourth-floor toilet at the *Eagle* tonight. By midnight, police had narrowed the list of those they thought might have committed the crime to eighty-six suspects, all of whom had worked for Murphy at one time or another." He would then pass the gem around to the rest of the staff.

Forbes tried to avoid the night desk on Friday nights. Most of the seventy-odd games that Murphy was waiting for started about the same time, and naturally a great many of them ended simultaneously. About 10 o'clock every phone in the place would ring, perhaps twenty at one time. Murphy would drive his re-write squad to greater efforts, and Forbes would pick up his hat and retreat to the Hole in the Wall, a local bar, until Murphy's schoolchildren, as he called them, stopped telephoning.

Forbes thought all high school sports results were a waste of time and even charged that Murphy's correspondents made up phony scores for games that never happened and phoned them in so they'd be paid. Eddie thought that printing Murphy's school-boy lineups and scores made about as much sense as putting nursery rhymes in the paper beside the real sports news, and he wrote many hot memos to Crist trying to get the managing editor to cut the whole thing out.

The *Eagle* circulation department liked Murphy's coverage however. It said it sold a lot of papers out on the Island, and Jimmy couldn't have had a more powerful ally. So schoolboy sports continued very big in the *Eagle*.

Forbes took his revenge every time Murphy turned in a feature story of his own. Crist had ruled that everything Murphy wrote had to pass either Forbes himself or whoever sat in the Old Bull-dog's place. Thus, even though Murph technically outranked his night editor, he was at Eddie's mercy.

Of that, Eddie had absolutely none!

11. The Big Lie Saves Me

One night when the Old Bulldog, Forbes, was three sheets to the wind and running the night desk between growls, Murphy turned in a feature story on Eleanor Holm. She had just been kicked off the U.S. Olympic swimming team for guzzling cham-pagne on the ship taking them all to the games.

Eleanor had attended Erasmus Hall High School in Brooklyn like so many other big-name athletes and movie stars, and Murph had written many pieces in his column about her when she was a schoolgirl swimmer. Now he needed a fresh new story angle.

Jimmy devised a dreamy lead-in that pictured La Holm as a little girl idling away her lunch hours in front of Oetjen's well-known restaurant around the corner from Erasmus on Church Avenue. Oetjen's, being a seafood house, had for years kept a sparkling tank of live fish in its window.

Ah, that was it! Eleanor had observed the fish, and copied their movements, and that was the secret of this slim mermaid's speed, or so Murphy typed the story. Jimmy got so carried away at the height of one of his simile binges that he wrote about Eleanor "emulating the finny beasts she saw in the Oetjen's window."

All afternoon Murph had polished this yarn, showing it around the office to the young writers. One after another, they nodded approvingly; why should they tell him the awful truth and get their ears burned?

Forbes came across this classic in his copy basket about mid-night. He gave it a swift read-through, rolled it into a tight knot the size of a golf ball, and fired it into his wastebasket, which was full of stale coffee grounds and tobacco juice as usual.

Murphy saw this little tableau from a distance but didn't let on. He outlasted Forbes that night, and, after the old gent had grouched his way home, Jimmy rescued his gem from the wastebasket, smoothed it out, and personally wrote a two-column head. He took the whole thing to the composing room to have it set in type for the next day's paper. In his heart Jimmy thought he had composed a classic.

I was in the city room the next day when Crist's eyes lit on Murphy's masterpiece about Eleanor and the finny beasts. The managing editor went up off his chair as if the seat were afire. He had the story yanked out after the first run, and clippings from that bulldog edition got to be collector's items around the office.

Of course, Crist demoted Murphy. Again. But this time it was really serious, because he went outside the *Eagle* and brought in a yachting expert to be sports editor. Paul Warburg was one of the worst misfortunes ever to befall the paper.

Warburg's first mistake was to fire Tommy Holmes for talking

back to him. Holmes had been the nationally known *Eagle* correspondent covering the Dodgers for years and years. In fact, only
four experts had been appointed—anointed is a better word—
by the editors of the *Eagle* to cover the baseball beat since Brooklyn had its first team in Organized Baseball in 1877. The first of
these was Father Chadwick, the inventor of the box score, which
should give you an idea of the weight of the assignment. Holmes
was the fourth in the line, and he had been following the Dodgers about twenty years. He was respected as a baseball historian
and analyst, and the *Eagle* had plastered all its delivery trucks
with his name and picture only a month before.

Crist called me over to his desk the morning after the big firing
and told me to catch a plane that night to Miami, where the
Dodgers were in the middle of spring training at the sumptuous
Miami Biltmore Hotel. He then summoned Warburg and told
him to draw $500 expense money for me as an advance.

This shook up the staid old *Eagle* something awful. Sacking
Holmes was bad enough, but putting a green pea writer like this
into Tommy's big shoes to fill the biggest job on the paper—well!

However, nobody dared argue with Crist, and that included
the owners and big stockholders of the *Eagle*. The orders stood.

They stood, that is, until my mother heard of them.

Crist had reckoned without her.

She called the old tyrant the next morning and informed him
that the airplane was absolutely out of the question as far as any
son of hers was concerned; those contraptions didn't always stay
up in the air the way they were advertised to.

Furthermore, she was dead against any silly assignment that
took her boy Harold so far away from his nice home in Howard
Beach. She had heard Miami called the Paris of this hemisphere,
and she had a pretty good idea what that meant. She admitted
the Miami part of it hadn't been settled yet, because my father,
who had always been a big league baseball fan, was siding with
me. All in all, she was a match for Crist.

Much to my surprise, the crusty old editor backed off and told
mother that I could go to Miami on the train, if she preferred.
And when I came into the office that day he asked, with a twinkle
in those feared eyes, how the "battle" was going at home. He said
he needed my decision in twenty-four hours, because with Holmes

canned the *Eagle* was using rewrites of the morning papers to fill in, and that wasn't going to satisfy the avid Dodger fans for very long.

Mother had kept me under glass, so to speak, for the first twenty years of my life. Here I was, a college graduate with two degrees from St. John's in Brooklyn, but I hadn't even taken a girl to my junior or senior prom in college. Mother had zealously shooed away all the girls, with their built-in temptations, and tried to insulate her darling against evil. I had attended the dances alone and watched the older boys play.

The good lady had had great misgivings about my working at the *Eagle* right from the start. She was an incurable playgoer, and I think we saw every one that opened on Broadway in those days, except of course the skin shows like the *Follies*. She had seen *The Front Page,* in which booze and broads figured heavily. As far as she could tell, newspapermen seemed to be drunk most of the time, talked with limp cigarettes drooping out of the corners of their profane mouths, slouched with their feet up on the desks, and grabbed feels from the hussies who flounced around the editors trying to make it as girl reporters.

Just a few doors down from the *Eagle* on Jay Street she had spotted the Star Burlesque Theater, and the undressed ladies on the billboards outside had shocked her. I suspect she thought the Star was some sort of annex to the *Eagle*.

What kind of life was this for her little boy Harold, who had been brought up to say his night and morning prayers, avert his eyes when he spotted some unspeakable words the local toughies had chalked on the sidewalk, and avoid playing with all the roughest boys on the block?

I was heartbroken. How was I to convince this good woman, short of moving out, that I desperately wanted this top assignment on the *Eagle,* that it was the chance of a lifetime?

I couldn't leave home, for mother had convinced me that if I did she would die within the hour. I think my father believed that, too.

Just when all seemed lost, I hit upon a plan that saved the day.

I phoned Tom Meany and Bill McCullough, both well-known reporters who were then in Florida writing baseball, and talked them into calling mother. They were to impress on her what fine, hard-working and virtuous characters newspaper writers really were. She had known Meany and Mac as star athletes at St. John's, which she firmly believed was the best high school in the country, and she admired them tremendously.

Both pulled this trick off well. McCullough assured her that composing baseball essays every day for his Brooklyn *Times* required a sharpness of mind that would have been lost with alcohol. And Bill said that he and his wife, Gladys, would keep an eye out to see that no harm befell her little boy.

I knew that Mac had been a heavy drinker since the days when he was arching those high set shots through the hoop for St. John's, and that even then he had kept a bottle of gin stashed in the water tank atop the toilet in the bathroom, so the priests wouldn't find it if they searched his locker.

Meany laid it on even thicker. He didn't know where all those ridiculous stories about hard-drinking writers came from, he said. And he told mother that he worked practically from dawn to dusk, interviewing players and writing pieces for *The Tablet*, a Catholic weekly my mother liked. Of course, not all the pieces appeared under his name, he said. His paper, the *World Telegram*, wouldn't allow that.

Actually, Meany had been a tough kid when he played quarterback ahead of Eddie Dooley (later a Dartmouth All-American) at St. John's Prep and with pickup teams on the Brooklyn Parade Grounds. But he was witty and had read a lot instead of going on to college. Now butter would have melted in his mouth as he charmed my mother right out of her resolution to keep her little boy at home.

The truth was, Meany and McCullough drank enough between them, in the course of a week, to float a small boat; it eventually killed them both.

And Gladys McCullough sure did keep an eye on me when I got to the Dodger camp! She came looking for me every evening about six to see if I could "help" Bill with his story. Bill was always beyond help by then, drunk as a lord. He knew he had a stand-in ghost, and he could lean on me after the favor he'd done for me with mother.

But Meany and McCullough saved my life—my life at the

Eagle, that is—and plunged me headlong into the unreal world of Babe Hoiman and Boily Grimes and Uncle Robbie and Casey Stengel.

When I got to the Miami Biltmore, I found that Dodger bumpkins like these, and Van Lingle Mungo and Chick Outen, the catcher who could not find any ball hit above his head, were as much out of place in a hotel like that as a hippie in cut-off jeans would be at a debutantes' party.

But at least I was getting to meet the journalistic giants, the guys who could really put words together, like Grantland Rice and Dan Parker, the slapstick satirist, John Kieran, Damon Runyon, Ring Lardner and Bugs Baer, Sid Mercer and George Phair, the wizard who started each story with a stanza of poetry he could turn out in sixty seconds flat, although it was never flat and he was seldom sober. Later in Philadelphia, I was to discover the trenchant pen, currently active on the *New York Times,* of Red Smith, whom I wanted to add to the *Eagle*'s fine staff. "What makes you think anything is closer to Broadway's big time than Philadelphia is, even if it is just across the river?" Smith was to ask me quizzically. I had no good answer, and "Coach" Stanley Woodward landed this talent for his pages in the New York *Herald Tribune,* where Smith began to prod the "badgers" and stuffed shirts just as W. O. McGeehan had earlier.

Meany and McCullough had "sprung" me out of Brooklyn into all this.

Except for them, I could never have started on the road that was to lead up to MacPhail's punch on my nose.

12. When Ebbets Field Was a Bad Joke

Hunting material for my column and as a backup man for Holmes, I had poked around Ebbets Field enough to learn that you could find more action in Mme. Tussaud's Wax Museum. Some of the characters with the ball club, like "Judge" Steve Mc-

Keever, who held court daily in a specially constructed armchair in the last row of the grandstand behind home plate, looked ready for the waxworks, at that.

The Judge was one of the McKeevers who had helped build the Brooklyn Bridge and had been warring with the Ebbets family for control of the ball club for years. In his seventies and decked out in a black derby hat and gold-handled cane, he accepted daily homage from droves of police captains, fire inspectors, and ward-heel politicians, for he was the one who handed out passes to the Dodger games. The genial old gent also had a colostomy, and he gave demonstrations of this surgical novelty along with the Annie Oakleys, if you could stand it.

Old Man McKeever was the only visible sign of a Dodger front office, except for a figurehead named Dave Driscoll who was allowed to do little else but worry. Once in a great while Joe Gilleadeau, a dapper hat manufacturer, or Jim Mulvey, who was into movie-making as Samuel Goldwyn's right-hand man, would surface. But they were from rival factions in the club ownership, and they would pass each other silently, as if embarrassed to be connected with a team that lost and lost and lost again.

On the field, things were run by a little round man with a tummy that looked as if somebody had shoved in a pillow to make him pass for a department-store Santa. Uncle Robbie, as Wilbert Robinson was called by one and all, was more of a habit than a manager. He had been managing the team since 1914, and here we were in the thirties, and nobody had asked him to leave.

Robbie couldn't remember his players' names, much less spell them. But so many came and went, you couldn't blame the old fellow. The Dodgers picked up every bit of baseball flotsam that floated past on the waiver lists.

One day I was in the dugout hunting a story when a complete stranger shuffled up to Robbie and introduced himself as the newest Dodger outfielder. He looked more like somebody trying out for the Salvation Army than for a major league outfield. An all-night bus ride had left him rumpled and bleary-eyed. Robbie called him by a name that sounded something like a vegetable: Rutabaga, or close to it. We found out later his square name was Roettger, Oscar Roettger.

Apparently on the theory that any new talent would be better than the veteran stumblebums, Robbie told the rookie to suit up, that he would play that afternoon. "You're in right field today, kid," said the manager, pointing vaguely out toward the famous Abe Stark sign that said "Hit Sign, Win Suit" in large letters. The sign was barely four feet off the ground, and a Lilliputian out-fielder with only one leg could have kept any line drive from hitting it; not once in all my years at Ebbets Field did I see Abe Stark give up a suit.

Roettger was taking his practice swings in the batting cage a few minutes later when Tom Meany, struggling with the day's lineup, asked Uncle Robbie how the new man spelled his name.

The roly-poly manager made several brave passes at it. "R-o-t . . ." he began, then backed up. "R-u-t-t . . ." he said, trying again; but it didn't look right as Meany copied it down.

"Hell's fire," said Robbie finally, with the satisfied smile of a man who has just solved a very large problem. "Put Boone in right field!"

That was pretty much how that hopeless, hapless team was run from day to day. Yet the little round manager bubbled with endless enthusiasm. After six or seven straight losses he would grin and say, "Don't worry, men. Daz'll stop these guys tomorrow!" If the Robins—called that by most papers because of Robinson's long tenure—were steamrollered by ten runs in the first game of a doubleheader, Robbie would chirp, "The Babe'll hit a couple in the second game."

"Daz" was Dazzy Vance, a pitcher who could strike out just about anybody he pleased, and "the Babe" was Herman, the only authentic Babe as far as Brooklyn was concerned, the Yankees' Ruth notwithstanding.

The Babe could hit in the dark, or falling out of bed. He clouted .393 for the full 1930 season, yet didn't win the batting title because Bill Terry picked that year to hit .401.

Herman could also run well and throw, although usually to the wrong base. But the big hayshaker seemed to have bad luck every time he pulled on a fielder's glove. He had trouble locating any ball hit higher than the button atop his cap; and line drives that ricocheted off the tricky right-field wall at Ebbets eluded him like a cake of soap in a sudsy bathtub. Legend had it that Herman had been hit on the head by several high flies, causing the absent-mindedness that made him run bases like a man blind-folded.

This the Babe denied emphatically when I brought it up re-cently at an old-timers' game. He attends those because he likes to show he can still hit.

"Never once did I get hit on the head by a fly ball," he insisted. "Wunst or twice on the shoulder maybe, but never on the head!"

I also ran down the vicious rumor that the Babe, who was their true Casey-at-the-Bat to all Ebbets Field fans, had stroked a clean double one sorry day, only to have it wind up as a triple play.

"Another lie!" stormed Herman, "How could I of done that when they was one out areddy? Chick Fewster an' Daz was on base when I hit the ball, but Chick held up to see if it would be caught, an' I never noticed an' run right by him. Daz ran back to thoid to tag up, an' we all met there. I remember the thoid base-man tagged all tree of us—but oney two tags counted!"

Vance was a late-blooming pitcher who had been pushed off on the Dodgers because every scout in the game had said the big guy with the windmill windup would never overcome his wild-ness. He led the National League seven straight times in strike-outs; but the Brooklyns were strictly sixth place in an eight-club league most of the time, except in 1924, when Vance did a Her-cules number and lifted the whole team into a shot at the pen-nant. He won twenty-eight and lost only six that year, and they might have won the whole thing had the Dazzler agreed to pitch in crackerbox Baker Bowl in Philadelphia. But he would never take his turn there. "Might hurt my record," he would say, in all honesty. And Uncle Robbie would not order him to pitch, for he was Robbie's pet.

Never mind! Vance became a household word in Greenpernt and Gowanus and Lon Guyland (Long Island), as Dan Parker kiddingly called the Dodger precincts in his column in the *Mirror*. Vance was still pitching for the Bums, as they got to be called, at forty-five years of age; which should give you an idea of how Flynn's, the bar across the street, preserved Ebbets Field's heroes in those days. Two more years on the mound and the Dazzler would have been stuffed and put on exhibit in the famous Brook-lyn Museum over on Eastern Parkway.

As it was, Dazzy barely missed the coming of MacPhail, and the Dodger Resurrection, in 1937.

But in the years just before MacPhail arrived on his white horse, the rest of the owners surely must have winked at the downhill slide of what should have been one of the richest franchises in the National League, where they should all have been picking up fat visiting-club checks.

They ignored it because in this setup they could shove their own rejects off on the defenseless Dodgers at holdup prices. There was no general manager in the nonexistent Brooklyn front office to stop this sort of thing, and Uncle Robbie was a patsy. He once traded a fine pitcher, Jess Petty, for a shortstop the Dodgers needed badly. But only after Glenn Wright arrived in Brooklyn was it discovered that he had hurt himself and was in fact a one-armed ballplayer. He could not throw across a room, much less an infield. But the fraud went uncorrected. Pittsburgh got away with Petty Larceny, and the Dodgers were stuck again.

Branch Rickey, who had seven hundred ballplayers in the minors, knew his lemons, and he selected some of his ripest for the Dodgers. One was Long Tom Winsett, who came to Brooklyn at a fancy price, billed as "the next Babe Ruth," amid terrific ballyhoo. Nobody thought to ask why Rickey didn't keep Winsett for his own Cardinals if he was that good.

During batting practice, the other ballplayers stopped whatever they were doing to stare at Winsett's beautiful swing, a classic stroke that was as much admired as Sam Snead's is in golf today. Not only that, but the Dodger rookie pumped ball after ball out of Ebbets Field, across Bedford Avenue into a parking lot where he created a windshield crisis until the attendants started parking the cars backward. Some of the balls were hit so high and far they vanished in the general direction of Canarsie.

But that was in batting practice. Once the game started, poor Tom couldn't get the bat and ball together.

To the ballplayers, Winsett was known as a "two o'clock hitter." All the games were in the afternoon then, and they started at three to get the "Wall Street crowd." Batting practice, where Long Tom put on his daily show, was at two.

Curious, I asked Rickey about Winsett's problem the next time the old horse-trader came to Brooklyn to peddle another junk ballplayer. I had grown friendly with Branch because of some magazine pieces I had written about his St. Louis Cardinal dynasty.

Mr. Rickey—as even his veteran employees addressed him— swore me to secrecy and explained.

"Watch that beautiful swing, my boy," he chuckled, "Mr. Winsett sweeps that bat in the same plane every time, no matter where the ball is pitched!"

Rickey let that sink in and then went on.

"Woe unto the pitcher who throws the ball where the Winsett bat is functioning," Branch said, sounding every bit like the psalm-singer the writers pictured him to be, "but throwing it almost anywhere else in the general area of home plate is safe!"

Safe, indeed! The pitchers grew to love Long Tom, who hit only eight home runs in almost five hundred at bats during three years of high hopes in Brooklyn.

One of those who held those high hopes until the bitter end was Max Carey, who had become the manager when Uncle Robbie's comic term ended in 1932.

Carey was a God-fearing, college-educated man out of Concordia Seminary, and the warring McKeever-Ebbets factions one day got together in a civil conversation that lasted long enough for them to agree on him.

Max had played sixteen glorious seasons for the Pittsburgh Pirates, but then wound up with the Dodgers, as all broken-down ballplayers seemed to. Even though his legs had started to go, Carey stole thirty-two bases in his first full year with the Brooklyns, and they hadn't had anybody who could move that fast unless it was the Ebbets heirs, who had to keep ducking the sheriff.

But most of all, Max was well-scrubbed and polite, and didn't chew tobacco, so he was given the job of banishing buffoonery and imparting some decorum to this undisciplined crew.

It just didn't work. One of the first problems Carey had to wrestle with was Hack Wilson, and Max flunked badly. But then Wilson might have defeated anybody, including Billy Graham, Savonarola, and a whole platoon of Alcoholics Anonymous.

Wilson had been nicknamed after Hackenschmidt, the famous wrestler. Hack was a barrel-chested little (5 foot, 6 inch) two hundred-pound outfielder with the muscled arms of a smithy and the feet (size 5) of a ballet dancer. This cameo Hercules had hit fifty-six home runs and driven in the unheard-of total of one hundred ninety runs for the clouting Chicago Cubs in 1930, just two years before, and that is a record that may stand forever. Where Wilson himself seemed to stand forever was at the handiest bar. He guzzled booze day and night, and as soon as he started to slip, the Cubs shipped him to—where else?—Brooklyn.

Carey, the preacher, tried a few fire-and-brimstone talks, but his words seemed to roll right off fun-loving Hack's broad back. So Max called a meeting of the entire team. A hitter as good as this—even hung over, Wilson was hitting .300 for the Dodgers and pumping out homers—had to be saved somehow! So Carey tried the psychological approach: health, doctors' warnings, and all that.

As he called the player meeting to order, Max stood at a table on which he had placed two glasses and a plate of live angle-worms. One glass was filled with water, the other with gin, Wilson's favorite elixir.

With a flourish, the manager dropped a worm in the glass of water. It wriggled happily.

Now Max plunged the same worm into the gin; it stiffened and expired. A murmur ran through the room, and some of the players were obviously impressed.

Not Wilson. Hack didn't even seem interested.

Carey waited a little, hoping for some delayed reaction from his wayward member. When none came, he prodded: "That mean anything to you, Wilson?"

"Sure, Skipper," answered this sawed-off tree trunk of a man, anxious to oblige. "It proves if you drink gin you'll never have no worms!"

Wilson burned out almost as fast as Max's demonstration worm. He was washed up at thirty-four after three rollicking seasons with the Dodgers, and dead at forty-eight.

Max Carey's reform ideas weren't working, and the looting of the Dodgers continued, as the other owners shoved off on the Brooklyn team all the over-the-hill ballplayers they had.

This made for pretty grim reporting in the *Eagle*, and for Mc-

Cullough's paper, too, for he was drinking heavily, and I had to cover him most of the time. Many people tried to talk some sense into Bill, for he was a pleasant fellow, and they felt sorry for his embarrassed wife.

On one of his frequent visits from the Cardinals' base at Bradenton to the Dodger camp, Branch Rickey, a teetotaler himself, talked McCullough into taking the pledge.

A week later Rickey was back again, peddling another lemon, and he sought out Gladys McCullough. "Bill isn't drinking anymore?" he asked hopefully.

Gladys thought a minute and then said, "No, Mr. Rickey, but not any less, either!"

With Carey's head obviously on the chopping-block although his contract still had a full season to run, there wasn't one of the twelve reporters in the Dodger camp who had the foggiest notion of who his successor would be. For a solid month I did two headline stories a night: one for the *Eagle,* and a completely different second-day angle for the *Times* under McCullough's name. I was just as proud of my handiwork for the rival paper as I was of what appeared under my byline.

McCullough was nice about it, too. When copies of his paper caught up with us at training camp, he often complimented me on stories that he saw under his name. But as long as Bill knew he had me as a pinch hitter, he drank more and more and wrote less and less.

The Dodgers were so dull under Carey that they helped drive more than McCullough to drink. Brooklyn fans had shown they could forgive errors in the field and incompetence, but they wouldn't stand for dullness, and Carey had no color, no flair as a leader. The fans were clamoring for a return to the rollicking days of Uncle Robbie.

Names, big baseball names, were bandied about by all the writers like confetti in a wind tunnel. I would give one of them the inside track for the job when I wrote my piece for the *Eagle.* Later that night, when I ghosted for McCullough, I would nominate somebody entirely different in the *Times.* Who would it be? We were all guessing.

One morning while he was still sober, McCullough got a penny postcard from Glendale, California. The message on it was just,

"Leaving for Brooklyn on business." It was signed by Casey Stengel, whom Bill knew very well from his daffy days as a playing Dodger, when Casey let the bird out from under his baseball cap at home plate to ridicule an umpire.

Bill didn't bother to show me this postcard, and I thought it was odd that he wrote his own story that night. It was the first time in a week I hadn't had to pinch-hit.

McCullough had been smart enough to put two and two together. He went out on a limb with a story in his Brooklyn *Times* saying Stengel would be named to succeed Carey as Dodger manager in a day or two.

When Casey did indeed get the job, it was a clean beat for McCullough and the *Times,* and all hell broke loose at the embarrassed *Eagle*.

For a while, it looked as if Mrs. Parrott would get her wish, and her little boy Harold would be saved from the pitfalls of the sinful newspaper game, his journalistic career at an end. I should have been fired.

But I was saved by Harris Crist.

I was still Crist's pet.

Part III

✕✕✕

The Redhead, the Mahatma, the Lip, and the Black Ty Cobb

13. MacPhail and the Rhyming Reporters

Stengel gave no hint in Brooklyn of the wizardry he was to show years later as the leader of great Yankee teams. As manager of the Dodgers, Casey made wisecracks instead of the reforms Carey had tried. Neither changed the sorry Brooklyn team, which lolled around the bottom of the league.

I can't forget the very first question I put to Stengel at the 1934 Dodger training camp. He had just received another reject, an outfielder named Frenchy Bordagaray, who had been bumped out of the American League. Bordagaray reported to the Dodger camp with a mustache and a violin, two questionable assets.

Seeking to put together a hopeful story about the "new speed" in what had been for years a slow-footed Dodger outfield, I asked Stengel if Bordagaray were the fastest man on the team, or perhaps even in the whole National League.

Casey went into one of those pantomimes with accompanying doubletalk that he was to make famous later.

"You might say that, Parrott," the Professor finally blurted. "But you'd be even righter if you wrote Frenchy wuz the fastest man—*runnin' to the wrong base!*"

That was indeed the book on Bordagaray, but you couldn't write jokes like that in a newspaper in Brooklyn, where the Dodgers were more of a religion than a baseball team.

Stengel's jokes got better, but the team didn't. The warring owners of the team canned Casey and put in a rough and tough ex-pitcher, "Stubble-Chin" Burleigh Grimes, who never shaved for two days before he was due to take the mound. Now they had to pay two managers, for Stengel had another year on his contract. And there wasn't enough money in the till to pay one, let alone two.

Crist got so annoyed at these front-office antics that he called me off the Dodger beat. Warburg, the Johnny-come-lately sports editor, had assigned himself to cover the America's Cup yacht races. He made such a mess of it that the managing editor cut him adrift while he was still at sea somewhere off Newport, Rhode Island.

Crist talked me into taking the job as sports editor, at twice the salary I was making as a writer. I didn't like the idea of staying in the office, but with Murphy to help, I thought I could get the *Eagle* sport pages back on the track. They had become a shambles under Warburg.

The first thing I did, now that I had some muscle, was to hire Holmes back on the paper to write about the Dodgers.

Tommy had plenty to tell about. The Ebbets heirs, borrowing and borrowing against their stock in the Brooklyn Baseball Club, finally reached the point where the Brooklyn Trust Company, which held the mortgage on the club, threatened to foreclose.

The McKeever faction had held on; in fact, they're still holding on today, and the one-third of the franchise that does not have the O'Malley name stamped all over it belongs to the two daughters (one of whom, Ann, is married to ex-pitcher Ralph Branca), and Bud, the only son of old Judge McKeever's daughter Dearie. Her husband was Jim Mulvey, the movie man, and it was Mulvey who grew alarmed when George V. McLaughlin threatened to sell the ball club out from under them all to redeem all the loans his Brooklyn Trust Company had made through the years to keep the leaky, drifting Dodger ship afloat and on course.

Mulvey and McLaughlin, a former New York City Police Commissioner, went to Ford Frick, the National League president, to get his advice on a strong general manager who would stop the looting of the franchise by the hungry other owners.

Frick consulted Rickey, the master mechanic, who advised that Larry MacPhail was the only man for a job like this.

MacPhail had come back to Rickey on his knees after being bounced out of Cincinnati. "I'm not going to take another drink for a year," the Old Man's pupil had vowed.

"Why not make that a lifetime, instead of a year?" Rickey had said.

But the Mahatma regarded MacPhail as his most precocious protégé, and he talked the Brooklyn group, as well as Frick, into installing Larry to pump some life into the dying Dodgers.

The Redhead roared into the *Eagle*'s territory like a hurricane.

I was writing a sports column, as well as running the sports pages in the office, and I made it my business to be with MacPhail when he went out to look at rundown Ebbets Field, which he had not visited in years.

Larry gasped at what confronted him.

When we walked into it, the entrance rotunda to the old ballpark echoed to our steps like some vast underground cavern; the mildewed, peeling ceiling brought to mind an overage Italian opera house.

The place was built like some giant cornucopia, and for years it had funneled the faithful of Flatbush into comically small entrance gates, where they struggled past the turnstiles to watch a fumbling team that was more of a headache than a pleasure.

It was even more difficult to escape from this monstrosity than it was to enter, and after a disappointing game fights often broke out among the Brooklyn bugs who were hurrying to put behind them the trauma of still another fiasco—perhaps a base-running goof by Babe Herman or a pitching blowup by Boom-Boom Beck or Van Lingle Mungo.

So there was something symbolic about that dreadful lobby, which curved inward almost to the home plate area, enmeshing like some giant fish trap the fans who thrashed about, frantic in their frustration. Elation, the kind that comes with winning, or even simple peace of mind had eluded these good folk for more than a dozen years. Ebbets Field and the ballplayers in it were like an insidious habit that would not let go until it had hurt you or bent you out of shape.

As we stood there that day, I felt this depressing spell working on MacPhail. And as I look back now, I know that it eventually broke the Redhead in half, too, despite his bravado and his temporary successes.

Out on the pock-marked diamond, a few of the Dodger players who had been invited to this informal press conference stood around in street clothes, obviously suspicious of the new broom,

MacPhail, who was talking very big. They all wondered if they'd be kept, or swept out. If they *were* kept, they'd have to talk contract to this new guy soon.

The Dodgers had been a rag-tag team in 1937, losing three games for every two they won and finishing with a slide that saw them lose sixteen of their last seventeen. How could you sell tickets to see a bunch of bumblers like this?

MacPhail tried to divert attention from the gloomier aspects—the humpty-dumpty players and the rundown ballpark—by talking grandly about the new $30,000 paint job, which had already started. Larry waved at the chipped and blistered paint on the splintered seats that surrounded him; even on the ones that were intact, the color had faded like last summer's flowers. "We'll paint every seat in the park," he promised, "every girder, every post, every wall." The job had already started in right field, and the section the painters had done stood out like an eyesore; it was a brilliant shade of blue.

"Can you believe they're painting it all turquoise?" said a writer, trying to strike up a conversation with Blimp Phelps, the overweight catcher.

"Don't try to kid me, mister," the Blimp replied, menacingly. "I know that ain't no color, it's a animal!"

The bankers—George V and his Brooklyn Trust chorus—screamed to high heaven when MacPhail spent the $30,000 on paint.

Larry's answer was to put $50,000 into Dolf Camilli, a home-run hitter who was also a dancing master around first base. The Phillies had been peddling him all over. MacPhail bought. The bankers roared louder. Wasn't this new guy hired to *save* money? All he seemed to be doing was *spending*.

When gigged about this, the Redhead changed the subject and talked grandly about the arc lights he was putting in. Night baseball would cure everything!

The Baseball Writers' Dinner, featuring a show that poked fun and venom at all the moguls in baseball, picked MacPhail as its No. 1 target in 1938. One of the reporters, dressed in the loud clothes that Larry seemed to love, and with radio antenna and light bulbs sticking out all over him, came on billed as "Mac-Phailure" and sang:

When mortgage-holders squall,
I introduce a yellow ball . . .
Oh, I've got a pocket full of schemes!

When there's no one in your park,
I can fill it after dark . . .
Oh, I've got a pocket full of schemes!

It was the age of rhyming reporters, and the very best of the breed were Grantland Rice, Bugs Baer, Dan Parker, and George Phair. As you look back at their stuff now, it scanned perfectly and fairly jumped off the page at you to tell its message.

When Jack Dempsey won the heavyweight championship in his famous brawl with Luis Firpo, he came back to New York City to be honored by a big parade. Jack, really a country bumpkin then, marched up Broadway at the head of a small army of broken-nosed trainers and seconds, lawyers, publicity flacks, and assorted hangers-on and grifters. George Phair, knowing these leeches were bent on separating the young man from his newly won dollars, summed the story up in a couplet at the head of his column in the next morning's paper:

Hail, the conquering hero comes—
Surrounded by a bunch of bums!

Dan Parker, a giant of a man (6 feet, 6 inches), who wrote a laugh-a-line sports column in the tabloid New York *Mirror,* seized on MacPhail as the butt of his jokes about the Daffy Dodgers, as he called them. Accompanying Parker's prose and poetry were deft cartoons and caricatures by artist Fred Weatherly, and MacPhail often came out looking like a clown.

It was mostly in good fun, although there were some sharp barbs. Larry did not resent it in the least; in fact Joe Williams of the *World Telegram,* one of his more caustic critics, drew a personal letter from the Redhead that contained the supreme insult, or perhaps two of them. "You copy all the mistakes in Parker's column," wrote MacPhail, "but he manages to keep his stuff interesting. Yours is dull as dishwater!"

Hardly a day passed without Parker devoting a few paragraphs

to the Barnum of Brooklyn. When star pitcher Mungo came up
with a sore arm and couldn't throw for two months, Parker diagnosed it as the direct result of landing on his shoulder when the
ace of the staff had to leap out a window at midnight in spring
training to escape the irate husband of a dancer with whom he
was having a romantic fling. Accompanying the piece was a
caricature of MacPhail throwing hundred-dollar bills to the
winds, while all Mungo could do was hit practice flies to the outfielders. This two-liner told it all:

> I pay fifteen grand to Mungo
> Just to hit an occasional fungo . . .

Of course jibes like this brought the banker bloodhounds down
on MacPhail even harder, but they never slowed him up. He ran
to the bank to borrow money for the steel towers and transform-
ers, lamps and bulbs he needed for night baseball; they complained. He brought in Babe Ruth as a coach to divert attention
from his sorry team; the money men threw up their hands. He
had to put money into a deal with Rickey to get Durocher out of
St. Louis to play shortstop; they groaned some more. This was
early 1938, and there was no money coming in. The team's biggest
spring training crowd in Florida was two thousand. Back in
Ebbets Field, they lost fifteen of their first twenty; and when they
went on a western trip, the top crowd was 6,800 in Pittsburgh on
a Sunday. MacPhail had to fire Burleigh Grimes, the manager,
and pay him off for an unserved year. Worse, he now had to
choose—and pay—another manager.

Larry leaned toward Ruth, who still had a magic name, although he was a tragic figure. Those closest to MacPhail, notably
John McDonald, the pal he had brought with him from Cincinnati, talked it up for Durocher.

Leo didn't help his cause when he had a fight with Ruth and
pushed the Babe into a locker in a crumpled heap. It was as un-
thinkable as pulling a crutch out from under your grandfather.

Still McDonald pushed for Durocher every time he had Larry's
ear. He pointed out Leo knew how to win, had been the 1934
champion Cards' kingpin.

MacPhail scoffed at the idea. "The guy can't even manage himself," he snorted. "Look at all the bouncing checks, the unpaid alimony—"

Things went from bad to worse, and the players started to lie down on Grimes. The new leader had to be picked—fast. But who?

One evening MacPhail and McDonald were riding in a taxi, and Larry suddenly sat bolt upright. "I've got it," he said. Then, "The guy's a leader of men; he'll do the job!"

"Who are you talking about?" McDonald asked.

"Durocher! He'll be our manager for 1939!"

No mention of the fact that Leo had been McDonald's candidate all along; not even a hint that the name had ever come up before.

MacPhail was as unpredictable as a gust of wind.

He struggled night and day to get that team up out of the depths. It seemed he just couldn't exist without success.

Worse yet, he couldn't live *with* it.

When his big moment came, he would invariably throw off sparks, blow a fuse, and go off on a ridiculous tangent, like an unharnessed bolt of electricity.

Never did that become more clear than on June 15, 1938.

It should have been Larry MacPhail's most triumphant night in baseball: an Ebbets Field overfull with 38,748 fans, for a game that would have drawn five thousand that afternoon; an eloquent answer to the writers, who had been saying night baseball was no longer a novelty (since MacPhail had started it in Cincinnati in 1935) and would leave sophisticated New Yorkers cold. A beautiful evening, with a second-straight no-hitter by Johnny Vander Meer. Vandy was from neighboring New Jersey, near enough for Dodger fans to adopt—for this one night only—and they were rooting on every pitch for him to get this gem, even when he walked the bases full in the last of the ninth.

It was everything that Barnum or De Mille could have hoped for. It should have been MacPhail's most satisfying night. Instead, he was hating every minute of it.

It took me two hours to find out why. And when I did find out, I still couldn't believe it.

14. Grantland Rice and George Phair

MacPhail went on a rampage at Ebbets Field the night of Double No-Hit Vander Meer's classic; I mean raging, wild-eyed mad.

He was tearing phones off the wall trying to fire a guy in Zanesville, Ohio, whose name was Ducky Holmes; he was screaming at long-distance operators and supervisors over the phone from the press bar he had built up in the rafters, out of sight and sound of the classic he should have been watching out where his customers were.

Who was Ducky Holmes, and what terrible thing had he done in Zanesville, Ohio? If the Holmes affair was more important than all that had happened to MacPhail this night, it had to be a helluva story, I reasoned. It should make a great column for to-morrow's *Eagle*.   .

Every single thing had gone right for MacPhail, and not the least of them was this night's gate, just over $100,000, which would turn things around for the Redhead and a team that had been starving to death. You could read all the signs that night: It was to mean an average of twenty-seven thousand fans a night for the seven night games he had had to beg from skeptical National League owners who had been predicting night baseball was just a passing fad. It meant the Dodger attendance would jump from 450,000 to 633,000 on this man's inventive courage alone, and that a team that had been to the bank forty times in the last ten years for loans totaling $1.5 million would make money for the first time since 1920. The Bankrupt Brooklyns were out of the woods!

Every detail had come off right. Even the $4,000 for a pregame show the bankers said he was squandering to get Olympic hero sprinter Jesse Owens to run a pregame race now seemed well spent; and there was another race between the popular announcers, Red Barber and 300-pound Al Helfer. The fans ate it all up. Every soul in the ballpark—save three—hung goggle-eyed on every pitch in this once-in-a-lifetime ballgame.

The three were in the otherwise deserted press bar, a saloon far up in the attic behind home plate. One was MacPhail, who was raging as he jiggled the telephone receiver with no results. How could he get an outside line when Willie, the old gal who had run the switchboard since the place opened, had deserted her post to run up for a glimpse of history in the making?

The second man in the place was the bartender, known only as Hymie, an old MacPhail spar-mate. And of course there I sat, trying to fit together the odd pieces in this weird tableau.

Hymie, tethered in his isolated saloon, couldn't see one inch of the playing field. But he had learned to read the crowd noises that flowed up through his open window from the fans below as unerringly as a tribal chieftain gets the news from his drums in the jungle. He could distinguish between a strikeout with the bases full and a fine running catch that ended the inning. He also had the benefit of a human chain of communication on the big plays. It went from Benny, the pressbox porter, to Slattery, the special cop at the press bar entrance, and thence to Hymie. He kept their larynxes properly oiled.

By now the little bartender was as completely immersed in the no-hitter as if he'd been pitching himself. Vandy, tiring fast, had walked the bases full with one out in the bottom of the ninth and the crowd groaned when Ernie Koy, always a Vander Meer nemesis, strode to the plate.

"Strike two," Hymie announced, "Now trow 'im a coive, Vandy."

MacPhail, still wrestling with the dead phone, paid no attention at all. He was still screaming for Holmes in Ohio and God above.

"Struck 'im out!" yelled Hymie triumphantly, jumping straight up and down, "Alls he's gotta do now is get Durocher." Leo was indeed the twenty-seventh out Vandy needed for immortality.

The Dodger manager squibbed a puny fly to short center that the Reds' speedy Harry Craft raced in to take at his shoe-tops, holding the ball aloft for all to see.

"Got him!" exulted Hymie, who couldn't have been happier.

MacPhail? He cursed bitterly, giving up the phone as a bad job now, for he knew the writers would swarm in soon. When he poured himself a fast double brandy it gave me the chance to pump the Ducky Holmes facts out of him. He responded with a roar.

"Four years ago that dumb son of a bitch released Vander Meer outright when he was managing one of our farms teams. Without permission, too. Except for that fathead, Vandy would still be a Dodger, and the *whole* show would have been ours tonight—"

MacPhail spun on his heel, trying to escape Dan Parker and the rest of his critics, who were filling up the room fast now. His way was blocked by a little old man in a Western Union uniform, leather puttees and all. The wizened one was forcing the familiar yellow envelope on MacPhail. Larry tore it open, and his eyes raced through the message, which seemed to make him even madder. Rolling the telegram into a compact pellet the size of a large marble, he let out a roar like a wounded water buffalo and looked around for a target.

Nothing better being available, he hit Hymie right on the forehead and, still raging, fled the room.

The bartender retrieved the missile, and together we spread it out on the bar to see what had so ticked off the Redhad. It said: "CONGRATULATIONS ON YOUR BIG NIGHT GAME SUCCESS. HOPE YOU WIN. DUCKY HOLMES."

Instead of congratulating MacPhail on his first extravaganza under the lights, the bankers complained about the $10,000 electric bill. But nothing ruffled Larry. He kept right on promoting and filled Ebbets Field again with a "musical depreciation night" —any fan who brought a musical instrument of any kind, whether it was a kazoo or the baby grand piano that two musclar fans from the waterfront showed up with, got in free. Again the bankers moaned about the money lost on the free admissions.

Treasurers, accountants, and bankers are like that the world over, I was to learn. I remember what happened when I arranged the Angels' first "two-tickets-for-the-price-of-one" game in Anaheim, with a comedy ballgame between Gene Autry's KMPC disc jockeys and a well-put-together team of airline stewardesses as an added attraction. It was a poor date on the Angel schedule, and we drew fourteen thousand more fans than would have come normally.

Before the game that night, I was jabbed by Francis Xavier Leary, the team's bookkeeper. "I see you gave away seven thousand tickets tonight," he accused.

I was stunned. I felt we had sold seven thousand extra seats, besides getting fourteen thousand people into the park who might return another time. And far be it from Leary to think about all the hot dogs, beer, and parking spaces those seven thousand people paid for.

It's a difference in point of view. Some pessimists always feel that the gas tank is half empty. MacPhail and the optimists believe the same tank is half full.

When he heard the bankers beef about the electric bill and the passes he had given away on musical night, Larry pointed to the "service charge" he was collecting at the pass gate, the famous Gate 19, where a little bulldog of a man known only as "Clarkie" had repulsed all kinds of gate-crashers through the years. Clarkie hated all pass-grabbers. He had turned back everybody, from the notorious One-Eyed Connolly to a young man who had appeared with a 50-pound block of ice, supposedly for the players' clubhouse, on a 100-degree day. The ice melted, but Clarkie's heart didn't, and the would-be crasher succeeded only in getting himself soaking wet before he gave up.

Old Judge McKeever was handing out passes like confetti, and the newspapers got whole pads of them, which copy-boys and some of the writers used as barter with the butcher and baker. This had been going on for years, but what could MacPhail do about it? Never mind, he'd think of something!

He came up with another "first," a fifty-cent "service charge" for all those who came in "free." And this was all gravy, for neither the visiting club nor the National League, not even Uncle Sam, shared in it.

This was great stuff in Dan Parker's typewriter, and the *Mirror* columnist immortalized in rhyme the shock that Clarkie was said to have suffered when he saw the pass-grabbers actually *paying* to enter:

> Limp and broken and unconscious,
>   There's a human form revealed
> In the marble-tiled rotunda
>   That leads to Ebbets Field . . .
>
> Faithful he had been to duty,
>   But the shock was too extreme:
> Clarkie fell across his turnstile,
>   Passed out, not in, at Gate 19!

The sports pages of that day carried a rich harvest of rhyme, which is in itself a rebuttal of young Mr. Shaw's put-down of the writers as semiliterate. Consider this, called "The Two Sides of War," which Grantland Rice used to lead off his column on the day of an Army-Navy football game:

> All wars are planned by older men
> In council rooms apart,
> Who call for greater armament
> And map the battle chart.
>
> But out along the shattered fields
> Where golden dreams turned gray,
> How very young their faces were,
> Where all the dead men lay.
>
> Portly and solemn in their pride,
> The elders cast their vote
> For this or that or something else
> That sounds a warlike note.
>
> But where their sightless eyes stare out
> Beyond life's vanished joys
> I've noticed nearly all the dead
> Were hardly more than boys!

Granny Rice, whom I got to know quite well, was a charming Southern gentleman of many skills. It was he who first called the great Notre Dame backfield—Miller, Layden, Stuhldreher, and Crowley—which killed so many great opponents, the "Four Horsemen," after war, death, famine, and pestilence in the Apocalypse. But there is a mania now for tearing down the old heroes, and recently I read—in Jerry Holtzman's fine book *No Cheering in the Press Box*—that a writer named George Strickler claims to have invented the Four Horsemen.

Two of the most quoted lines you'll find anywhere are the last two in Granny's "Ode to an Alumnus" about an old football idol returning to his campus:

> Keep coming back; and though the world
> May romp across your spine,

> Let ev'ry game's end find you still
> Upon the battling line.

> For when the Great Scorer comes
> To mark against your name
> He writes—not that you won or lost—
> But how you played the game.

Granny told me many times how he envied Dan Parker and George E. Phair for the light and fluffy stuff they could turn out in verse. I remember how we both laughed at Parker's account of the night he turned drama critic to review the serious acting debut of Slapsie Maxie Rosenbloom, the former light-heavyweight champion. It was a parody done to the tune of "Love in Bloom," a song hit of the day:

> Can it be the cheese that fills the breeze
> With rare and magic perfume?
> Oh, no, it isn't the cheese,
> —It's Rosenbloom!

Rice would tell you that the best of all the sports page poets was Phair, who worked for Hearst and covered the Dodgers in the thirties. This whimsical composer never let down the fans who turned to sports as an escape from the front-page stories of war, inflation, rape, and other assorted atrocities.

Phair covered the Dodgers when they trained in Orlando, Florida, an exercise that George considered sheer nonsense, and never once during the entire month of March did he leave his room in the San Juan Hotel to go to the ballpark. We would cover for him with the needed paragraphs about the game itself, but not one among us could produce the lines of verse that George always led off with. Accordingly, we would have to rush back to the hotel and sober him up, at least partially, to get him in tune.

I remember one particular day on which the Dodgers had been shut out by Guy Bush, a Chicago pitcher with long sideburns that made him look like a Mississippi riverboat gambler. Told what had happened, Phair dashed this off with hardly a quiver:

> A long and lanky lad named Bush
> Wore sideburns on his mush;

> Between his whiskers and his curves
> He wrecked a lot of Dodger nerves.

Another time, arriving toward the end of a benefit banquet for the widow of extremely likable Manny Vaughan, who had been a sportswriters in Milwaukee, Phair was pressed to produce a few lines that would climax the events of the evening.

The dear departed Manny had a gruff and grouchy brother, Irving Vaughan, who reported on the Cubs for years and years in the Chicago *Tribune* and was still grousing at everybody in the Wrigley Field pressbox at the time of his brother's funeral.

Three sheets to the wind, the obliging Phair nevertheless rattled off this jingle in jig time:

> Manny Vaughan, dead and gone,
> Leaving us to carry on;
> To his ideals he was unswerving,
> Too damn bad it wasn't Irving.

There were other poets of note. A lot of the older writers of that day, like Roscoe McGowen, the gentleman from the *Times,* were as familiar with Shakespeare and sonnets as they were with jockstraps. They could dash off a sparkling couplet or quatrain in half the time it took David Shaw of the Los Angeles *Times* to throw a harpoon into a whole generation of sportswriters.

Tom Meany, who had taken a dislike to Bill Terry, then the manager of the Giants, collaborated on a skit at the writers' show that probably led to Terry's being fired. Meany thought Memphis Bill was crude and rude to writers in general, and pompous on top of it.

I didn't go along with this, for Terry went out of his way to be nice to me and taught me a lot of the inside baseball that led to the Giants' 1936 and 1937 pennants.

In the Meany skit, a writer made up to resemble Terry was conducting a press conference to describe his latest triumph. I remember the details well, for I was one of the actors. This jingle set the scene:

> The Tennessee colonel,
> flushed with success,

> Was tossing his pearls
> To the swine of the press . . .

That and several more verses like it brought down the house. It put Terry in a bad light, and Stoneham eventually canned him, installing Mel Ott. Ott was as bad a manager as Terry had been good, but the writers had had their way.

MacPhail got more headlines and more ink and radio time in his first three years in Brooklyn with his ragamuffin team than either the staid, pinstripe Yankees or Terry's Giants. This despite the fact that the Yankees were on a streak that netted seven pennants in eight years. The Giants too were always contenders at that time.

How did he pull this off?

15. MacPhail Raids the Scrap Heap

MacPhail was carrying on a running gum battle with writers, cartoonists, editors, photographers—and, of course, with his bankers, who were still on him for overspending to snap up every reject who came down the waiver pipe.

Now and then Larry would get a gem off the scrap heap: Dixie Walker, who played the outfield like a man walking on eggs, was one. Dixie's American League history read like a medical book, he had been sewn together so often in the shoulder and patched up in the knees. He developed into a stylish hitter, one of the best I ever saw against lefties, although he swung left himself. Moreover, he kissed babies, gave autographs, went to fan club meetings, and had numberless pictures taken with politicians. Dan Parker dubbed him "The Peepul's Cherce."

But for every Walker, there were flops like Roy Cullenbine, Melo Almada, and Ernie Koy.

"Hot Potato" Luke Hamlin was awful when MacPhail first bought him from Detroit. Luke seemed unable to keep the ball inside the park, and got his nickname from the sad fact that when it was hit where it could be reached, it was often too hot to handle. On top of that, Hamlin was wild. Once, after he had walked home the winning runs in two successive games, Tom Meany wrote, "Hamlin is so wild, if he fell off the Brooklyn Bridge, he would not hit the water." That infuriated MacPhail, who wrestled briefly with Meany the next day.

But the fact was that the sports editor of every Manhattan daily had to assign a man to cover this circus and follow MacPhail around, for the man made news, and usually in time for the early editions.

In what amounted to a daily newsreel of Dodger antics, Dan Parker began playing with MacPhail's initials, L.S., for Leland Stanford.

If Larry let loose a particularly withering blast at some other owner or perhaps at a reporter, Parker would report that "Lucifer Sulphurious" MacPhail had spouted sparks and flames and scorched somebody.

After that first night game in which Larry crammed more than thirty-eight thousand souls into a ballpark that had less than thirty-two thousand seats, he became "Letemall Standup MacPhail" in Parker's column.

The Great Man was borrowing, borrowing all the time—at the bank or from the ball club treasury. If anybody objected, MacPhail roared. I think his roars intimidated the bankers eventually. There was no doubt that, when he roared in the Dodger office, everybody jumped, particularly a nice little man named Bill Gibson, the Dodger treasurer.

One day, heading for the racetrack as usual, Larry noticed that his wallet was thin. Over the office intercom he commanded the treasurer to meet him in the lobby of the building in five minutes with five hundred-dollar bills. He was late, and he didn't want to miss the first race.

Gibson, a milktoast, started to shake. He had incurred the wrath of this big blowhard before, and he wanted everything perfect this time. He opened the safe, extracted the greenbacks, and got to the lobby before his boss. Little Billy was smiling the smile of those who have followed orders to the dot when he handed the

Redhead 500 *dollar* bills, neatly wrapped, a hundred to the packet.

MacPhail looked at the singles as if they were slime; he flung the five packets of bills right into Gibson's face. Two of the wrappers broke, and there were dollar bills all over the lobby. The burst of air that blew in when the Redhead, still roaring, spun the revolving door on the way out to his waiting taxi didn't help the worried treasurer retrieve his airborne money.

Whitlow Wyatt arrived in 1939 and developed into the best MacPhail bargain pickup of all. But for every Wyatt there were three expensive lemons like Newt Kimball and Mace Brown and Cletus Elwood Poffenberger; they didn't add up to one pitcher among them.

Poffenberger, called the Baron, was the worst of all. He could throw hard, but he drank even harder. He was always missing whenever Durocher wanted him to pitch. Strangely, he brought out the tender side of the gruff MacPhail.

One stifling day in Philadelphia, when it was his turn to work, the Baron stayed at the hotel and gave a message to the players on the bus to carry to Durocher: It was just too hot to pitch that day, he said.

Leo was still fuming about this when he got back to the hotel. But now Poffenberger was missing.

The manager waited up in the lobby until almost two before his quarry showed up, weaving and bleary-eyed.

As they stood in front of the fancy hand-carved front desk at the rococo old Bellevue-Stratford, Durocher challenged: "Do you know what time it is?"

Poffenberger pointed to a row of clocks above the desk; they told what hour it was in Hong Kong, London, Hawaii—and Los Angeles. "Thasha one I'm goin' by," he mumbled, indicating the L.A. time, which was 11 o'clock.

Durocher canned him on the spot and sent him home.

The next day it was the old softy, MacPhail, who phoned Durocher and begged for another chance for Poffenberger. Perhaps it was because Larry had scouted the Baron when he was pitching for Detroit and had seen a good arm that could help the club, if its owner would go to bed once in awhile. But more likely it was the sentimental side of Larry, who had hoisted a few too many himself more than once and knew very well how the unfrocked Baron felt.

Durocher relented, and they sent Poffenberger a check for $150, his air fare to the next Dodger stop on the road.

But the Baron never came back. Neither did the check.

When the story of this heart-warming little episode leaked into the newspapers, MacPhail completely denied the whole thing. In those days, he was denying almost everything that did happen, because so much of it was negative.

This led Dan Parker, his number-one biographer-critic at the time, to write, "The Redhead is so careful of the truth, he uses it very sparingly." The truth was that this Jekyll-Hyde fellow seemed to have a built-in disconnecting gear that he could use at will to sever himself from reality.

Never was this gizmo used better than the day in 1940 when Ducky Joe Medwick was skulled by a beanball at Ebbets Field.

Medwick had just come to the Dodgers in a most mysterious deal involving $132,000, a fortune in those days. Part of this was heartbreak balm to Branch Rickey in St. Louis for losing Pistol Pete Reiser in a cover-up attempt that failed—and could have gotten both Rickey and MacPhail kicked out of baseball for life. We'll get to the details of that caper later.

There had been bad blood between Medwick and pitcher Bob Bowman when both were with the Cardinals. Now the two met in an elevator in the Hotel New Yorker shortly after Medwick was traded to the Dodgers. The third party in the lift was Durocher, in the middle of things as usual.

Bowman started it with a snide crack about Durocher's light hitting; Medwick chimed in to indicate the pitcher would never be in that afternoon's game long enough to face the eighth-place hitter, which was Lippy. "We'll have you out of there before you get anybody out, gutless," said Ducky, who made a move at his foe. Bowman wisely backed off, adding significantly, "I'll take care of you this afternoon, Medwick!"

First time up, Medwick got a Bowman fastball on his left temple, and he went down as if pole-axed. There were no protective helmets in those days, and the impact of the pitch made a sickening sound. The large Brooklyn crowd reacted angrily, because one of their favorites, Pee Wee Reese, had been put on the shelf for three weeks earlier in the season by a Jake Mooty beanball.

While they were still carting the unconscious Medwick off on a stretcher and an angry buzz was going through the crowd, who should burst out of the Brooklyn dugout but the fiery MacPhail. He had broken all speed records getting down to the field from his private box, suspended under the upper deck behind home plate.

This was unprecedented, the president of a ball club invading the playing field. But the Redhead went further; he advanced toward the mound, lecturing Bowman, who gripped the baseball he held a little tighter, as if preparing to let go another duster.

Finishing with Bowman, MacPhail went over to the Cardinal dugout and challenged the whole team, until Charley Dressen and Hugh Casey dragged him away.

It was an ugly incident. The head umpire, in his report to the National League office, mentioned MacPhail for possibly inciting a riot. And my paper, the influential *Eagle*, blew the whole thing up into the proportions of a holy war. It was a premeditated attempt at murder, the *Eagle* screamed, because of the incident that morning in the hotel elevator. An *Eagle* editorial called for District Attorney William O'Dwyer to investigate and put an end to "Beanball Incorporated," just as he had done to "Murder Incorporated." O'Dwyer was quite a Dodger fan, and he ate up that kind of publicity. It was eventually to make him a popular but highly controversial mayor of New York.

After MacPhail had left the Dodgers, *Sports Illustrated* sent a staff expert, the late Gerald Holland, to do an in-depth profile on the exuberant genius. This biography would run through three issues, and Holland had to do a lot of exploring.

One of the first questions he asked was about MacPhail's extraordinary excursion onto the playing field in Brooklyn the day Medwick was beaned.

Right here Larry threw his disconnecting gear into action. "I never went on the field that day," he said.

Baffled, but not stopped, Holland read from the report of the *New York Times*, which had a man there, as did a dozen other papers. The *Times* piece mentioned that Larry had shot from the dugout like a racehorse out of the starting gate. It described his stop at the pitching mound and his visit to the Cardinal dugout.

"I tell you I never went on the field," MacPhail said, his voice tinged with annoyance. "I went right from my box to the dressing room to see how Medwick was."

They were chatting in the living room of MacPhail's horse ranch, and his daughter was playing the piano. The piece ended, and there was an awkward silence.

Holland shuffled the sheaf of clippings he had and tried again. This time it was the piece from the *Journal*. Different writer, but the details were the same. "How," said Holland, "do you account for that?"

"He made it up," Larry said, gulping a drink.

Holland was not easily defeated. He read MacPhail another newspaper clipping, and then a piece in the *Saturday Evening Post* by Tom Meany. Each reporter had the same facts, in the same sequence.

Now MacPhail rose angrily from his chair and strode toward the writer. "Are you going to pay attention to all that garbage?" he asked with an edge on his voice. "Or are you going to believe *me*?"

Holland dropped the subject. He wanted to stay around long enough to get his magazine piece.

MacPhail frequently suffered from spasms of forgetfulness when stories of his other bouts in baseball come up.

He always denied the incident in which he punched a detective in Cincinnati in 1936. That story got a big play in the Cincinnati papers. Thinking Larry would be distraught, Frank Conroy, a member of the Reds' quite proper board of directors, hurried to MacPhail's office to console him.

There, with all the clippings spread before him on a large table, sat the Redhead, grinning from ear to ear.

"How do you like *that* for publicity?" he asked the amazed Conroy.

Larry refused to talk about punching Powel Crosley, owner of the Reds, in 1936, which caused him to leave Cincinnati in a hurry. But why else would a man quit a winner he was building, a young team that was to take the 1939 and 1940 pennants, with others getting the credit?

MacPhail also scoffed at the fact—and fact it is—that he was asked to get out of Brooklyn in 1942 after putting together a year earlier that city's first pennant-winner in twenty-one years.

In the season following that pennant, MacPhail's Dodgers had a thirteen-game lead in August but then started to slip. Larry summoned key players, the coaches, and manager Durocher to an extraordinary after-game grilling in the Ebbets Field pressroom. The whole thing was as solemn as a grand jury session. It was another MacPhailian first, as well as last.

The skid continued, and the Redhead paid $40,000 for Bobo "Road Map" Newsom, a large-mouthed pitcher who had knocked around both leagues for years. This purchase was against the explicit orders of the Dodger board of directors; for MacPhail had already spent the expected profits from a pennant, and more.

Newsom was a resounding flop. When the Dodgers were nipped at the wire by the Cardinals, all Brooklyn went into mourning.

Not MacPhail, however. He could jazz up a double funeral, this man!

Suspecting that he was about to get his walking papers from the Brooklyn board of directors, the Redhead went marching off on his own—to war! His country needed him, he said, although he was past fifty.

You could almost hear the drums and the martial music at Larry's last marathon press and drinking conference in Joe's Restaurant, in the shadow of Brooklyn's Boro Hall.

A mere lost pennant, what was that? Our Barnum was off to battle Hitler and Tojo, single-handed if need be!

Once the foreign enemy was disposed of, MacPhail returned to battle on the baseball front. He bought the Yankees in 1945 at a bargain price, with Dan Topping and Del Webb as his partners.

Only thirty-two months later, he fought Topping and punched himself out of a triumphant Yankee ownership. Typically, he did it on the day his Yankees took a dramatic seventh-game World Series victory over the Dodgers and his one-time godfather, Branch Rickey, whom he now hated.

Larry was moving under a full head of steam that day. First he fired George Weiss, who had been the key talent man in the Yankees' domination of all baseball. Next, he grabbed the micro-

phone in what had been a riotously happy Yankee clubhouse and
threw over them all the stunning wet blanket that he was quitting the Yankees and leaving baseball for good. It was the most
outrageous bit of scene-stealing in sports history.

Topping and Webb rehired Weiss within the hour, giving
George a raise. What they gave MacPhail was a nudge out the
door—plus, of course, $2.2 million for his stock, almost all clear
profit.

That was a bad mistake for the Lords of Baseball. They should
have given this unpredictable genius $5 million to stay in their
game. With him aboard, there would have been no Finley fiasco
and no Arnholt Smith disaster either, for MacPhail would have
had the gumption to stand up to O'Malley and fight against bringing the swifty in.

Even when he stole that final scene in the Yankee clubhouse,
MacPhail came off like the Barrymore he was. Next to him Finley,
when Charley mugs with that ridiculous mule of his or does that
silly tap dance on his dugout roof in front of the TV cameras,
shapes up as a baggy-pants burlesque comedian.

While writer Holland was back in his magazine office putting
together that serial on MacPhail, Larry happened to be jailed for
cop-fighting. The Redhead had disagreed with the way a Maryland State Trooper was directing traffic at the racetrack.

Holland had to rush to Baltimore to get the facts so he could
revise his story.

Just a week later MacPhail was named to head a drive of so-
cialites to save the Baltimore Symphony Orchestra.

Holland had to do another rewrite. His subject had so many
sides, it was like interviewing three people. Would the *real* Leland Stanford MacPhail ever stand up, Holland wondered.

Larry had made many a similar about-face on the Brooklyn
scene.

One time, when the Dodgers were in a painful slump and the
writers had been knocking his ragamuffin ball club, the Redhead
suddenly decided to change the angry face he had been showing
his critics and make peace.

The newspapermen had been poking fun at Blimp Phelps, the
fat catcher, and Hot Potato Hamlin, the home-run pitcher. It had

begun to hurt at the gate. And Larry badly needed the gate to keep his bankers at bay.

MacPhail decided to charm them all. He would take this anvil chorus on a cruise down New York harbor and along the Jersey coast. Picking a date when there was no ballgame, he loaded the handsome sixty-foot yacht he had just bought with the very finest in foods and booze. He invited every one of his critics, and that was a boatload.

The name of MacPhail's fancy yacht was the *Mariposa*. For the writers aboard, it came close to being another *Titanic*.

16. The Buried Ballplayer

The good ship *Mariposa,* flying a jaunty burgee telling the world that owner Letsallgo Sailing MacPhail was aboard, hummed down New York harbor toward the open sea this July afternoon in 1939.

On the bridge was a hired skipper in a captain's cap that fairly dripped with gold braid.

MacPhail had a full cargo of baseball writers, and he had decided to be the perfect host. There was no doubt the man could charm a cobra when he put his mind to it, and there were a few of those on the boat. They had been knocking his brains out because of the way his Dodger team had been floundering, and it made him furious. However, he had no intention of drowning these knockers at sea, unless it be in scotch or bourbon.

"Not bad!" the Redhead murmured as he surveyed his slick craft as it purred past the Statue of Liberty. "Of course this thing would look like a lifeboat alongside Tom Yawkey's yacht, or that ocean liner Jake Ruppert had. But it's a start, it's a start!"

Tom Meany of the New York *World Telegram,* and later *PM,* Marshall Field's rag, nodded agreement. Up until this moment Tom's entire marine background consisted of a few rowboat trips on Prospect Park Lake in Brooklyn, and he was not of a mind now to rock the boat with any of the one-line zingers he liked to aim at MacPhail and his players.

Roscoe McGowen, the gentleman from the *Times*, Herb Goren of the *Sun*, and Gus Steiger of the *Mirror*, whose boss was Dan Parker, were all aboard. So was Eddie Murphy, another *Sun* man who was the Ned Sparks of the pressbox, a real sourpuss.

Only a few days before, Murphy had commented on a six-game Dodger losing streak. "When this team blows," he cracked, "it is no peanut-whistle!"

These fellows had to be soothed, reflected MacPhail as he surveyed the boatload of knockers. He would ply them with the proper tranquilizers!

The writers circled MacPhail warily as his cabin boy plied them with drinks and hors d'oeuvres. Right now the Redhead was a perfect host, but they knew from experience how his mood could change in a flash, like a summer squall.

The scotch and bourbon flowed; so did the conversation, up to a point. The point was just about where the arm of Atlantic Highlands reaches out into the ocean. There things got rougher—both the waves and the talk.

Running for shelter into the mouth of the Shrewsbury, the *Mariposa* ran aground. MacPhail blamed his captain and fired him on the spot. The fellow steered the boat to Seabright, where he folded his uniform and his gold braid into a valise and caught the last train back to New York.

Nobody in the party was worried. Why worry, when you had one of the all-time free-spenders throwing a party like this? The writing boys were enjoying themselves.

True, a search of the Seabright docks and bars failed to turn up a substitute captain, but there was time for that later. Right now MacPhail had hired an entire nightclub for the dinner and show, closing the doors to the public. Instead of a new captain, he added the girl vocalist from the orchestra to the crew of the *Mariposa*.

Larry knew I had a small boat of my own, and as midnight approached he talked me into revving up the motors on the *Mariposa* and pointing her down the Shrewsbury, then out into the open sea and up toward Riverside Drive on the Hudson, where all our cars were parked.

Larry had such confidence in his new helmsman that he gathered up every available blanket, as well as his newest crew member, and retired to the semiprivacy of the front deck.

Picking our way along the river channel in the pitch-black
night was no cinch, and every time I turned on the *Mariposa*'s
big searchlight to pick up one of the marker buoys to starboard or
port, MacPhail would let out a bellow like the *Queen Mary*'s fog-
horn. He wanted to be alone; the hell with press relations for the
time being!

The writers sobered up fast as we started to dodge the big
ferryboats, ablaze with lights, that were criss-crossing from Staten
Island and the Jersey shore to Brooklyn and Manhattan. Meany
and Murphy were visibly shaken when we missed a couple of
chuffing tugs that loomed up on our beam at the last minute as
we were picking our way around and between the rust-caked
tankers and freighters swinging at anchor.

It was 4 A.M. when we docked, with all hands grateful that the
peace voyage hadn't ended in pieces. But some of the gentlemen
of the press were pretty huffy toward MacPhail, who had completely ignored us all on the return trip. This was dangerous stuff,
snubbing the press.

Larry was skating close to the edge of the cliff in other ways,
too; much more scary ways. He and Branch Rickey had cooked
up a cover-up deal that could have had them both thrown out
of baseball, had Commissioner Landis gotten wind of it—thrown
out for life!

The crusty old Landis, bent on breaking up Rickey's domination of the market in young playing talent through his "chain-
gang" farm system, had cut loose one hundred of the Old Man's
phenoms in March of 1938, in his famous "Cedar Rapids" decision.

Above all others, Rickey wanted to retrieve a special one of
these young prospects, a high-school boy he had found on the St.
Louis sandlots. The Mahatma and his chief scout, Charley Barrett, had used the boy to chauffeur them around, the better to
keep an eye on him until they would start him out in the Class D
Three-Eye League.

Rickey, owed a favor by his pupil, phoned MacPhail and told
him to corner the boy; then the Old Man told the youngster to

sign for whatever the Brooklyn Club offered. Would you believe
a mere hundred bucks?

The deal was that MacPhail would keep the kid buried in the
low minors until 1940, when he could be legally traded back to
Rickey.

The Mahatma believed this boy would become the greatest
player in the history of the game. He could run with the speed of
wind and make a tap to the pitcher's box close at first base. He
could throw from shortstop with either arm, and in the outfield
he would climb fences to get the ball for you. On top of all that,
he was a switch hitter with home-run power from either side.

The young phenom's name? Pete Reiser.

How close was Rickey's estimate of the young man's greatness?

Three years later Reiser was to hit .343 to lead the National
League, and eventually he would steal home seven times in one
season, a record.

They should have known, these two connivers, that it would be
easier to hide an elephant in a phone booth than throw a blanket
over a talent like this. But they tried to pull it off.

Elmira, New York, a whistle-stop in the Eastern League, was
the cubbyhole where they planned to hide the boy and where he
eventually was sent. But Leo Durocher, MacPhail's manager, was
the one who blew the cover on the cover-up; Leo had spotted
Reiser working out with Brooklyn's main farm team, Montreal,
during spring training and before his eventual assignment to
Elmira.

Naturally, Durocher was not in on the whole MacPhail-Rickey
caper; you couldn't trust a touchy secret like that to a man whose
mouth flapped as much as Leo's.

One look at this kid in a game on a diamond near where the
varsity worked had been enough for the Lip. He kidnapped
Reiser, brought him over to the Dodger camp, and put him in
a ballgame that very afternoon to show the fourteen New York
newspapermen his "discovery."

Merriwell and Superman combined couldn't have done better
than Reiser in the first two days; he stroked hits in his first seven
times up and was on base eleven straight times. The amazed reporters started calling him "Pistol Pete" for the bullet shots he

cracked out over the infielders' heads, and their columns in the New York papers were full of the new sensation.

Naturally Rickey thought he was getting the doublecross when he read these stories about the boy he wanted covered up.

MacPhail was near apoplexy back in Brooklyn. He fired off a wire to Durocher: "UNDER NO CIRCUMSTANCES PLAY REISER; HE IS PROPERTY OF MONTREAL CLUB."

The Lip had other ideas. He had been bragging about his "find" day and night, sounding very much like a superscout. Hell, what did MacPhail and that scouting staff of his know about young talent, anyway? How could they have overlooked a star like this? Leo gabbed endlessly about the million-dollar baby he had found in the minor league five-and-ten-cent store.

Even after getting MacPhail's wire, Leo went on playing the kid. After all, he had been bragging that Reiser would lead the Dodgers to the 1940 pennant, just twenty years after they'd won their last one, and he couldn't very well bench the new sensation now for any reason less than a broken leg. Durocher was determined to play the best nine guys he could get his hands on. Anyway, he might as well find out right now who was the manager of this team, MacPhail or himself!

He found out in a hurry!

MacPhail took a plane out of New York to Camp Wheeler in Georgia, where the Dodgers were scheduled for two weekend exhibition games. He sent his traveling secretary, John McDonald, to bring Durocher up to the MacPhail suite for a showdown. McDonald warned his friend that the boss was loaded for bear.

Larry started to berate his manager the moment Leo entered. He didn't get much beyond the word "stupid" before Leo swung; Larry went backward over a bed and landed on the floor. He propped his head up with one arm and bellowed to McDonald to begin typing a press release.

He was firing his fiery manager—again!

McDonald sat on one bed with his portable typewriter on his lap. MacPhail began dictating with the speed of a machine-gun: "Leo Durocher was dismissed today as manager of the Brooklyn Dodgers, it was announced by—"

McDonald was fumbling with the keys, trying to buy time for

Durocher. He knew from experience that these "firings" sometimes blew over as quickly as they had arisen.

As McDonald pecked at the keys and changed the paper several times, MacPhail's temperature went up instead of down. Still
on the floor, with his head propped in the palm of one hand,
Larry barked, "You are incompetent too, McDonald. Include
yourself in that announcement. You are through, out of this
organization."

There was a pause, and the Redhead added, "But be sure to
put Durocher's name first in that press release!"

The press release was never finished. Neither were Durocher
and McDonald, who carried on business as usual the next day.

Instead, MacPhail worked on Leo, saying he needed the manager's help to persuade young Reiser to go down to the deep minors "for more experience." Larry never dropped a clue about the
real reason. "If we keep him in the lineup now, we'll never be
able to talk the kid into going down later, and he may be ruined,"
MacPhail purred. Leo was flattered by the "we." He gave in, and
the Dodgers distributed one of the most extraordinary press announcements ever made: The phenomenal Pete Reiser was being
optioned all the way down to Elmira, where Clyde Sukeforth,
who was in on the whole caper, would "bring him along slowly."

How deep in sleep must have been the other six general managers in the National League, their scouting staffs, their bird
dogs! How dense must have been the owners, not to have at least
been suspicious! They had been reading about this new superstar
for weeks, and suddenly Reiser was whisked out of sight.

All of them hated the firebrand, MacPhail, for the way he had
stomped on their gentlemen's agreements and pushed radio and
night baseball on them against their will. A lot of them envied
and disliked Rickey for the man's far-flung chain gang and the
prices he charged them for overballyhooed ballplayers. They had
secretly applauded Landis's Rickey-busting Cedar Rapids bomb-
shell. They knew MacPhail had been a Rickey protégé at Columbus and that the Old Man had put him in at Cincinnati and again
at Brooklyn.

Wouldn't you think they'd have suspected something was rot-
ten in Denmark, or at least in Elmira?

No. That was the way they ran their businesses. It wasn't that they looked the other way. They just didn't look at all. Or, looking, they did not see.

The little drama of the buried ballplayer was far from over.

No blanket was big enough to hide Reiser, even in Elmira. He began 1940 by stealing twenty-eight bases in the early part of the Eastern League season; he made a joke of the pitching there, clouting the ball at .378.

Rickey wanted his superbaby back, as they'd agreed. Right now, before Reiser attracted any more attention. It was 1940, and the time was up.

The Mahatma offered MacPhail a whale of a deal; it was so big they hoped that Reiser's name would be lost in a crowd of guys named Carl Doyle, Sam Nahem, and Bert Haas, who were slated to move from Brooklyn to St. Louis. The Dodgers were to get a real slugger, Ducky Joe Medwick, who was having trouble with the St. Louis manager, Ray Blades.

Medwick had led the league only two years earlier, hitting .374 and driving in one hundred fifty-four runs. In 1939 the so-called Hammering Hungarian had clouted .332. And he was from nearby Joisey, which made the Dodger bugs welcome him as one of their own.

But the baseball writers had gotten another glimpse at Reiser in 1940, after his exile to Elmira, and they had fallen in love with him all over again. They were starting to ask embarrassing questions: When was Pistol Pete going to get his chance? Wasn't he better than some of the relics in the Brooklyn outfield, like Old Joe Vosmik, who had to wear a corset to keep his back together and couldn't bend over to pick up a rolling ball?

MacPhail realized by then that he had to renege on returning Pistol Pete.

He called Rickey, pleading, almost in tears: "Branch, they'd lynch me here if I traded Reiser away for Medwick right now, even up. Durocher has talked too much, and the reporters have written every word. The fans here are so excited about the kid there would be a scandal. I just can't give him back to you."

Naturally, Rickey was in no position to complain, being a co-conspirator.

But the Old Man would have to get cash, lots of cash, instead of the superbaby. They couldn't pass the money under the table; and to partially "explain" the $132,000 that would appear on the Cardinals' books after coming out of the Brooklyn Trust vaults, Rickey sent Coonskin Curt Davis, a thirty-eight-year-old pitcher, to the Dodgers along with Medwick. Ernie Koy went along to St. Louis with Nahem, Doyle, and Haas, hardly Hall-of-Fame material.

Somehow Rickey, the old hoss-trader, knew that Medwick was through when he made this deal.

Even Durocher didn't realize it, and he was rooming with Ducky.

It began to dawn on MacPhail; one southpaw pitcher after another was tying up Camilli and Walker, the heart of the Dodger batting order. The right-handed Medwick would have eaten them alive when he was right, but now he was pulling away from the plate instead of stepping into the ball. Perhaps the beaning by Bowman had ruined him.

MacPhail announced that Medwick should be benched.

The bankers down the block hopped on the Redhead with both feet: Imagine spending all that cash for a bench-warmer! They didn't know the inside of the Reiser story.

Durocher still refused to believe all the thunder had gone out of his pal Medwick's bat. He kept playing Ducky day after day, and it led to another big flareup with MacPhail.

One afternoon the Redhead blew up because Medwick's name had just been announced in the starting lineup at Ebbets Field again, after all his lectures to Durocher. Larry stormed into the press bar yelling that he wanted a paper and pencil.

He moved down to the far end of the bar, away from the prying eyes of the writers, who would have given anything to see what he was putting into this war communiqué. Larry was so mad he ground his teeth as he bore down hard on the paper, printing the words. He folded it so hard he almost tore it in half. Then he summoned Benny Weinrig, the pressbox messenger, and bade him take it down to Durocher on the run.

That afternoon, the late editions of the New York *Journal* reached Ebbets Field before the ballgame was over; a scare headline screamed that Durocher had been fired again. The reason: keeping Medwick in the lineup.

MacPhail immediately accused Durocher of giving the story to Hugh Bradley, the *Journal* reporter.

Lippy hurled the charge right back at his boss, insisting that the Redhead had popped off in the press bar over a few brandies.

For a while it was the big unsolved mystery around Ebbets Field. How did Bradley get his hands on the exact wording of MacPhail's latest death sentence to Durocher? Even Benny the messenger boy was a suspect. Had he peeked at the war bulletin on the way down to the dugout to Durocher, and then sold out?

There were bad feelings on all sides, including the writers who had been scooped and were in hot water with their editors.

Only one thing was sure: The handshake truce between Mac-Phail and Durocher, which Dan Parker had called in Brooklynese "the dawn of a new area" was over, kaput, dead.

As usual, Hymie the bartender had the solution, and he cleared up the mystery after things had cooled down.

The *Journal* man had seen MacPhail bearing down so hard on the sheet of paper on the bar that he felt sure indentations had been made on the mahogany. About the fourth inning, after the room and the smoke from MacPhail's anger had cleared, Bradley came back with a piece of tissue paper and a soft pencil. As Hymie watched, he stroked delicately on the paper, which he held over the right spot on the mahogany. Gradually the printing emerged, just as MacPhail had impressed it there in all his fury: "For continuing to play Medwick against my orders, you are hereby fired—MacPhail."

The gabby manager was back on the job again the next day, of course, just as if nothing had happened, so the headline and story really meant nothing. It was just firing No. 9 for the unfireable manager. Or was it No. 10?

Of course, it had been a neat scoop for Bradley, the *Journal* man, for that afternoon at least.

Not as neat a scoop, however, as MacPhail was putting together right under the noses of the fast-asleep National League moguls, Rickey included.

Coonskin Davis turned out to be a real steal. The gaunt old sinkerball sidearmer pitched well enough in 1940, but the two hundred innings he was to hurl in 1941 were to be almost as decisive a factor in the theft of that pennant as Whitlow Wyatt's clutch pitching.

That brings us to how MacPhail almost lost Wyatt, along with his temper, when he punched me on the nose and shook up the whole Brooklyn *Eagle*.

※※※

17. A Shortstop Gets Punched

The old curmudgeon of the *Eagle*, Harris Crist, had run across a sports column in the New York *Sun* that he fell madly in love with.

This thing, appearing daily by an author identified only as "The Old Scout," was a patchwork of baseball gossip, quotes, and dugout chatter lifted from out-of-town newspapers. It was pirated from the stories of byline writers in other cities who were following their own major league teams.

The rehash was put together by an old geezer on the *Sun* copy desk for the few extra bucks he earned by his thievery. When Sam Murphy passed on, a bright-eyed kid named Herb Goren, who must have been all of twenty, aged abruptly and became "The Old Scout."

This hodgepodge column was utterly despised by the front-line writers of the day as the lowest form of journalism, on a level with stealing from poor-boxes. Frankie Graham, the ace columnist of the *Sun*, openly called it his own paper's "disgrace." You didn't write a thing like that, Graham snorted, you composed it with a scissors and a paste pot.

Tommy Holmes thought that, if the *Eagle* were planning a similar atrocity, "Cook" ought to be in the phony byline. "It's just a rehash column," he sneered, "and you know what warmed-over hash is like!" There were plenty of other irreverent suggestions from all over the city room when word got around that Crist had asked me to start stealing this secondhand stuff from the papers on our exchange desk. "Why not head up the column with the name 'Clipper Smith'?" said Eddie Forbes wryly. "If they come looking for you on a burglary rap, the name 'Smith' can never be traced; and you'll be 'clipping' everything, won't you?" There was an All-America end at Villanova named Clipper Smith at the time, and that's where Forbes got the idea.

But Crist wanted something like "The Old Scout" in his *Eagle,* and what the old tyrant wanted, he got.

I was elected. There were no other candidates.

I remember being summoned to the almighty editor's desk and waved into his first-degree hot seat while we both tried to hit upon a name to compete with "The Old Scout."

As I sat there glued to his bolted-down chair, Crist looked out over the city room, searching for the new byline. Suddenly it hit him. "Shortstop!" he cried, pleased with himself. "That's it! We'll head it up 'By Shortstop.' Start the column as soon as you can. We'll advertise it on all our trucks next week."

I had always liked to rummage through the out-of-town papers on the exchange desk at the *Eagle,* for the different type styles and makeup had fascinated me, and of course I held some of the big-name writers in awe. Now the table became my headquarters, and I sometimes raided the *Eagle* mailbags in the early morning hours to get the latest editions of the St. Louis *Post-Dispatch,* the Boston *Transcript,* or the Cincinnati *Enquirer.*

If H. G. Salsinger, who followed the Detroit Tigers for that city's *News,* found out something unusual about Schoolboy Rowe or Charley Gehringer, I seized on it. If Roy Stockton in St. Louis had some Dizzy Dean quotes about an older brother Diz insisted was "better'n me and Paul put together," they became mine for the Shortstop column. If a kid left-hander was told not to throw a trick pitch that broke weirdly down and away like a reverse curve because it would "ruin his arm," I would steal that story about young Carl Hubbell from John Carmichael in the Chicago *News.* There was nothing that Sid Ziff wrote in Los Angeles about some hotshot hitter in the Coast League or that Chilly Doyle dug up about the Pirates in the Pittsburgh *Sun-Telegraph* that I didn't know a few days later.

It was a story that Shortstop fished out of a newspaper in Milwaukee, then a minor league town, that ignited MacPhail like a four-alarm fire and made him try to waffle my nose. Ironically, the story was about pitcher Whitlow Wyatt, one of the mildest men you could meet in a year's travel; the gracious, gentle Georgian with the charming drawl would be the last who'd wish to stir up such a rhubarb.

Wyatt had been one of a dozen over-the-hill ballplayers that MacPhail had retrieved from the American League garbage can. The big pitcher's fastball was a zing of the past, and nine solid years of breaking off big league curves for the White Sox, Tigers, and Indians had left the thirty-year-old Georgian's elbow sounding like a dice box when he flexed it for curious bystanders. Whit had been dropped through the waiver trapdoor down to the minor league Milwaukee Brewers, where they tried a last-chance operation on his salary wing, as the writers of that day liked to call a man's pitching arm.

Now, MacPhail got a tip that the Wyatt wing was showing signs of returning life after a postoperative layoff of a year, so Larry took the gamble: two unwanted Dodger players plus $22,000, which was to be paid in installments, for the contract of the comeback pitcher.

Wyatt at once seemed to find new life in Brooklyn. Pitching more than a hundred strong innings in the second half of the 1939 season, he won eight of eleven games, with a very low earned-run average. He was pitching the best ball in the National League, although the Dodgers were already out of the race. He was a strikeout pitcher, too, and that excited the Dodger fanatics, who saw in Whit their new Dazzy Vance—sure, Vance had been a late-bloomer, hadn't he?

Wyatt had been another of those gambles, like Poffenberger and Hot Potato Hamlin and Vito Tamulis, that had MacPhail in continual hot water with the bankers. But this big guy was something else, the way he was firing the ball. For MacPhail he was a lone ray of hope, the light at the end of the tunnel, the water hole in the desert for a very, very parched Redhead. He'd show them all yet, Larry murmured this afternoon as he watched his big comeback ace overpower the Cincinnati hitters.

The late editions of the *Eagle* hit Ebbets Field that day just as Wyatt was putting the finishing touches on a four-hit shutout; it had a 40-point Bodoni bold headline that fairly screamed: "DODGERS MAY LOSE WYATT." The newsboys soon sold all their copies, and fans who couldn't get one read the story—by "Shortstop"—over a neighbor's shoulder. The subhead had more bad news: "LANDIS MULLS VOIDING MACPHAIL DEAL."

I had spotted the original yarn, by a baseball writer named Sam Levy, in the Milwaukee paper. Levy had a lot of hot quotes in there from Henry Bendinger, the owner of the minor league Brewers, who was griping that MacPhail had welched on the deal and never paid him for Wyatt. More than that, Bendinger was on his high horse because Larry had been ducking his phone calls for a month or more. Now he had taken his beef to Kenesaw Mountain Landis, the crotchety old commissioner.

MacPhail had been in hot water before, over some charges that he had paid some of his ballplayers under the table—thus exceeding the minor league salary limit—when he was president of the Columbus club in the American Association. He had been forced to resign under a cloud.

Now it seemed that Landis might come down hard on the Redhead again and give Wyatt back to Bendinger; that's what the minor league owner wanted, for he knew he could now get five times what MacPhail owed him for this rejuvenated winner from any one of a half-dozen clubs in the majors.

MacPhail grabbed a copy of the *Eagle* in the press bar, where he had been having a happy afternoon while Wyatt was spinning another masterpiece. In fact, everybody in the ballpark had been having a happy day; the fans were delirious about their "new Vance," and the writers were glad to have some good news to write about for a change: Wyatt's comeback. Even a couple of the bankers from Brooklyn Trust who were there seemed overjoyed, for the money that had been laid out for Whitlow would now be recouped at the turnstiles.

While MacPhail was reading the story by Shortstop, his face deepened into a scowl. Those around him could tell there was a big storm coming.

When the Redhead finished reading, he tore the *Eagle* into shreds and went stalking "Shortstop," who he knew very well was Parrott.

He found me sauntering out of the pressbox, quite unsuspecting. That's the way Lucifer Sulphurious popped me, too—quite unsuspecting—right in front of a few hundred fans who were still in the upper deck behind home plate, buzzing about Wyatt's shutout and the story in the *Eagle*.

Of course, the impulsive Redhead could have handled the Wyatt crisis differently; even though he was temporarily broke, he surely could have dug up the money somewhere to pay for a pitcher who had suddenly become this important. And he could have rushed the castoff players he owed Bendinger, along with the cash, to Milwaukee to appease the minor league owner.

Instead, MacPhail punched me first and then got the payment off in time to save Wyatt. The man moved in fits and spurts, weaving in and out of trouble. He seldom did anything the easy way.

MacPhail's punch, and the way it aroused the editors of the *Eagle*, brought a quick reaction from George V. McLaughlin at the Brooklyn Trust. The former New York City Police Commissioner was a large man with a very red face and a roar as loud as MacPhail's. What enraged him was that two of the Brooklyn Trust's loan accounts should be squabbling with each other. The *Eagle*, like the Dodgers, was deeply in hock to Brooklyn Trust because of a Communist-inspired Newspaper Guild strike against the paper two years earlier, in 1937.

McLaughlin immediately ordered MacPhail to apologize to everybody.

Larry gave in to the banker, probably because he needed to borrow more money at the moment.

George V. set up the luncheon with his usual show of class, engaging one of the swankier parlors at the prestigious Brooklyn Club so that the outraged *Eagle* editors would be properly soothed.

The Redhead's ruffling of the *Eagle* feathers, not to mention my nose, was in all the Manhattan papers by now. Dan Parker in the *Mirror* referred to MacPhail's punch as "the boff on the Parrott's beak."

George Barnewall, who was on the board of directors at both the Brooklyn Trust and the Dodgers, was toastmaster at the kiss-and-make-up lunch. It was his job to get everybody talking to each other again.

After four MacPhail martinis, the "peace luncheon" almost broke out into another war.

Larry had been talking rapid-fire and nonstop for more than an hour about the next deal he had on the fire and the Dodger pennant he was planning, when Barnewall reminded him of his promised apology, the one the *Eagle* editors were waiting for.

It would have taken a straitjacket to get an apology out of a MacPhail with that much fuel aboard.

The Redhead jumped to his feet and strode toward the door. "The hell with an apology," he said. "I'm willing to forget the whole thing!"

End of "apology." End of luncheon. But not by any means the end of MacPhail's antics.

One by one he was capturing the players he needed to win the 1941 pennant, and he had to use bribery and booze and perfect timing to bring it off.

18. MacPhail Hijacks Two Stars

In early 1941 Horace Stoneham of the Giants thought sure he had bought a strong-armed young pitcher named Kirby Higbe from the Phillies in a handshake deal. They had haggled over the price, but Horace felt it was positively set at $65,000.

But when MacPhail laid a check for a hundred big ones on Gerry Nugent's palm, the money-hungry owner of the Philadelphia team suffered a severe attack of forgetfulness. Horace who? What handshake?

After this bit of bribery, MacPhail swore the hungry Nugent to secrecy—that suited Gerry fine, too—because he had to get a catcher out of Branch Rickey before the Higbe deal came out. Some of the brothers in the National League lodge were getting nervous about that upstart in Brooklyn, who might be getting too strong for 1941. Rickey had already contributed Medwick and Coonskin Davis for $132,000, and now Branch was trying to jack up the price on Mickey Owen to $50,000 more of the Brooklyn Trust Company's cash.

This was pretty sweet pickings for the Old Man, who got 10 percent of all the cash that came in to the Cardinals in such deals. And he knew he had a big, strong kid in Walker Cooper who was going to be a better catcher and power hitter than two Mickey Owens. Not only that, Cooper could run faster than any man that size should be allowed to.

When it came out that MacPhail had landed Higbe, Phil Wrigley in Chicago began to catch some flak in the press because he had not won any pennants lately and Brooklyn was basing its flag hopes on two stars that the gum genius had let slip away: Camilli and Higbe. Alarmed, he called Rickey, the acknowledged wizard in such matters.

"Pooh for MacPhail," answered the Old Man, using one of his strongest epithets. "In fact, two poohs for him and his Brooklyn ragamuffins."

Trying to soothe Wrigley, the Mahatma denounced the Brooklyn team as much too ancient. "They will fall apart in the dog days of August," he predicted.

Rickey was thinking of the aged Dixie Walker and Whitlow Wyatt, as well as Durocher, who was past thirty-five now but still playing short as well as managing because young Pee Wee Reese was still a question mark.

Despite the baseball writers' jokes, MacPhail's pickings off baseball's scrap pile had yielded some prizes. Walker had cost only $10,000 plus the miles of adhesive tape needed to keep him together over the course of a season. Dixie was now a solid .300 hitter, and undoubtedly Dodger No. 1; he could have been elected Borough President in a landslide. Reese, adjudged too frail by the Boston Red Sox, who had reared him in Louisville, was to be worth twenty times his $35,000 tab. Even Hot Potato Hamlin had come around and won twenty in 1939; now he was about to pitch on the 1941 team that MacPhail bragged would be his first pennant-winner.

Larry's mouth, always in motion, didn't make things any easier. When he taunted Horace Stoneham in Toots Shor's about missing out on Higbe, the aroused Giants knocked off the Dodgers three straight in their first series of 1941.

Then there was Durocher's mouth. The Lip kept nagging at MacPhail that he needed a solid second baseman to steady the shaky rookie Pee Wee at short and to turn the double play. Petey Coscarart, who had played one hundred forty games there the year before, just couldn't do it, Leo said.

Billy Herman, who had been an All-Star for so many years, had been benched in Chicago, and Durocher kept drumming it into his boss: "Get me Herman and I'll win the pennant for you!"

MacPhail carefully laid his plans to extract Herman from the two green peas owner Phil Wrigley had just put in charge of his Cubs: Jimmy Wilson, a rookie manager, and ex-reporter Jim Gallagher, who had unbelievably been named general manager.

Gallagher and Wilson were staying at New York's Commodore Hotel with their team when MacPhail pounced. The three of them haggled for hours after dinner about the cash and Brooklyn players the Chicago club should get for Herman, who they thought was washed up. The scotch was flowing freely, and Wilson dropped out about three and went to bed.

MacPhail and Gallagher matched drink for drink until five, when the deal was made. But there was one difference: Larry was pouring his scotches down the sink, much as it pained him. Thus the booze that had betrayed him so often proved to be good medicine for him and his ball club this time.

Billy Herman was one of the all-time steals at about $90,000, if you figure along with the $60,000 cash the two mediocres the Cubs picked in return: washed-up Johnny Hudson and Charley Gilbert, a little outfielder who never made it.

Parched after the long palaver, MacPhail now put Gallagher to bed and celebrated, as the clock climbed toward 6 A.M. He found Herman, who very probably hadn't yet retired, and the two of them roused an indignant Durocher on the phone.

"This is your new second baseman speaking," Herman purred into the mouthpiece. That woke Leo up fast.

MacPhail had done his part, delivering Herman; Durocher now did his, producing the 1941 pennant.

But, true to form, Larry fell flat on his face in what should have been his finest hour ever. He publicly fired his manager—again!—only seven hours after Leo had clinched the flag in Boston.

This fracas involved a triumphal welcome in Grand Central

Station in New York, which MacPhail missed. He and his companion had taken a taxi to the One Hundred Twenty-fifth Street
station, the last scheduled stop before the team's train rolled into
Grand Central. Larry had intended to board there and get in on
all the huzzahs, but he was left standing in the dust as the train
roared by at full speed. Leo didn't want any of the players to get
off, so he had told the conductor to skip the stop.

Durocher and his conquering heroes, entirely ignorant of the
fact that they had passed up the big boss, roared into Grand
Central to take the bows as the cameras flashed and the bands—
including Shorty Laurice's own Sym-Phony band from Ebbets—
blared loudly.

MacPhail's one companion on the lonely train platform at One
Hundred Twenty-fifth Street that night was the Mahatma himself, Rickey. It was the last time pupil and godfather were to be
that close, or even civil, to each other.

The welching on the Reiser cover-up had opened the split, but
MacPhail's reckless destruction of Pistol Pete in 1942 widened
it beyond repair. Destruction, I said. It was as heartbreaking
and messy a thing as I had ever seen pulled in any sport: Mac-
Phail, the hungry magnate, bending and breaking a crippled
superstar like a kid in a tantrum might twist out of shape an expensive toy because it wouldn't work just that minute.

Remember, Reiser was Rickey's dream come true of the all-
time "perfect" ballplayer. Not a donkey who would perform
satisfactorily day in and day out during the one hundred-fifty-
four-game grind, but a one-in-a-million Whirlaway—a finely-
tuned combination of muscle, sinew, and grit who could break
up a game at any moment.

It's surprising that Reiser, who scrambled his brains on the
center-field wall in St. Louis that July day in 1942 and then was
played again and again against doctors' orders, is still around to
talk about his nightmare. But he is, working in the Cubs' minor
league organization under Salty Saltwell.

How does Pete remember the smash-up that started it all?

"Some of the blame is mine," he cautioned. "In those days, I
believed I could catch any ball hit anywhere near me. I was only
twenty-two, and I had been proving myself since I was twelve.
The kids I played with had all been five, six years older, and I

always felt I needed to prove I was as good as my older brother had boasted, good enough to play with them."

Pete is bald as a bowling ball now, and if you look hard you can see some of the embroidery the surgeons left on him. But the smile is the same as it was on the apple-cheeked kid who was so abused by baseball's front-office greed. It's surprising that there is no bitterness in the man as he looks back now at the boy who was.

"I was on one of those hot streaks when we came into St. Louis late that July," Pete told me. "I'd had nineteen hits in twenty-one at bats in the two series before that, in Cincinnati and Chicago. I was right around .380 and there wasn't the slightest doubt in my mind I was going to hit .400 that year, it was all coming so easy for me. And to make it all the better, we were thirteen and a half games ahead."

The thing sounded like a rifle shot, but for Reiser it turned out to be the crack of doom. Country Slaughter hit the ball. "It was a line drive and I knew it was going over my head," Pete said, "but I thought I could get to it. I felt I had to. The game was scoreless, last of the thirteenth, it was getting dark, and Whit Wyatt had been pitching his heart out against Mort Cooper. I was running all out in dead center, and when I just grazed the flagpole, I thought sure I could get to the ball. I did, too. But as I took my leap and gloved it the wall came out and hit me, or so it seemed. The ball fell out of my glove; inside-the-park home run for Slaughter, and we get beat, one to nothing."

"My head?" he said, repeating the question slowly. "Why, it felt like a hand grenade went off in there."

Worse was to come.

When Pete woke up in St. John's Hospital in St. Louis, an old friend, Dr. Robert Hyland, was hovering over him, breaking the news that he was through for the season. Hyland was a noted surgeon as well as the Cardinals' team doctor. Fractured skull, severe concussion, he said. Nothing to do but rest, hope, and pray. But no exertion whatever.

Back in Brooklyn MacPhail hit the ceiling when he heard that—harder, maybe, than Reiser had hit that wall.

Larry saw it as a plot by Rickey's doctor, and Rickey himself, to remove the Dodgers' star player so that the Cardinals would have a chance. The hell with all of them, roared the Redhead. He would have his own doctors examine Reiser in Brooklyn.

Reiser had smashed himself on a Sunday, and by Tuesday the kid had talked his way out of the hospital. He was supposed to go directly into Brooklyn, but he was eager to catch up with his team, which had left St. Louis without him. "Hell, you gotta go through Pittsburgh to go to Brooklyn," he told me with a twinkle, "an' I wanted to see the guys."

It was the seventh inning when he walked into the ballgame at Forbes Field in Pittsburgh and sat down in the Brooklyn club box, right behind the dugout.

"Leo spotted me first," Pete said. "He figured I must be okay if I was out of the hospital, I guess. He told me to put on a uniform and come sit on the bench."

"I told him I couldn't play. I was seeing things double and having those shooting pains in my head."

But you know Durocher. He urged some more. "Come sit down here with us," said the Lip. "I won't use you."

You can guess what happened. In the thirteenth inning, with the winning run on second base and nobody left on the bench, Leo looked at Pete. The question was in his eyes, if not on his lips: "Wanna go up there an' hit one for us?"

Pete remembers the pitcher was Ken Heintzelman, the left-hander. Line drive over second base, and the run came in. But as Reiser tried to make the turn at first base, he fell flat on his face.

This time they rushed him back to Brooklyn, and a whole committee of doctors said: "No more! Sit the kid down for the rest of the year."

You think MacPhail would listen? No chance. Things were going bad now: The Dodgers were falling apart, blowing their big lead. This was when Larry held that grand jury session in the press room at Ebbets, in front of the astounded writers, and accused some of the older players of lying down. Privately, he told Reiser he needed him to set the example.

The kid belonged in a wheelchair, not a uniform, but he gave it the big try.

"Get him outta there," said a frightened Babe Pinelli, the umpire. "I can tell he's not seeing the ball when he's at bat. He'll get hurt!"

By now, Pete was only a shadow of himself. His average sank to .310, which meant that he was hitting a bare .200 after the smash-up.

Whirlaway didn't have the strength to be a donkey.

MacPhail had blown the whole thing, including the pennant, and was then asked to blow town himself by the angry Dodger directors. But, most important, Larry had wasted Pete Reiser, the perfect ballplayer, and in St. Louis, Rickey anguished over it. Oh, Pete had a hitch in the service, and after that put in a few pitiful .270 years and had another collision with the Ebbets Field wall in 1947, but mostly it was all over for Pete as early as 1942.

What MacPhail had done to Rickey's superbaby galled the Old Man deeply. "That character," the Mahatma told me, "should never have been entrusted with anything so fine—" There were tears in his eyes.

On top of all this, it was a bitter, bitter pill MacPhail was asked to swallow when Rickey took over Larry's massive desk under the enormous moose head in the Brooklyn front office. The Mahatma had finally come to claim superbaby, but now it was too late.

At this point, there were many bitter words between Rickey and MacPhail. They were moving, these two, closer to the day when each would fling mud at the other, and all of baseball would get splattered!

$$\times\!\!\!\!\times\!\!\!\!\times\!\!\!\!\times$$

19. The Powerhouse: A Column for Rent

The telegram addressed to John McDonald was simple enough: "ST. MATTHEW, CHAPTER 26, VERSES 14–16. MACPHAIL." John couldn't make head nor tail of it; the thing might as well have been written in Chinese. "I thought," he said with a nervous little laugh, "that Rickey was the only one allowed to quote the Bible."

"That's an idea," I said. "Let's take this thing to the Old Man and get him to decipher it."

McDonald was a big, ambling sheepdog of a man who had been MacPhail's punching bag for eight tough years. Larry seemed to stir up trouble everywhere he went, and McDonald collected it. John had patched up more squabbles and soothed more stepped-on toes than he could count. He had forgotten enough shenanigans and under-the-table deals to put the Redhead in jail, had Mac been a tattler.

When MacPhail was blown out of Brooklyn by the backdraft from the loss of the 1942 pennant, he had left McDonald behind. Rickey found John on the premises and decided to put him in charge of the Dodgers' No. 1 farm team, Montreal.

In Rickey's book, this was a splendid position in baseball; but to a Broadway guy like McDonald, anything north of Times Square was exile. John's "banishment" landed the Old Man in his first hot water with the writers in the big city.

McDonald liked a drink, and when the newspapermen joined him at the bar he always picked up the tab. This did not sit well with Rickey, who regarded booze as the devil's tool. More than that, it was expensive.

Jerry Mitchell published a little skit in his column in the New York *Post* purporting to give the details of McDonald's assignment to Montreal.

According to Mitchell, Rickey had been cleaning out the impressively large desk in the Dodger offices that had been MacPhail's. Helping him had been his only son, Branch Junior, known as the Twig ever since Tom Meany had decided any smaller Branch should bear that title. Rummaging through the drawers, the two of them were giving away all the odds and ends MacPhail had left behind. Suddenly the Old Man—according to Mitchell's version—had stood up and asked, "Who will take the Canadian club?"

Before the Twig could answer, McDonald raised his hand and stepped forward. He thought he was getting a case of booze. Instead, it was exile in Elba—Montreal!

McDonald was obviously uneasy as we walked in on Rickey and showed him MacPhail's telegram. What kind of caper, John wondered, was his erratic ex-boss pulling now?

Rickey's heavily forested eyebrows went up a few notches when he read the wire. He needed to consult no Bible to get the message. "General MacPhail," he rumbled, with elaborate emphasis on the "General," "refers to the passage in which Judas Iscariot took the thirty pieces of silver for betraying Christ."

McDonald sucked in his breath. John had collaborated on a feature piece for the *Saturday Evening Post* under his own name, and it had hit the newsstands that very week. He had absolutely nothing to do with the choice of a title for the article, but unfortunately for John, it came out as "Fall of the House of MacPhail."

In it he had told frankly how he had pushed hard for Durocher to be the next Dodger manager, once it was decided Burleigh Grimes was through. Larry, according to McDonald, was hot for Frankie Frisch. John went to bat for Leo. After a week MacPhail had cooled on Frisch and was now touting Jimmy Wilson. Again McDonald spoke up for Lippy, who eventually got the job.

After Rickey decoded the telegram, McDonald was shaken. He had been called the lowest type of traitor, a Judas. As for me, I was more impressed by the novelty of MacPhail's message; I wondered out loud, to Rickey, how anybody could answer such a slur.

"Quite easily, my boy," said the Old Man, rotating a cigar under his thoughtful gaze. "Just consider that our egomaniac friend is appointing himself as Christ Almighty in that telegram!"

It was the first inkling I had of a real falling out between these two giants. Now they were on a collision course, as we shall see, toward the 1948 "Trial by Fury" in front of Unhappy Chandler, the puppet politician MacPhail had helped put in as commissioner.

These two brilliant men were almost exact opposites.

Rickey seemed like the father-figure, being almost ten years older, a mild speaker of parables who had been married to the same plain Jane of a wife all the way. He was a dispenser of paternal wisdom, and he had all the phobias against spending money that linger from a dirt-poor childhood.

MacPhail was the errant child: rash, impulsive, a banker's

spendthrift son who had an overactive mind and fists to match. He had uncoupled the lovely lady who was the mother of three spectacularly successful children—Lee MacPhail is today the president of the American League—and married Jean Wanamaker, a switchboard operator in the Dodger office.

MacPhail was a big spender, a high roller all the way. Rickey was never one to belly up to the bar and buy the boys a drink or ten, as Larry would. For this shortcoming, the Mahatma got to be known as some sort of bluenose who piously avoided the contamination of a ballpark on the Sabbath, only to sneak a peek at the game from behind drawn curtains in a YMCA across the street. He was pictured again and again, by those who didn't bother, for one reason or another, to dig for the real man under this defensive façade, as a sort of nutty reformer who thought racetracks were evil and card-playing was Satan's game. That was all pure hokum, and Rickey was partly to blame for its spread. The truth was that he had locked himself into the straitjacket of a very square, Puritan image, and he did not know how to wriggle out of it without scandalizing people.

Mrs. Rickey explained this to me one day when she and the Mahatma and I were having dinner in Joe's Restaurant. She began: "Harold, will you order me a Manhattan cocktail, please? I know *he* never will . . ."

This charming lady, who could have been any man's ideal of the All-American mother, looked over her glass at me with a twinkle in her eye as she sipped. "Would you believe," she went on, "that every year he used to take me to the Kentucky Derby? We had such fun . . ."

Here she hesitated to steal a glance at the Old Man, who was boring into the menu with such fervor that you'd swear he hadn't heard a word.

With a little sigh Mrs. Rickey added, "But that was before all this silly talk started about Branch being cheap, and a religious fanatic. Now he's afraid to be seen at the track for fear somebody will make a big story of it."

The "somebody" who hadn't wanted to dig out the real Rickey, the "somebody" whom Rickey feared, was Jimmy Powers, the jaunty, irresponsible sports columnist of the tabloid New York

Daily News. "The Powerhouse," this pillar of supposed wisdom was called.

Powers and Branch had never met, although Rickey did his best to arrange it several times through me and others. Jaunty Jimmy never let fact interfere with a good story; he followed the gospel of journalism according to Arthur Brisbane, for years one of the wildest headlined columnists in the rival Hearst stable.

Powers was certainly not alone in making a villain out of Rickey. Modern cartoonists who lament that they cannot get a "handle" on President Ford because he is a stereotyped, plastic middle-of-the-road man would have enjoyed kicking around Rickey the pinchpenny. Certainly the talented cartoonists of that day had their fun at the Old Man's expense. The pens of Burris Jenkins, Jr., in the New York *Journal American,* Pete Llanuza and later Willard Mullin in the *World Telegram,* Tom Paprocki, who just signed "Pap" to his drawings that appeared daily in the New York *Sun* and for the AP syndicate, and Ed Hughes of the *Eagle* all made fair game of the old gentleman. In those days cartoonists were given plenty of space for their flamboyant creations. Jenkins's cartoons usually filled six columns at the top of the page, sometimes even eight. Rickey became a miserly Scrooge in a stovepipe hat who lured unwary million-dollar ballplayers out of the canebrakes to sign on the dotted line by dangling in front of them a shotgun or a fancy fishing rod. The legend went that he then kept these fuzzy-faced kids laboring like slaves in his minor-league chain gang, underpaid and even underfed until the bloom of youth had vanished from their cheeks and they were old and wrinkled and flat-footed, at which time Rickey turned them out into a cruel, heartless world.

All this stuff completely baffled Rickey and his wife. Jane had bled through the years as she saw and heard her man scourged in print and on the airwaves. It puzzled and amazed them that these so-called journalists could grind up half-truths, mix them with garbage, and serve up a lot of baloney that the public apparently ate up. Stung again and again, the Rickeys moved farther and farther away from the press, which of course made them even more vulnerable. Any newspaperman will tell you it's much easier to knock some faceless guy you've never met than a man you've sat down and talked with. That was the Powers battle plan to pillory and destroy Rickey. Jimmy seldom visited Ebbets Field, never attended Rickey's press conferences, and furiously fought off all the efforts I made to get him together with the Old Man. Powers told me once he was afraid he'd be charmed out of his socks, and out of his handiest target.

The baseball writers on other papers usually sang this same theme song about Rickey's chain gang at their $25-a-plate dinner every January at the Waldorf Astoria; but in their case it was more in fun than fury.

I remember one skit in which Eddie Dyer, the Cardinal manager, looked hungrily at a rookie who had hit .385 on one of the Redbird farm teams in Rochester or Columbus or Houston, meanwhile performing incredible feats in the outfield. The frog-voiced Arthur Mann, who was taking Dyer's part, sang longingly: "Gee, kid, I could use four of ya—" But then the scene shifted to early May, cutting-down time for the Cardinals, and the unhappy rookie lamented in song: "—here I am back in Peoria!"

There was some truth to this big fable—there always is—but largely it was pure bunk. The truth was that Rickey, the reputed slavemaster, did have seven hundred ballplayers under contract when he was masterminding the St. Louis farm system. The same was true later at Brooklyn.

That made the odds against any fuzzy-chinned youngster who thought he could take the job of Pee Wee Reese or Duke Snider about five hundred to one.

But the big lie was the charge that these starry-eyed kids rotted away as they were kept chained down in the farm system. Rickey sold off like hot-cakes the ones he didn't want; the prices, as you shall see later, were outrageous, and the master salesman kept 10 percent of the proceeds.

Rickey skillfully showcased a half-dozen young Dodger shortstops in the 1950s. Each was touted as "Pee Wee Reese's successor." That billing naturally jacked the price up considerably. But did Gene Mauch, Rocky Bridges, Bob Ramizzotti, Bobby Morgan, Danny O'Connell, Stan Rojek, and Eddie Miksis rot away in the minors because they failed with the Dodgers? Hardly. All were sold to major league clubs, and all had their chance to make it big, although none did. How did Rickey know these things? It was just one man's uncanny skill at appraising ballplayers, that's all. Rickey himself called it "putting a dollar sign on a muscle." He was unbelievably accurate at it.

The Mahatma's blueprint for finding and developing raw talent—sign 'em cheap and put them on the assembly line through Class D, C, and then on up to AAA—was there for all the owners to see. But they were too lazy or too proud to imitate, so there was only one handy defense: knock Rickey and his chain gang as cruel and inhuman and a disgrace to baseball.

Yawkey and Wrigley and Galbreath could have signed the same kids who became the Country Slaughters and Slats Marions and brothers like the Deans and Coopers, but they didn't. All their scouts seemed to have patent leather shoes and silk shirts and wouldn't think of sloshing through the canebrakes where Frank Rickey, Branch's brother and great scout, worked in a frayed windbreaker, searching among the mill teams and around the semipros.

Only George Weiss of the Yankees copied Rickey's plan, and he did pretty well with it for the Yankees, if you remember.

Joe Williams, the *World Telegram* columnist, slammed Rickey unmercifully for his chain-gang ideas, charging at one point that the Old Man intentionally spurned the 1946 pennant by keeping Robinson down on the Montreal farm team. Milton Gross, writing in the New York *Post,* took a lot of pot shots at the Rickey methods, and even the mild John Kieran and Arthur Daley, both authors of the sports column in the *New York Times,* wept occasionally for the poor wretches down on the farms. Dan Parker, the *Mirror* expert, would not join this chorus, one big reason being that he was certain any anti-Rickey campaign engineered by Jimmy Powers had to be strictly phony.

Parker used to attack his opposite number on the *News* by name, something you seldom see now in journalism. Dan called him "Junior Jimmy Powers, second-string columnist on the *News.*" Jack Miley was doing the lead column at that time.

This was in a free-swinging period when writers took clouts at each other in print. The attacks Westbrook Pegler made on Heywood Broun, and vice versa, made spicy reading on the split page of the *World Telegram,* for which they wrote adjoining columns.

But Powers was the loudest, lowest slammer of them all.

The *News* columnist hung the "El Cheapo" tag on the Old Man in 1943, when Rickey unloaded Medwick, Camilli, Wyatt, and other washed-up veterans who had folded in the big collapse of the summer before, after leading by thirteen games. B.R., as we sometimes called him, was making room for a new crop of youngsters—the Furillos, Erskines, Sniders, and Hodgeses.

Powers made a litany of it, hammering on the "El Cheapo" theme in his powerful paper with more than 2 million circulation. Everywhere Rickey took his family, that jibe was shouted at them. An angry crowd of fans even lynched Rickey in effigy in front of Borough Hall in Brooklyn, in full view of the Old Man's office.

Powers was an unusual fellow. He had a "zero rating" among his fellow newspapermen, as Arthur Daley once wrote in his *Times* column, but he flung those harpoons of his with a purpose. For months Jimmy had ridiculed Stoneham of the Giants as "Horace the Hoople," until a spot in the Giant broadcasting booth opened up. Hoping for the appointment, Powers suddenly began to refer to Horace as a shrewd baseball operator.

You could have the use of the powerful Powers column for a day if he trusted you, and if you supplied a neatly typed, newsy interview for him that was just the proper length. I remember writing a folksy column about Walter O'Malley cooking, and then carving, a turkey in his Amityville home, while wife Kay built a salad and his two fine youngsters helped.

Daughter Terry was then seventeen, and Peter, now the Dodger president, was thirteen, it said in the column. The piece appeared under Powers's name in the *News* of November 12, 1950, and included a cameo cartoon of the man who had just pushed Rickey overboard in one of the most bitter power struggles the world of sports has ever seen.

The theme of the column was that the brand-new owner of the Dodgers was really a simple homebody who had no butler, no cook, nor even a maid. The Big Oom was quoted as saying he was not in baseball to make money and—God help me for ever writing it—would, with the widow Mae Smith, plow the profits right back into the team for the benefit of the Brooklyn fans he loved so very, very dearly.

Walter never thanked me for the column. Perhaps he chose to believe that Powers was hiding under his settee that day and really did write all that malarkey.

When Rickey accelerated the Dodger farm system, he had more than thirty teams operating in the more than fifty minor leagues that existed then. Of course the old fox kept the best of the crop for his Brooklyn team and sold the surplus for more than enough cash to support the whole operation. It was just what he had done so successfully in St. Louis, in a dynasty he had built even before the days of the Gas House Gang.

For this, Powers pictured Rickey as a swifty who signed innocents to miserly contracts and kept them enslaved in the minor leagues. The Old Man was made to look like some kind of desperado—half Scrooge, half Simon Legree, and all bad.

As I said, Rickey and Powers never met. One night at the mayor's charity game in Yankee Stadium, I whispered to Branch that his persecutor was sitting nearby. "Describe what he's wearing," said Rickey, "so I can turn and see what he looks like."

At one point the abuse from Powers became so bad that Rickey decided to sue for slander and defamation of character. He had Arthur Mann and me get back issues of the *News* and collect Jimmy's dirtiest shots as evidence.

Naturally the Old Man had to tell the Dodger lawyer—O'Malley —of his plans.

The slick Irishman talked Rickey out of the suit. "Laugh it off," was his benign advice. "Roll with the punches. If you sue, every newspaperman will turn against us all."

That was bunk, of course. Very few of the writers had any respect for Powers, and none would have taken his side.

So Jimmy went on hammering away, and this fitted in perfectly with the O'Malley long-range game plan; the Powers pot shots, however untrue, upset bankroller and partner John L. Smith, annoyed the bankers, and kept Dodger fans hollering for blood.

How I got into the corporate shin-kicking between Rickey and O'Malley, and out of the minor rat race of writing a daily column for the *Eagle* and being punched by MacPhail, makes a story in itself.

Rickey lost Mel Jones, his traveling secretary, to the wartime Navy in 1942. The Old Man's first choice for the job was a furtive-looking fellow whom he had brought to Brooklyn with him from St. Louis. Durocher called this character "Stables," but his real name was Ed Staples.

Staples got into hot water with Durocher on his first road trip with the team as a combination troubleshooter and nursemaid, which is what every traveling secretary really is.

On trains, the traveling sec was supposed to share a drawing room with the manager. This was protocol on all big league clubs, and the Dodgers were no exception.

On the first night out "Stables" retired early. Leo stayed up to play poker with the newspapermen, the conductors, and even the umpires, if they happened to be aboard.

One night Lippy was in high good humor because he had sat—purposely—in the seat directly ahead of Roscoe McGowen, the scholarly gentleman from the *New York Times*. Durocher kept raising outrageously, even when he had nothing, scaring McGowen and some of the others out of pots they should have won. Roscoe was cursing the manager colorfully in Shakespearean epithets, but he knew that Leo would find a way on the morrow to give the money back, either by buying drinks or by having a party.

Leo would rake in a big pot and exclaim, with a sly look at McGowen, "This will buy a nice frock for Edna." Edna was Durocher's best girl, a long-legged beauty from the front line at the Copacabana.

Roscoe would grind his teeth at such moments, because the stately Mrs. McGowen always cautioned him—in front of the other writers—not to play any poker on the upcoming trip. "If I had the money *you* lose at cards," she shrilled, "I could be the best-dressed woman in New York."

When the poker game broke up about three in the morning, Durocher went to his drawing room to find, to his amazement, that "Stables" had taken the lower berth.

Lippy let out a roar that could be heard above all the railroad noises, including the locomotive whistle. The Lion, as some of his players liked to call him, had not slept in an upper since he played in the Eastern League in the twenties, and he was not about to climb into one now. He woke the conductor, who had to find him another room.

The new traveling secretary slept blissfully through the whole row, but he found out about it the next afternoon when the rattler ended its thirty-hour run to St. Louis. Leo eyed the new man up and down as they stepped down to the platform.

"No wonder they call you Stables," rasped the manager, "you're a horse's ass!"

Now Rickey called me in. He knew I traveled with the team a lot on my *Eagle* job as columnist, and he trusted me because I had done some magazine articles that he liked when he was still with the Cardinals. He had another candidate for the traveling secretary's job, he said. It was Emil "Buzzie" Bavasi, a wealthy boy who had powerful connections in baseball. Buzzie had roomed with Freddy Frick, son of the National League president, at DePauw University in Indiana. Frick's son chose a position teaching psychology at Harvard, but Buzzie opted for baseball. He asked Frick to get him a job in the game.

Ford called MacPhail, who started the boy in the low minors. Valdosta, Georgia, I think it was.

Bavasi would get along with Leo—Rickey knew that. How did I think Buzzie would handle the press? Or should he stick with Staples, give him another chance?

I was flattered that Rickey asked me all these questions, but I begged for time to consider all the angles. Who would make the better information pipeline to Rickey if the job included checking up on the players and Durocher as well, as I supposed it did? Who would do a better job working with the hotel managers? The railroads always gave you skilled men to work with, like the Pennsy's Don Fagans and the Central's Jack Sweeney, so there was no problem there.

I told Rickey I would have a report ready for him the next morning. I worked on it that night and brought it in to him like a little boy turning in a composition to Teacher. As I started to read from it, the Old Man held up his hand.

"I might as well tell you," he said, "that *you* are the one I really have in mind for this position, but I did want to get your ideas on how it should be handled. Now, please continue with what you have written."

This was the man's trademark: going the long way round to get others to collaborate on something he could have told outright any one of a dozen people to do for him.

For this, Rickey was charged with being devious, a double-talker, a slicker, and a con artist.

All I can add is that his roundabout methods worked. He had everybody working with him, including the elevator operators in the Dodger offices on Montague Street, the cabdrivers, the post-men. And everybody seemed flattered to be included in the act by Rickey.

A perfect example was what might have been a very touchy press conference in Montreal. The Dodger team badly needed an outfielder named Luis Olmo, but the Puerto Rican Perfecto, as the colorful French press and fans called him, was walloping the ball at a sensational rate for the Royals, the Dodger farm team. Every time Looey came to bat he got a standing ovation.

It was against all Rickey's policies to rape his farm teams in the middle of the season, and it was a double no-no when the team was drawing four hundred thousand-plus fans, as Montreal was.

The Mahatma didn't want to get raked in the Canadian press, either, and he knew that would happen if he just walked in and snatched Olmo. But this was an emergency, so the wily old gent took another tack.

"I need your help," he told the Montreal journalists. "You watch this team every day. You're my scouts. Tell me, is there a bat on this team that is ready for the major leagues?"

Columnist Al Parsley fell for it, and blurted "Olmo."

"Hmmm," mused Rickey. "I do not think that boy is ready yet."

Baz O'Meara, a respected columnist on the Montreal *Star*, jumped to his feet to defend the Cuban Perfecto. Pretty soon the Montreal writers were falling all over each other to push the Puerto Rican on Rickey. At the end of the press conference, Rickey would have been marked as a villain if he had not given the Latin outfielder the promotion all the writers insisted he deserved.

So, in the roundabout way he loved to pursue, the Mahatma got what he wanted: Olmo. He also got great notices in the next day's papers.

Back in Brooklyn, however, the wise-guy writers knew very well what was going on. "Olmo is the first ballplayer ever smuggled to the major leagues by a committee of sixteen newspapermen," cracked Eddie Murphy in the *Sun*, "who didn't know what they were doing!"

When Rickey finished reading my comparison of Staples and Bavasi, he looked up and said, "Will you take the job?"

I would, indeed. He was offering $100 a week, almost twice what I was getting at the *Eagle*.

"And remember, son," he said, "there will be, in the very near future, a reasonable expectancy of added emolument."

The Old Man liked to roll phrases like "added emolument" around on his tongue. He had thrown one like that at Furillo one day, and Carl had asked, with a frown, "You mean more moola, doncha, Boss?" What Rickey referred to with me was the share of the players' World Series money that always went to traveling secretaries on the winning teams.

One of my first tasks, when we went to spring training before the 1944 season, was to keep track of Durocher. It wasn't easy.

Our training camp was at Bear Mountain, up the Hudson near West Point. Ball clubs were forbidden to travel to Florida as they usually did because of the wartime transportation shortage.

The keeper of Bear Mountain Inn, where we were quartered, was John Martin, an exceptional man who had offered both the Yankees and Giants rooms in his empty establishment, plus meals that included steak every night, for only $4 a ballplayer per day.

More important than that, Martin had, through his friends at the Military Academy, wangled the use of the West Point field house, a huge heated structure the size of an aircraft carrier. It had a dirt floor where a ball club could run off regular infield drills and even batting practice into massive net backdrops. It was wartime, and the Cadets were more involved with mock battles and war games than with their normal sports.

The stuffy Yankees and Giants snubbed Martin, not even bothering to look at what he was offering. Rickey snapped up the deal.

As soon as the first wave of ballplayers moved in in February, the transformation of what had been a rustic retreat in the woods high on the left bank of the Hudson was immediate. The inn, which had been slumbering like the Rip Van Winkle of legend who had made the area somewhat to the north famous, was suddenly alive with players, newspapermen, and fans. Half of Brooklyn, it seemed, drove up every weekend to gawk and rub shoulders with their beloved Dodgers.

Martin's business zoomed from $400,000 a year to a million and a half. He bought more drinks than McDonald ever had. He never charged a newspaperman or a photographer a cent.

Durocher was not much for this wilderness bit; snow scenes and the tall pines didn't charm him. We tried to keep him happy in one of the three suites the inn boasted. More than that, Martin had a new door punched through from Leo's quarters to still another room, so that some of the lovely creatures who sashayed through the Lip's life would be able to visit—with the proper decorum, of course.

Even so, Durocher headed for the Big City every chance he got—and a few more that he took when he shouldn't have. We were only forty miles from Broadway, and the bright lights drew this guy as if he were a moth.

20. Inside Leo the Lip—
with Berle and Benny

One afternoon Rickey was bellowing like a wounded water buffalo for Durocher, but the dandy little manager had jumped the training-camp stockade as soon as the day's workout was over. Bear Mountain wasn't his speed.

It was a raw, blowy day in late March 1944. The Old Man needed Leo for decisions on cutting down the big team. Montreal and St. Paul had to be stocked with whichever fuzzy-faced kids Leo didn't insist on holding.

Somebody said the Lip had gone down the river to New York to rehearse a guest shot on Milton Berle's radio show. The week before, he had been on "Duffy's Tavern," with Ed Gardner. Two weeks before that it had been the Jack Benny show.

They paid him $1,500 a shot, sometimes even "two big ones," as he called them, and he was in big demand. There was no competition: The Yankees' Joe McCarthy was as somber as an undertaker, and Mel Ott, the Giant manager, was a shy man who would have come apart trying to read a gag-writer's script.

Leo had an easy ballplayer's way that lent itself to these things. He came on strong, and he would say anything they put into the dialog, even about the umpires. His battles with George Magerkurth and Beans Reardon, Jocko Conlan and Babe Pinelli were famous, and the gagmen played them up to the limit. Umpires were always fair game.

Some big oaf they brought in from Central Casting to be an umpire on the show would say in menacing tones: "Did I hear you call me a blind bat, Durocher?"

Leo would snap back, "What, can't you *hear*, either, Magerkurth?" and people would break up in Anaheim, Azuza, and Cucamonga, not to mention the Bronnix, Lon Guyland, and Greenpernt, as Dan Parker loved to call those precincts in his column.

To Benny, Berle, and the rest, Durocher was authentic Brooklyn in an era when mention of that village or the Daffy Dodgers they rooted for was a sure-fire laugh-getter.

All of this was no laughing matter to Rickey. When Leo's frequent absences came up that night at a press conference, the Mahatma cleared his throat and sounded like a judge pronouncing sentence: "That young man," he boomed, "will have to make an election of professions!"

It was pure Rickey lingo, and the Old Man rolled it around his tongue the way he had played with "reasonable expectancy of added emolument."

The writers loved it. Bad Boy Durocher was in trouble again. That night, the *Mirror* and *News* had it in their early editions, which hit Times Square a little after ten, so Leo had read all about the new rhubarb before he started back across the George Washington Bridge and up Highway 9W at midnight.

The next morning he was resplendent as usual when he came down to breakfast. The silk shirt bore no trace of a wrinkle, and you could have suffered a severe cut on the crease in the perfectly tailored slacks. Just a trace of Chanel No. 5 wafted along with him, and the grin was ear-to-ear as he sought out Rickey's table.

The Old Man looked up from his morning paper like a startled owl.

"You won the election, Mr. Rickey," said Leo mysteriously.

"What election?" Rickey seemed puzzled.

"You were running against Milton Berle, and I voted for you, that's all," said Lippy with some bravado.

Rickey snorted. But before the Old Man could say any more, his gabby manager added, "What I mean is, I like this job, and I won't leave camp any more without your permission."

He had beaten Rickey to the punch, taken away his ammunition.

I had seen it happen once before, the time Leo had played hooky from an exhibition game in Kingston, a bus ride up the Hudson from the city. He was supposed to take a good look at Eddie Basinski, a new infielder. Lippy had taken a quick dislike to the kid because he had thick eyeglasses and a violin. "Betcha he can't hit the ball with the broad side of that fiddle!" he said in an aside to Charley Dressen.

Leo decided to skip the game as well as Basinski and leave the coaches in charge. He figured nobody but the villagers would be there, anyway.

I was aghast when Rickey and the Twig showed up at Kingston. They had driven all the way up in a limousine to see Basinski in this little burg where the ballpark lights were so poor you could barely read the scorecard.

Rickey was furious. He suspended Durocher on the spot, making Clyde Sukeforth the manager "until further notice." Sukey was in power and out again more often than a South American dictator.

I had to call a dozen newspapers to protect their writers who hadn't bothered to make the Kingston trip. Then I sent the bus on its way with the players and coaches, and drove the Rickey limousine. Branch Junior was trying to cool the Old Man down in the back seat, and every once in a while I managed to slip in a word or two for Leo.

Finally the Twig grinned at his Dad and said, "Why do you keep on talking about being 'through' with Durocher? You know you'll never fire him permanently—"

"Indeed?" said Rickey. "And why not?"

"Because he's your favorite reclamation project. It's not enough for you that he's a good manager. You want to make a good person of him, reform him, and you'll never give up!"

Rickey let out a big "Harrrrummmph!" But that was all.

What the Twig had said was 100 percent true. Rickey had a deep feeling for Durocher, who had come out of the school of hard knocks after a tough childhood in Springfield, Massachusetts. He also had a very deep affection for his only son, who had had a rough time growing up in the midst of five sisters.

Branch Junior had left St. Louis early to get out from under the shadow of his famous father, and MacPhail had given him a job with the Dodgers. It was tough for young Rickey to take when the Old Man had followed him to Brooklyn.

Both Durocher and the Twig were rebels at heart. The younger Rickey was to die while still a young man, because he refused to give an inch and take medication for the diabetes he had contracted winning a $5 bet that he could take off 30 pounds in a month on a crash diet.

Durocher? He led a charmed life, walking the tightrope across problems with women, money, umpires, and Unhappy Chandler.

After playing hooky from Kingston, Durocher was dressing the next afternoon in the paneled room that he used for an office off the main Dodger clubhouse at Ebbets Field. Rickey stormed in and put it to him fast: "Where were you yesterday?"

Without batting an eye, Leo said, "I went to the racetrack."

The Old Man pulled his expensive homburg down over his ears in frustration, ripping the lining. "If you had told me anything but the truth, you'd have been finished for good," said the Mahatma, his teeth clenched. "I knew you were at the track."

Durocher got a good dressing down and promised never, never to leave the team again. But he got his job back, and manager pro tem Sukeforth faded into the wings again. He didn't mind. No manager ever had a more loyal pair of lieutenants than Sukey and Charley Dressen, Leo's enforcer.

Durocher had more unpolished brass than Muhammad Ali, and he came on stronger, louder, more abrasively than Howard Cosell. There were times when the guy didn't know what he was talking about, but even then he sounded impressive. If he wanted to he could walk into a room full of atomic scientists with some scrap of information he had picked up in the men's room, and hold them spellbound.

He is a superb card-player whose card-index mind keeps track of every spot on the pasteboards as they are played, just as he can recite, play-by-play, every inning of ballgames played months, even years ago.

But as a bridge player Leo is hard to live with, because he must always be the star, the center of attraction. Be dummy once in a while? Not Leo! The hell with it, if he had to sit there while his partner played a big hand.

At Bear Mountain Inn, the card games in front of the big fireplace in the lobby, after the workouts and meetings were finished, were better than vaudeville. One night Durocher and Rickey were partners against Bob Cooke, sports editor of the New York *Herald Tribune*, and me. Ballplayers, rookie and veteran alike, photographers, writers, and just plain fans ringed the table, straining for a look at Rickey and an earful of Leo. The latter was easy to come by, even if you were at the other end of the inn. He was always broadcasting.

As far as Rickey knew, the game was for small stakes, like the tenth of a cent he and I always battled for. Actually, Durocher had thirty times that much action; he was betting three cents a point against Cooke, another born gambler.

Rickey picked up a handful of aces and kings, and the crowd behind him pressed in closer to hear the bidding. The Old Man opened, and after a pass Durocher raised him. Cooke stuck in an overcall. The auction went at a lively rate until Rickey bid four no-trump, the Blackwood Convention that demands a bid from partner that will disclose how many aces he holds.

Instead of bidding, Durocher said, "Pass."

"My boy, you cannot pass," said Rickey, looking over his glasses in a pitying way.

"But I just did!" snapped the Lip, defiantly.

Rickey was patient, but firm. "When you are playing in civilized company, and you are aware of the rules and conventions that have been agreed on, you *must* reply."

"You're wrong," barked Leo in tones that had made many an umpire cringe. "I know all about Blackwood, and I do not always have to answer. What's more, I can prove it!"

"You can?" said Rickey, softly, "I'd like to read *that* rule, if you can produce it—"

"Better than any rule book," crowed the Lip, "I got the world's greatest card-player. He's having dinner here at the inn right now. I'll bring him in and prove to you you're wrong!"

Rickey sat bemused. Who was Leo's "greatest card-player in the world?"

Some two-bit card shark, perhaps?

In a few minutes Leo returned with P. Hal Sims in tow. The man was undoubtedly the No. 1 bridge authority and all-around plunger of that day, and perhaps any day. His head-to-head battles with Culbertson and Lenz were legend. Sims's meal had been interrupted—who could put off a Durocher in full cry?—and now he stood patiently while Leo gave him the facts, the question at stake, and his orders.

"Tell them," commanded Lippy, "that I don't have to reply to the four no-trump bid!"

Sims looked at him as one would an obstreperous child. "I'm sorry, Leo," he said with a frown, "but you're wrong!"

Durocher dismissed him with a wave. "What the hell do *you* know about it, anyhow?" he barked.

Durocher oozes confidence at all levels of competition, but at cards particularly, he honestly believes he should never lose. If somebody does beat him, it is because some lucky guy has, to use one of his own favorite expressions, "caught lightning in a bottle." This assurance at cards comes partly from the fact that he has a gambler's wits. But usually he also has some little edge going for him.

One night after we broke camp at Bear Mountain, he got locked in a head-to-head gin rummy game at a nickel a point with a millionaire by the improbable name of Horace Schmidlapp. We were at New York's swank Mocambo nightclub, and the clock's hands were climbing that last half hour toward midnight. The Dodgers were booked on The Owl, the midnight train to Boston, which was due to leave from Grand Central Station, just a few blocks away. Leo was $400 in the hole and playing as if his life depended on each pick off the deck.

I tried to get him to wrap it up for the night and run for the cab I had outside. I'm not sure he even heard me, although I was right next to him.

In a minute or two I tried again. I pointed out how enraged Rickey would be if he found out his manager wasn't with the team. "There'll be a next time," I said. "Forget it for now. This just isn't your night—"

I should have skipped those last five words. Leo took them as a challenge.

"You take the team up to Boston," he said, biting the words off through clenched teeth. "I'll fly up first thing in the morning, and you can stall the Old Man if he calls."

Schmidlapp was shuffling the cards now with a smug look on his face; he reached for another scotch.

Leo walked me out to the doorman, who was holding the cab open. "No way that I can lose to a clown like this," he hissed, gesturing back over his shoulder as he slammed the cab door.

I had barely checked into the Kenmore Hotel in Boston with the rest of the sleepy group that had tumbled off the train at Back Bay Station when here came Leo, waving eight hundred-dollar bills. He had chartered a small plane, too, and paid for that out of his winnings. He had taken Schmidlapp for a bundle.

This made me curious: Why had Durocher been so sure he was going to win?

"Ain't no livin' human bein' gonna beat me in a game like that," the brassy manager explained. "First off, he's havin' another drink at the end of each game we play, an' that's an edge for me. Then the dum-dum is lettin' me see the bottom card every time he cuts the deck. How could I lose?"

The Lion, as Eddie Stanky liked to call him, got away with playing hooky on that night train to Boston. Still, he always seemed to be walking the very edge of the cliff as far as Rickey was concerned. With one leg dangling out into space, too.

There was the day that the Old Man had warned him to be punctual for a very important press conference in the Dodger offices on Montague Street in Brooklyn. The Mahatma had kept Leo hanging on tenterhooks for months, and many of the writers were speculating that Dressen, or maybe Sukeforth, was finally going to get Leo's job as Dodger manager.

The press conference was to announce Leo's reappointment as manager. He was broke—as usual—and badly needed the job.

"Remember," the Old Man cautioned, "not a minute before noon, because they'll be waiting downstairs for you, and some of them will have a scoop if you're early. But, Judas Priest, son, don't be a minute late, either!"

Yet here we were, with the clock barely five minutes before noon, careening down Broadway on the left side of the street, running red lights as we raced toward the approach to the Brooklyn Bridge. He had dallied too long with a piece of fluff in the office of Schenley Distillers, who were paying him a bundle for a billboard ad.

Durocher was driving his Merc, but it might as well have been Barney Oldfield or Ralph DePalma. He gunned it up to 70 as we zipped past the gold dome of the old New York *World,* right beside the bridge.

I loosened the death grip I had on the right-hand door long enough to steal a look at my watch, which said it was three minutes to noon. I cupped my hand to shout to him as he leaned hard on the horn and weaved between two trucks.

"I believe we're going to make it, Leo," I yelled. "Barring the unforeseen—"

He glared at me because I had the nerve to doubt him. "Ain't gonna *be* no unforeseen, kid," he snapped, waving to all the cops who recognized his streaking black coupe. "I got everythin' figured!"

It was this kind of outrageous gall that Rickey seemed to look for in ballplayers, possibly because he was short of it himself. All his life, but particularly after his arrival on the New York scene, he was pilloried as a double-talking obfuscator whose "evasive phraseology" left interviewers groggy. His press conferences were called sessions in the "Cave of the Winds," as Rickey's office came to be known, or in his "Gas chamber," a term that Hitler had made odious. The reporters would stagger out after an hour and a half—so the stories went—to ask each other, "What did he *really* say?"

Rickey had run across a brash rookie of the Dean and Durocher type years earlier, in St. Louis. He fell for Heinie Mueller head over funnybone. Incidentally, Heinie played eleven good years in the bigs.

But he was only a raw rookie when he pestered Charlie Barrett, Rickey's chief scout, so much that Charley asked the Old Man to take a look at this fresh kid.

"Son, they tell me you claim to play the outfield as well as Tris Speaker," said the Mahatma.

"Yes, Mr. Rickey, I can!"

"They tell me you say you can hit like Home Run Baker."

"Yes, Mr. Rickey."

"And you say you can run bases like Ty Cobb?"

"No doubt about it, Mr. Rickey."

"Judas Priest!" gasped the Old Man.

"I never seen him," said Heinie, "but I'm as good as he is!"

Rickey saw that Dizzy Dean was overstocked with this special kind of confidence the very first day he laid eyes on the big hillbilly. Dean just struck out everybody who came to bat in that tryout camp, throwing strike after strike with his pinpoint control, and laughing uproariously as they waved at his curve. He had pitched his allotted three innings, but Rickey had the supervisor keep him on display longer.

Most rookies held the Mahatma in awe and gave him a wide berth, for he seemed formidable in his pulled-down fedora, the imposing cigar, the array of papers and charts he always had with him. Not so Jerome Herman Dean, of the Oklahoma or Arkansas Deans, whichever yarn you chose to believe. That very evening Diz sidled up to the Old Man: "Branch," he said, taking a liberty that many who had been in Rickey's employ for decades would not dare, "am I goin' to St. Louis with you?" He wanted immediate promotion to the Cardinals.

Feigning ignorance, Rickey said, "I don't believe I know you, *Mister—*"

"You know right well I'm the one who was foggin' that ball past all them good hitters this afternoon," Dean retorted. "You wanted me to strike out more of them after my time was up—"

"You brag a lot," said the Mahatma, "for one so young."

" 'Tain't braggin'," corrected the rookie with some finality, "if you kin really *do* it!"

In Rickey's book, ballplayers were either this "take-charge" kind he liked so well, or "pantywaist" players, which he sometimes called "pussycats." The Old Man had a wide lexicon of terms that were like a code to his intimates. So-and-so looked adequate at a glance, but he had a "dead body"—which meant no reflexes, poor reactions. Poor whoozis was now an "anesthetic," by which Rickey meant an over-the-hill ballplayer who had lost a step, or maybe more, in the field or on bases. The Old Man knew most managers favored this kind, who knew all the right moves in the field from long experience and would never disgrace you with a bonehead play.

Rickey preached again and again that if you used the "anesthetic" players day after day, you'd be weakening the team in the field without realizing it. Ordinarily, B.R. traded these has-beens off his team as fast as he could to force his manager to play the rookie who might embarrass you now and then, but had to be broken in for a job he would hold for the next ten years.

But Rickey's 1944 Dodger team was a strange—for him—mix of beardless youths who hadn't yet been called by their draft boards and spavined veterans who were either 4F or had enough kids at home to make them exempt. This nondescript aggregation drove Durocher up the wall, and he shuffled them into the lineup and out of it with scornful abandon.

On my first western trip as Dodger road secretary, we had lost seven or eight in a row when Durocher decided to juggle the lineup again. It was Sunday, and we were in Cincinnati for a doubleheader. I had already posted the berth listings for that night's hop to St. Louis. They were tacked on the wall of our visiting clubhouse in Crosley Field, all neatly typed: regulars in the lower berths, subs got the uppers. We had only two berth cars due to the wartime transportation shortage, and there were twelve uppers and as many lowers in each car, along with the one drawing room Durocher and I shared. In our other sleeper, the newspapermen tossed for the lone drawing room and the lowers, while the trainer, clubhouse man, and more of the shock troops climbed into uppers.

When Durocher put Goody Rosen into the lineup, I thought nothing of it. Here was a little guy who had rattled around the high minor leagues for years. The stub of a foul-smelling cigar invariably stuck out of a face that was forgettable except for a nose that looked as if it had been broken half a dozen times, doubtless by direct contact with fly balls.

Rosen was a pretty good left-handed hitter, and in that first game he stroked three hits. Durocher pushed a hot hand and played Goody again in the nightcap. He rapped out two more, but I still didn't have any inkling of the problem that lay ahead.

Rosen didn't leave me in the dark very long. "You gotta mistake on that there list," he said, toweling himself and blowing cigar smoke over me from the ever-present stogie. My heart sank. The first road trip, and I had goofed?

"You got me in upper 12," he charged, "an' I'm playin' reg'lar. I wanna lower like the rest of th' reg'lars!"

I had assigned all the lowers, and couldn't snatch one back now from the outfielder Rosen had bumped onto the bench, for most of the players had left, leaving the clubhouse almost empty. This was a crisis for the new traveling secretary, and Rosen was making the most of it.

I took the problem to Durocher. He saw I was uptight and told me to relax. "I'll take him outta there," he rasped.

"Out of upper 12?" I said haltingly, "but—"

"Hell no," said Leo, making sure that Rosen heard him. "Outta the lineup!"

He did, too. We had lost two that day despite Rosen's five hits. Every day Roscoe McGowen or one of the other writers would compose a new stanza to a song called "Lose 'em All," which stretched out to seventeen stanzas before we finally won one.

Every day we found a new way to lose. That day I remember

Eddie Miksis, a boyish-looking shortstop out of Trenton, New Jersey, had kicked one in the clutch, and the winning runs came home. Roscoe wrote:

"Miksis will fix us,"
    Said Rickey the boss;
So Leo played Miksis
    —An' chalked up a loss!

Durocher had stormed into the clubhouse breathing fire after that one. "Tomato pickers!" he had roared. "That's all they are, a bunch of tomato pickers!" Then, turning to me, he had snarled, "Tell Rickey to back up the truck and bring in another load!"

The kids on the team didn't know what to make of this man who was transformed into a roaring maniac when we lost. Their coaches in high school and college hadn't carried on like this.

In the very first week of the season our ragamuffins had been no-hitted in Boston by Jim Tobin, a flabby old pitcher who threw knuckleball after knuckleball, teetering gently on the mound as if he were in a rocking chair, not even breaking into a sweat.

A youngster who had somehow retrieved a foul ball during this long forgotten no-hitter was unlucky enough to bring it to the Lip as we all waited for the train that would take us back to New York. A freight loaded with garbage was passing, and Durocher fired the kid's prize right into the lead dump-car, a perfect strike. "That's for Jim Tobin," he snarled. "No-hitter, my ass. Tobin couldn't get your mother out, kid! Here's ten bucks instead of your ball."

The night Miksis kicked the game away, Howie Schultz had struck out twice, leaving a total of five men on base. He was a very polite college boy who had hit .300 for a brief time after Rickey bought him for $60,000 to fill in at first base during the war years. No curse words passed Howie's lips, and he went to church regularly—which was the second reason they called him "Steeple."

Schultz was doing just fine as a regular until he got married; then his .300 batting average sank below .200.

After the game in which Steeple had left the five runners

stranded, two little old ladies came up to Durocher in our hotel lobby to ask how that nice Schultz boy was doing. Like Howie, they were from St. Paul, Minnesota.

Durocher was still fuming after the defeat. "I'll tell ya, ladies," he began. "Your boy Howard was a nice kid who didn't even know what it was for. Now that he's married, Howard's drillin' for oil. He's so weak he couldn't hit me with a paddle if I ran across home plate!"

The ladies were horrified. But they had nothing on Durocher, who was horrified in his own way at the manner in which his tomato pickers were throwing games away. He never did learn to accept defeat gracefully, even though he got a lot of practice at it that year.

In Rickey's vocabulary, Miksis and Schultz were "pussycats." The Old Man traded for the "glue man" he needed to hold his infield together and got Eddie Stanky. Military rank also cropped up often in shop talk between B.R. and his lieutenants. Dizzy Dean was a "captain," taking charge on the mound the way Durocher did with any infield he was a part of. If you were tabbed a "corporal" or, worse yet, a "private," God help you, there was no future for you in baseball.

It was amazing to be around Durocher and Big Dean to see how similar was their approach to the game, although I'm sure they never discussed it. Dizzy was a take-charge guy who stomped around the mound as if it were his own private porch. Sometimes he knocked down a hitter in the first inning just to show who was boss. He'd do the same if a hitter had the gall to scratch around in the batter's box, digging for a toehold, which was a definite taboo with Diz. More than once I saw him go right down through a nine-man lineup, throwing at each hitter, "putting some dirt on their numbers" as he laughingly called it when they went sprawling, cap flying in one direction and the bat in another.

If you ripped Diz for a base hit, you were glared at like a bill collector or any other lifelong enemy. Next time up, you were sure to get that good Dean fastball, high and tight, or "high neck in," as Charley Dressen used to call that frightening pitch.

Dizzy seemed to have worked up a special dislike for Bill Terry, one of the great hitters in the game who rose to be manager of the Giants. Dizzy knocked him down at least once in every game he pitched against New York.

I had been traveling with Terry's club as a writer at the time, and I asked Diz about it: "Why do you throw at Terry? He's really a very nice guy when you get to know him."

Dean just shrugged. "Could be," he allowed, "that he's a nice guy when you get to know him, *but why bother?*"

That was out of the same baseball catechism that produced "nice guys finish last," one of Durocher's bylaws. I was there when Leo said that for the first time, to Frankie Graham, the gentle, talented columnist of the New York *Sun.* That quote has haunted him ever since. But the way he meant it, it was absolutely true.

They were discussing Mel Ott, whose job as Giant manager was hanging by a thread. The Giant players were walking all over this quiet, self-effacing fellow who had been one of the greatest batting heroes in Giants history. This was during the 1946 season, and we were chatting on the steps of the Dodger dugout at the Polo Grounds.

Leo pointed over to the Giant dugout. "Ott's lost control of that team," he said. "There's no discipline at all."

"But Mel is *such* a nice guy," said Graham, who had been his long-time admirer.

The Lip gave the same kind of disdainful shrug that Dean had given me. "Nice guys," he said quietly, "finish last!"

Ott *did* finish last with a Giant team which should have done better. That Winter I ghosted a book for Durocher—it was called *The Dodgers and Me*—and we sold a chapter to *Redbook,* a national magazine, for $2,000 before the book came out. The chapter the magazine editors selected was one I had headed "Nice Guys Finish Last."

I enjoyed ghost-writing. Being an author under the pseudonym "Shortstop" had been a kick, but even before that I had been both "Carl Hubbell" and "Lou Gehrig" in the 1936 World Series. I ground out that daily pablum for the Christy Walsh syndicate, and it appeared in papers with a combined circulation of over 60 million; I slaved twice as long and hard over my stories in the *Eagle,* which had less than 100,000 readers.

During that period, too, I had been J. G. Taylor Spink and

every week filled a column called "Looping the Loops" under his name in his paper, the *Sporting News*, which was acknowledged then as now to be the "Bible of Baseball."

Spink was an eccentric editor who had an unerring nose for news but couldn't write a line. He would pick up the long-distance phone as if it were an intercom if an idea happened to come into his mind. He sent long telegrams the way other folks scribble notes. His code word for me in his ghost-writing operation was "Bonfire." He delighted in sending a wire with only that identifying name to the pressbox at Yankee Stadium or the Orange Bowl in Miami; and it tickled him twice as much when the telegrams reached me.

One day he sent this wire to a hotel in New Orleans where he had learned I was going to stay during Spring Training: "BONFIRE: THERE ARE NOW SEVEN INDIANS ON ROSTERS OF NATIONAL FOOTBALL LEAGUE CLUBS. CAN YOU DO ANYTHING ABOUT THIS?" By "anything," he meant any kind of a feature story.

Another time I put off doing a story for him, pleading illness. When he finally got the yarn, he wired back: "I HOPE THAT YOU WILL NEVER REGAIN HEALTH IF YOU CAN DO WRITING LIKE THIS WHEN YOU ARE SICK. GREAT STORY. TAYLOR."

What Spink wanted, he usually got. It was easier to give in to him than have this hawk-faced little gnome of a genius chasing you all over the country by telephone and telegraph.

In early 1946 Spink commissioned me to do a story about a Cardinal pitcher named Blix Donnelly, who had remained in a ballgame by threatening to hit manager Eddie Dyer between the eyes with the ball as Eddie advanced toward the mound to change pitchers. I had told Taylor the story in confidence, and I was soon to regret it.

Having just become a member of the Dodger official family, I did not think it would be discreet to write such intimate stuff about another club's troops. I declined. Spink came on stronger and stronger. If you told him he couldn't have something, that one thing became what he wanted most of all.

That weekend I was covering a big Army game in Michie Stadium at West Point, and a cryptic wire arrived at the military base up the Hudson. It said "BONFIRE: MUST HAVE FACTS ON BLIX REVOLT. YOU CAN SMELL OUT GREAT STORY FOR ME. WILL DOUBLE USUAL YELLOW PAPER." It was signed "Stinky," which had been garbled in transmission from "Spinky."

Army officials puzzled over this one for a long time, thinking they had uncovered a mutiny in the Corps, or at least an insurrection in some banana republic to the South. When Western Union, having handled many similar messages to "Bonfire" in the past, told Army officials who Bonfire was, they came to me. I told them "yellow paper" referred to Spink's paychecks, which were that color, and I had to explain that I was still declining to write the embarrassing piece for Spink's paper and trying to ignore all his messages.

Dismayed but never defeated, the demon editor dispatched a special messenger from his New York office to my Belle Harbor home with a yellow check for a hundred bucks, but it was made out to my seven-year-old son, Tod. Naturally, the youngster was delighted that Christmas arrived this early, although he couldn't explain Santa's generosity.

I still refused Spink, who then attacked anew by telephone.

Trying to explain to a teary-eyed little boy named Tod why he would have to return the mysterious check, I was making little headway when the phone jangled again. It was the angry editor, and when I declined again to write about Blix Donnelly's threat to brain his manager, Spink exploded at me. "You are a real pain in the ass," he said. "You mean you're actually going to take that money out of that nice little kid's pocket?"

At that point, I surrendered.

When he made that "nice guys finish last" crack about Mel Ott, how could Leo ever have dreamed that he was going to take the very job of the very same nice guy he was talking about?

But that's the way it happened.

When the Lip swaggered into the Polo Grounds, where he had been Public Enemy No. 1, he took charge there, too. Within three years he had won *them* a pennant.

This guy would take over a high mass, if only the priest would move over!

His knockers said Durocher was just lucky, that things seemed to break right for him again and again.

"But luck," Rickey liked to point out, "is the residue of design." That was one of his favorites. B.R. thought Leo had a sharp mind.

Durocher did seem to have a sixth sense: when to yank a pitcher, when to put on the hit-and-run, when to blurt the straight truth to the Old Man (although, like MacPhail, Leo used the truth sparingly)—these things he did by intuition.

Rickey defined "intuition" as "subconscious reaction in time of stress." Leo had that knack in trigger-quick decisions on the field, giving Dressen the sign for the next play while this one was still going on. He had intuition in card games, shooting craps, and about people, particularly women. Rickey envied his dapper manager's style with the stream of beautiful ladies who sashayed through the fast life he led.

Edna Ryan was a long-legged blonde stunner out of the front line at the Copacabana, then the top nightclub in the world. Being from Dan Parker's Lon Guyland, she talked fluent baseball to Rickey from the very first time they were introduced. She completely captivated the Old Man.

Edna was always there to wave a tearful farewell to Leo at Grand Central or Penn Station when the Dodgers left on those two-week Western trips. And, win or lose, she was always on hand with a hug and a kiss for her hero when he and the boys came marching—or dragging—home.

"What a wonderful helpmate for my manager," Rickey murmured to me one day when his glasses had steamed up watching this touching scene along with hundreds of commuters whose heads spun to watch. Many of them halted to stare. Edna was a one-girl traffic jam.

But the Old Man didn't know the half of it. No, not one-eighth!

⚔︎⚔︎⚔︎

21. Breadon's Dirty Trick and Lippy's Revenge

What Branch Rickey did *not* know was that Edna Ryan, the Golden Girl from the Copa, often flew out to St. Louis or Cincinnati or wherever, to root for Pee Wee and The Dook—but most especially for her fella, Leo.

Nanette Fabray sometimes joined us for a series in the West, too. She was a witty, clever girl whose cute nose would wrinkle every time Leo turned an umpire's ears red or got off a funny that flustered one of the opposing hitters. The Lip was good at that; all he had to do was yell "Pontiac!" and Hank Sauer, the Cubs' home-run hitter, would fall apart up at the plate and call for time until he could pull himself together. Sauer had a prominent nose that did seem to lead him around like the Indian's head radiator ornament on Pontiac cars at that time.

Kay Williams had also been Durocher's visitor at our Bear Mountain camp. A real beauty, she was in the process of divorcing Macoco, the Argentine sugar millionaire. She would later become Mrs. Clark Gable. Barney Stein and the other newspaper photogs who trailed the Dodgers ate this stuff up; it was like the icing on their cake after they'd been taking pictures of guys swinging bats and sliding in the dirt all day.

Leo kept all these lovelies moving from stop to stop as skillfully as he herded his runners around the bases or signaled for one to go from first to third. The ladies never crossed paths, and no two of them ever arrived embarrassingly at the same place at one time, the way early Dodgers like Babe Herman and Dazzy Vance had.

I knew the timetable and much of the detail, because frequently I had to meet Leo's charming guests at the plane or train. Unless, of course, we were in St. Louis, where Benny took over.

Benny was a burly, Brooklyn-type cabdriver who always had his black-and-white hack at whatever train station or airport we used to enter St. Louis. Sometimes we arrived later than planned, if we got tangled in an extra-inning game over in Chicago. Once in a while we detrained at an obscure railroad spur near the Chase Hotel, or we might even appear a day early because of a rainout. How Benny found out our movements, I never discovered; he would have been useful to the CIA in wartime. He never missed meeting us, and he stuck to Leo like a private eye for the entire series. For four full days, Benny and his hack would be parked in front of the Chase night and day until the master dismissed him in the small hours.

Leo threw money around like confetti, tipping doormen, bellboys, clubhouse men, cabbies, and porters. They still talk about him today, for he may have been the fattest tipper of all. He moved through the National League like an Arabian prince, complete with entourage.

Lippy took a wardrobe trunk on the road to protect the twenty suits he needed to get through a two-week Western trip. There were compartments in it for his silk shirts and linens.

Not to be outdone, Ducky Medwick, when he roomed with Leo, acquired a large trunk, as befits a batting champion. Senator John Griffin, the Dodger clubhouse man, warned the bell captain at every hotel we visited to be on the lookout for these two huge pieces of baggage.

Durocher's trunk was always quickly trundled up to his room, where there was invariably a fat tip waiting. Medwick's trunk never made it; it was always sidetracked in the freight elevator, or misplaced in the boiler room, or wherever it is that bellboys conceal the baggage of those foolish souls who have failed to reward them. I don't think the Hammering Hungarian ever figured this out.

Benny the cabbie was not in it for the tips or fares alone, although he got his share. He liked to sit in the club box at Sportsman's Park in St. Louis, where the crowds were extra hostile to Durocher and his team. The fans in St. Louis felt that Branch Rickey had deserted them to build in Brooklyn a juggernaut that would one day crush their Cardinals; they were systematically inflamed along these lines by Harry Caray, probably the most intemperate radio announcer who ever lived, until Howard Cosell came along to take over the championship.

On top of that, Rickey carried an open grudge against Cardinal owner Sam Breadon. The Mahatma had made millions for Breadon, auctioning off to other sucker owners more than $2.8 million in castoffs while keeping the players needed to win five pennants and four world championships. Rickey felt his reward had been to have Breadon betray him when he needed support to fight Judge Landis's vendetta against the far-flung "chain-gang" farm system.

These things made the Dodger visiting-club box in St. Louis's Sportsman's Park very much like a U.S. embassy in a hostile country. It was composed of eight railed-off seats so close to Brooklyn's dugout that you could look in and see and hear everything that went on, and plenty did go on. With Benny the cabdriver there, it was a fortress of security in the midst of enemy territory. Benny made it his business to quash any anti-Durocher comments, often with something stronger than his usual scowl.

I sat there with Benny on the eventful September night in 1945 when Durocher turned the entire National League pennant race around, because he felt his downtrodden Dodger team, hopelessly out of the race, had been humiliated and belittled by Breadon.

For Breadon, his doublecross of Durocher just to pick up a few more bucks in an illegal doubleheader was one of the dumbest blunders any one in baseball's House of Lords ever pulled off, and that is saying very, very much indeed. When you cross Durocher you had better be sure that your own jockstrap and cup are in place—that or a suit of armor.

The moment Leo got wind of Sam Breadon's dirty trick, he began acting like a crazy man; and he never stopped for the next thirty-six hours.

At the end of that time two men were dead in a flaming train wreck that very well could have snuffed out all the Dodgers in their sleep. Shaken by this nightmare, the Brooklyn bunch rolled over meekly a few hours later in an early afternoon travesty in Chicago, whose team then went on to win the pennant.

Only a few hours before that horrible wreck, in which we were all trapped because of Breadon's penny-pinching, Durocher had whipped his Brooklyn ragamuffins into a frenzy. He goaded them into twice upsetting the startled Cardinals, who shot their two best pitchers, Ken Burkhart and Charley Barrett, in that double fiasco on a rainy night. Leo was good at pulling off things like that.

Until that night, the Cardinals had been coming fast; they had streaked from far back in the race to a point where they would be only a game and a half back of the league-leading Cubs if they could trample the Dodgers twice this night.

That did not figure to be too tough, for Durocher and his team had been sauntering through September with a "who cares?" smirk. The Lip had originally intended to throw two "give-up" pitchers, Clyde King and Les Webber, against St. Louis in the last two games of this series. The Cards had chewed Ralph Branca to bits in the first game.

Leo was saving his two best, Vic Lombardi and Hal Gregg, to pitch against the Cubs in the next series in Chicago. The Cubs were staggering and had lost again that afternoon. That was Durocher's way: Save your best to knock off the guy on top.

But Breadon changed all that.

It had rained on our second night in St. Louis. And now, instead of playing the postponed game on the afternoon of our final day there, as the rules required, the owner of the Cardinals was forcing us to play a twi-night doubleheader. The old skinflint knew, because I had told him, that this night doubleheader—before the next day's afternoon game in Chicago—would cost us our Pullman sleepers on the regular night train and would force us into an all-night situp ride in a chair car at the end of a long freight.

Leo knew it, too, and he had blown up when I told him what Breadon was planning.

All night long the two of us kept calling Ford Frick, the National League president, at his Scarsdale, New York, home. The next morning we tried to corner him in his league office to complain about the dirty trick Breadon was pulling on us. A county-fair stunt like this wasn't legal even under the pathetically stretchable National League rules of the time.

But Frick wasn't answering his phone. He wanted no part of a hot potato like this, because Breadon was a powerful owner in league councils, and Ford needed his vote next time his contract came up.

I often wondered in those days why something big wasn't made of a dirty trick like this, which turned a pennant race around and made Death a passenger on our train to Chicago that night.

But the fact is, after it was over Frick couldn't afford to talk about it; and in St. Louis, Breadon was speechless with rage, because he was out of pocket hundreds of thousands of dollars of World Series money. Too, there were no journalistic gumshoes like Dick Young around in those days to expose the outrage.

It became clear on the sunny afternoon when we should have been playing that Breadon was going to get away with his night doubleheader; and Durocher got madder and madder instead of shrugging it off.

He got hold of Gregg and Vic Lombardi, whom he had been saving for the series in Chicago, and told them he was going to use them that night to "kill" Breadon and the Cardinals. He started to psych up his whole team in the lobby of the Chase Hotel before we left for the ballpark.

This wasn't easy. It was a joke of a Dodger team, a crazy quilt of has-beens like Dixie Walker and Frenchy Bordagaray and never-was ballplayers like Mike Sandlock and Eddie Basinski, the violinist.

Once at the park, the Lip strutted like a Napoleon in a baseball suit in front of his troops as they warmed up. "Look at that plush-lined bum up there in his private box," he stormed, pointing to where Breadon sat.

Old Sam was the perfect paunchy prototype of a magnate as he puffed contentedly on a big cigar, counting his money—the feudal baron living off the serfs below.

And Durocher never let the serfs forget. A steady drizzle was falling now, to make things worse, if possible. "Fuckin' Ol' Moneybags is makin' you risk your arms and legs—your very bread and butter—down here in this mud!" Leo screamed at his players.

Now the first game was under way, and as I sat there in the club box with Benny I could hear the Lip goading his men on every pitch.

I had heard Knute Rockne raise his whole team with one of those Notre Dame fight talks between halves, but I had never heard anything like this. It brought to mind Rickey's answer to a question about why he rated Durocher so highly as a manager. "Because he can steal a pennant for you with a third-place team," the Old Man had said, "if he puts his mind to it."

Nothing else mattered to Leo right now except knocking Breadon out of the pennant race. He had spent half an hour getting Lombardi keyed up to pitch this first game. The little left-hander didn't have a fastball that could black your eye, but he only teased the Cardinals with it. His curve was playing tricks in the damp night air, and he was getting them out with that.

Ken Burkhart was a sixteen-game winner, but Brooklyn hitters he could usually handle stomped all over him this night. Playing as if they were in the World Series, Durocher's men grabbed the first game, 7–3.

It was raining harder now, but that didn't cool Leo off. The Cardinals were stunned when they saw Handsome Hal Gregg, the big fireballer, warm up for the second game; they knew the Lip had been saving him for the Cubs the next afternoon. In the dugout we could hear the manager screaming, "Breadon took away your Pullman sleepers tonight. He's treating us all like animals, making us ride in a cattle car!"

The Dodgers climbed all over Charley Barrett right from the first pitch. The ace of the Cards' staff walked Eddie Stanky, just as the Lip screamed he would; then he blew sky high under the riding and never got out of the first inning. Gregg coasted to win it.

Breadon, instead of being on the Cubs' heels, was now three and a half back, and fit to be tied. The few bucks he had tried to make at the Dodgers' expense were about to cost him a bundle. Although he didn't know it right then, the pennant race was over.

It was long past a wet, cold midnight when the wrinkled, hungry Dodgers began to straggle onto the train platform. We usually went first class, with two sleeping cars, a diner of our own, and a baggage car for the equipment trunks. But wartime travel restrictions, plus Breadon's dirty trick, had changed all that.

Even so, the night freight was a complete shock. It was a collection of rolling junk: a few mail cars, some dirty, dimly lit smoke-filled coaches, and a long string of refrigerator cars filled with produce, but no diner. Up front, a huge locomotive eagerly panted to be out on the rails to Chicago.

Durocher stopped to chat with the engineer, who was already up in his cab, anxious to turn it loose. They were already more than an hour late as the big turnip of a watch in his palm told him.

Had Charley Tegtmeyer known, he'd have stretched out this little chat, instead of rushing it. It was to be his last night on earth.

⋉⋈⋉

22. The Train Wreck That Decided a Pennant

Charley pushed his blue denim cap back on his head. He had to smile as he gazed down at Durocher on the sooty platform. Leo was still dapper despite the rain and all the grime around him. The manager sported a silk shirt as usual, and patent leather loafers; and he was redolent, as always, of Chanel No. 5.

For all that, the old trainman thought, his sooty iron horse and the brassy Dodger leader were alike in one thing this night: Both were breathing fire.

"A dirty trick that was," Charley began. He lived in Chicago and was a double-dyed Cub fan; inwardly he was delighted at the double disaster Leo and his Dodgers had just hung on the Cardinals. "How could they force you to play two on a night like this when you gotta be on the field at noon today in Chicago?"

"We got even," fired back Durocher. "We give it to 'em good!"

"You just about killed the Cardinals tonight," Charley said. Then, after a pause: "I'll make up some time for you, Mr. Durocher; if you'll just get all your guys aboard, I'll get you over to Chicago so's you can catch a few hours in real beds before noon."

Durocher jumped at the offer and turned toward the back of the train to herd his stragglers into their "cattle car."

"Pour it to her, Dad," he threw back over his shoulder to the old engineer. "Like we poured it to Breadon tonight!"

It was the first time in two days that the Dodger manager had mustered even the semblance of a smile.

The smile vanished when Leo got a glimpse of the antique parlor car that they had tacked on the very end of the train for us. It had a huge observation platform whose tarnished brass must have been polished last in some long-forgotten day; inside the musky old mausoleum were two long rows of overstuffed velvet chairs and one drawing room. Lucius Beebe would have loved the old relic for its inlaid mother-of-pearl paneling and crystal chandeliers. But all the elegance of the old museum piece was lost on Leo.

"I seen pictures of Woodrow Wilson makin' speeches off the back of this old crate," he barked, shoving past the railroad agent who was apologizing for the fact that this was the best they could find for us on last-minute notice. They had to get the old girl out of mothballs, at that, he said; troop movements had just about cleaned all the rolling stock out of the yards.

Now the engineer, who should have been highballing on this main line to Chicago an hour and a half earlier, was pushing Old No. 70 to the limit. He was playing a happy tune on the throaty whistle, talking to the early-bird farmers who lived by his Wabash night freight as she raced toward the dawn. A broad smile lit his face, for he was sure his Cubs would get their pennant now, after the way this Dodger gang he was hauling had mauled the Cardinals last night. Might have been a lot different, he thought to himself, if Durocher had saved big Gregg to pitch against Claude Passeau today!

Back in their observation car, most of the Dodger players dozed fitfully in their rumpled clothes. The reporters from the New York evening papers, who would file their stories when they pulled into Chicago, picked at the bouncing typewriters they tried to balance in their laps. There weren't nearly enough chairs for all, so Basinski and Buckshot Brown and Ed Stevens, whose double had wrecked Barrett in the second game, stretched full length on the frayed carpet along the sides of the car, snoring intermittently. It looked like a scene from an all-night rescue mission, where bums come to wait for the soup line.

The railroad sounds were soothing: the crossing-bells, loud at first as they passed the car windows, then fading, and the rhythmic click as the spinning wheels counted off the rail joints. Only one card game was still going: In the one drawing room, the inevitable poker session that drew Durocher, the coaches, and those newspapermen who had finished writing was dragging to a drowsy close. Between hands, Dressen was telling how he'd played ball in just about every town in this Three-I League country: Decatur, Davenport, Terre Haute . . .

Roscoe McGowen, the dignified dean of the writers, was taking his customary bath in the game as Durocher, who always made it a point to get the place at table just ahead of the dignified old codger from the *Times,* raised on every card that was dealt. McGowen was cursing in Shakespearean lingua, as usual.

They'd used up most of the night and all of McGowen's money when finally they threw the cards aside. The thin glow that was the edge of dawn was beginning to show up ahead of Old No. 70, and she seemed to be leaping like a hungry horse nearing the barn. Even Durocher, his still immaculate silk shirt swinging crazily on a hanger above him, was catching forty winks; the flicker of a smile played around the corners of his mouth as he dozed, betraying his happy thoughts about what he'd done to Breadon.

When it happened, most of us thought it was the end of the world. Every window on both sides of the car lit up with that wild, dancing brightness you see in blast furnaces. Outside, an inferno was raging. The whole train, running full throttle a few moments before, was now bumping and swaying in a tortured way as the air brakes blew.

In the main part of the Dodger car, bodies were picked up and slammed into the front end along with uprooted parlor chairs, bags, and typewriters.

Looey Olmo, the calf-eyed Puerto Rican outfielder, clawed his way toward the narrow passageway outside Durocher's drawing room, screaming in panic. Charley Dressen, stunned from being thrown against the side of the car, fought to follow Olmo. All they knew was that the car's windows were cracking open, and the searing heat was stalking them. They wanted to be somewhere—anywhere—else.

Durocher was sure it wasn't the end of the world, because he hadn't agreed to it. Anything man-made, Leo always figured he could handle. He was wide awake as quickly as you could snap your fingers, and a glance told him the train's momentum had carried them through the fire and into the clear.

"Back, all you guys," he bellowed in that familiar brassy voice that topped even this din. "Get back to the open end of the car." He grabbed the wild-eyed Olmo's shoulder in a reassuring grip. "Out on the back platform, Looey," he coaxed. "Plenty fresh air out there—"

They didn't know it then, but up front half a tanker-trailer rig was astride Charley Tegtmeyer's locomotive, and the 2,000 gallons of gasoline it had spilled on the cab had cooked Charley to death before spraying aft to ignite the rest of the train.

The intense heat had welded together the big engine's pistons and brought those huge wheels to a halt. But Old No. 70 had stayed on the rails and thundered through that tunnel of fire before the air brakes blew. If she hadn't, they'd all have been crisped inside the old observation car.

As Durocher herded his charges like dazed children out the back door and down into the sharp morning air on the roadbed, they could look back at the death trap they'd all been carried through by sheer momentum, with a dead engineer clamped on the throttle. The lumber yard back down the track was ablaze, and the coal yard was going up now, too. This was Manhattanville, Illinois, about forty miles outside Chicago, and half the town was out gaping now at what had jolted them out of bed.

As the ballplayers sat there shaking in the morning chill, they heard a thin, pleading voice. It seemed to come from the smoking roadbed alongside their blackened car.

It was the fireman, who had been blown clear of the gutted locomotive, which rested now on its belly like a beached whale. Every stitch of the poor man's clothing, and most of his skin, had been burned off. Doc Harold Wendler, the Dodger trainer, tried to help with some ointment, but the man's pain was too great; he was walking, but he couldn't be touched. They all felt so helpless, just watching. And then the awful, pungent smell of burning flesh made Olmo and some of the others throw up.

All Durocher could do was to keep repeating, "Breadon . . .

that miserable bastard . . . Breadon . . . he should be here to see what he caused . . ."

In three hours the fireman was dead, and just about that time the Dodgers, not much better off, staggered out onto Wrigley Field.

Les Webber, dead on his feet, did the best he could with that overhand curve of his, but the Cubs ate him up.

Back in St. Louis, the Cardinals were also very, very dead. Run over, you might say, by Breadon's night freight.

⚬⚬✕⚬⚬✕⚬⚬✕⚬⚬

23. Some of Leo's Ladies

With the flower of journalism's intelligentsia taking up a lot of the plush rooms in the crowded Sheraton Hotel on the beach in Daytona, the stern edict had gone out from the top, at my urging: No women at spring training in 1946.

There was some grumbling from the players and their wives, but it subsided. However, it looked like an all-work and no-fun six weeks in Florida. We wouldn't even have the abundant charms of Edna Ryan in a skimpy swim suit to brighten up the beach in front of our oceanfront headquarters.

Bikinis hadn't appeared yet, but most of Edna had. She would have looked good in a burlap sack.

There was some betting between the writers at the cocktail hour in the press room over how long it would take Durocher to find a way around the "no women" rule.

I couldn't spend time worrying about Edna; I wasn't able to wangle enough rooms for the team at our hotel, which had a unique tunnel that took autos, bicycles, and sand-sailers practically through the lobby to the beach, where they were allowed to take a spin. I had to dig up overflow rooms at fancy prices at the Princess Issena, a wooden structure that looked minor league compared to the swank Sheraton.

I had to pamper our newspaper corps, who refused as usual to double up even though our traveling circus had grown to more than eighty that spring. One of the hardest to please was Mike Gaven of the powerful New York *Journal American,* so I assigned him to a large corner room that practically hung over the surf.

Gaven's mouth seldom remained closed. Not that he was that big a talker, but he seemed to spend half his time drinking and the other half shoveling down food. After a tremendous meal he would order two ponies of brandy. One he downed in short order, and the other he used to wet the tip of his after-dinner cigar. Eventually that too would disappear, and I knew it didn't evaporate.

All the provender that Mike put into his mouth made functions that are routine to most people the leading topic of conversation with him. He would entertain, if that is the proper word, his unwilling listeners in the press room with detailed reports of his bathroom movements, and he spoke of these things with as much delight as others would of an evening of bridge or a day on the golf course.

Within an hour of our check-in at our luxurious hotel on the famous Daytona beach, they were paging me in the lobby; it was Gaven on the phone, bellowing that he would have to be moved to another room.

But why? Wasn't his a corner room? Didn't it overlook the sea?

"Yes, yes, that part's all right," said Mike impatiently, "but they put the bathroom light in the wrong place; I can't see to read when I'm on the pot. I just can't live under conditions like this."

After about a week, Durocher carried a heart-rending plea to Rickey. Edna's mother, poor woman, was ill; she desperately needed some Florida sun and convalescence. Could Edna bring her Old Lady—that was the way Leo phrased it—down for a week and care for her as they roomed together? As I remember, Leo even went so far as to hint that we might save a life by this kindness.

Rickey melted. "Lovely girl, that Edna," he observed. "And you're a lucky man, Leo. Of course it must be done, and you tell Harold I said it was all right to give them a room."

Two nights later the Old Man and I were partners in a bridge game in the hotel lobby. We were playing Hector Racine and Romeo Gauvreau, two of the three Frenchmen who fronted for the Dodgers in Montreal. The third, who was kibitzing, was Lucien Beauregard. Not many of the world's pleasures had escaped these three adventurers.

There was a swish of satin and a hint of expensive perfume. The Ryan girl and her shapely companion were gliding through the lobby. "Good evening, Mr. Rickey," said Edna, dropping a pretty little curtsy. About this time Racine let loose a string of French words to his companions, which I assumed must be highly complimentary to Edna. The eyes of the Three Musketeers lit up at these two apparitions of feminine beauty; and Racine jumped up from his seat, and bowed gallantly from the waist. He was not staring at Edna, but at the lovely creature who was leaning on Edna's arm!

"Judas Priest, son, what is Leo doing to me now?" said Rickey in a hoarse voice, as the two ladies waltzed through a lobby that had been utterly devoid of feminine beauty in this wifeless year. All heads turned. "Who is the *other* one?" demanded Rickey.

When the Old Man got my signal that it was indeed Edna's mother, I thought he was going to swallow his cigar. Mrs. Ryan owned a face of an angel, and a figure to match; she must have been pushing forty, but who could tell?

Many months later, after the Dodgers had finished in a flat-footed, first-ever tie for the 1946 pennant with the St. Louis Cardinals, I was to think back to that touching scene: Leo's devotion to his girl Edna and her sick "Old Lady."

Something Durocher did the following November made me wonder if the strain of a wild pennant race and the wild life he led on the side hadn't gotten to him at last.

He had enough reasons to go bananas. Every other day during the season he had been pushing Rickey, pleading, cajoling, threatening to quit if the boss didn't bring Jackie Robinson up to the big team from the Montreal farm, where Jack had been running wild. The Negro was everything but the phony ball-player Bob Feller said he was: He hit .342, stole forty bases including home several times, and was a leader on the field. There was no doubt that his addition in the last month would have put the Dodger varsity over the top instead of in a tie, which they lost in a playoff.

Perhaps a month after that disappointment, I happened to be in Rickey's office when he took a phone call from Durocher. The talkative manager was up in Minnesota somewhere, making a speech that night. He was getting $2,500 a pop now and was much in demand with firms like General Motors and IBM as a sideshow to pep up conventions.

"Branch, I'm in love!" The unmistakable voice came through the receiver at Rickey's ear even louder than ever, more strident. I could hear every syllable, even from twenty feet away.

"Of course, Leo, I understand," the Old Man said very fondly, "Edna's a wonderful girl—"

"But it *isn't* Edna," the voice cut in. Leo was stammering now, he was so excited. "I met this girl on a short plane hop up here two nights ago. She's making a promotional tour for a movie she's in. She's a sweet girl, and she's got such a wonderful character that I have no right to be taking her out, much less marrying her—"

When Leo wanted to build somebody up to the Old Man, he always brought in "character." Rickey wasn't strong for movie actresses, but Leo had been around him long enough to know that he admired strength of character, whatever that was.

By now the receiver was dangling from Rickey's hand, with Leo's babbling still audible. There was a dazed look on the Old Man's face, and I thought he might be having another attack of the inner-ear dizziness—it was called Ménière's Syndrome—that had floored him several times and once put him in the hospital for a two-week stay.

"Branch, Branch, are you there?" The manager was screaming now, fearful that he had been cut off from his Father Confessor. The phone was dangling near the floor, the cord still in Rickey's hand.

The urgency in Durocher's voice brought the Old Man back to reality, and he reeled in the receiver in time to gather his wits and ask what had become of poor Edna.

"Oh, she's in my apartment," said Leo. "You know, the one on Sixtieth Street, up near the Pierre. We were going to get married until . . . well, until I met this other girl. You'll love this girl, Branch. And don't worry, I'll call Edna tonight and explain everything that's happened—"

The photographers and reporters got to the bewildered Edna before Leo's phone call, however. The newspaper guys had wire-photos from Minnesota, showing the two new lovebirds looking into each other's eyes. It was a tough way for Leo's long-time girl-friend to get the news that her Dodger Romeo had fallen for actress Laraine Day.

Shortly afterward there was a two-inch, blood-red headline across the top of the front page of Hearst's sensation-seeking *Herald Examiner* in Los Angeles, where the winter meetings of baseball were just getting under way: "DUROCHER BRANDED LOVE THIEF!"

It turned into a messy divorce case. Laraine, a strict Mormon, was censured by the California courts and forbidden to remarry for a year. Instead, she and Leo hopped over to Juarez, Mexico, and got a quickie divorce; she married her new manager on the spot, defying the courts.

Rickey sighed when he saw the headline. "This," he said, "should make great ammunition for Jimmy Powers, Joe Williams—and, of course, O'Malley."

The inclusion of Williams, the acid-pen columnist for the *World Telegram,* on the varsity of the wrecking team that was out for Rickey's scalp was a late development.

Williams had written in Memphis before escaping to New York, and he was obviously against the Black Experiment. He had also grown very pally with MacPhail, who by now was sniping at Rickey from every angle. So it was no great surprise when Joe printed a lurid, hoked-up story that just about accused the Mahatma of "throwing" the 1946 pennant race.

How? Williams charged that Rickey had intentionally weak-ened the Dodgers by selling second baseman Billy Herman (who at thirty-five had just returned from two full years in military service). Why would Rickey do such a thing? Williams had the answer to that one, too; he fanned racial animosities by charging that the Old Man was "postponing" the Dodger pennant until 1947, when Robinson would join the team to make it a "Negro triumph."

The flak that Rickey was catching on the Robinson issue was so idiotic as to be laughable, except that so many ignorant people swallowed it as the truth. It was about this time that Judge William Bramham, commissioner of baseball's minor leagues, gave out a lying, hateful statement that a shrine to Rickey was being planned in Harlem by the nation's "Nigras," as Bramham pronounced them. He was from the South, too, of course.

The truth was that I had probably been the one to "fire" Herman. The manager of the hotel where we stayed during a spring training weekend in Miami soaked me for damage to one of his rooms. Herman had obviously staged a wild party. Augie Galan, Herman's roommate, would gladly have chipped in with his share, but Billy, who had been a great star, got stubborn because he wanted to stick Rickey with the bill. He didn't think the Old Man was paying him enough.

I gave Herman a chance to pay for the damages quietly, but he refused. Once on the books of the Brooklyn club, the brawl, and the damages, soon came to light. Incidentally, it must have been a pretty good party; they had to get a plasterer to dislodge the whisky glasses that were imbedded in the ceiling.

When he learned of Herman's caper, Rickey acted fast. He had a young Dodger team and didn't want any night crawlers around to teach his kids bad habits. Within a week after the Old Man found out, Billy Herman was on his way to the Boston Braves. If indeed the pennant did turn on that deal—and it was unlikely, because Eddie Stanky was doing a great job at second for us—it was because of a measly $30 bill for damages!

Williams's story of the "thrown" pennant stung Rickey deeply, and he made a visit to the Dodger clubhouse—a very rare expedition for him—after the loss to the Cardinals in the playoffs.

With tears streaming down his cheeks, the Old Man told his young team that the Williams column was an out-and-out lie, and that he tried to win *every* year, as he hoped they would.

Because they had missed the World Series money by such a narrow margin after trying so hard, Rickey gave every member of that team, including the manager, coaches, and traveling secretary Harold Parrott, a new Studebaker. Cars were still hard to get because of wartime shortages, and these were the Studies that looked the same fore and aft. You couldn't tell at a glance whether they were coming or going.

That was exactly the way Rickey felt, too, when O'Malley let loose a blast that the Mahatma was "giving away" money that should have gone to the Dodger stockholders, including himself.

This was a first. Rickey had never been called a spendthrift before.

It was true that the Old Man had paid Dizzy Dean only $17,500 when he was in his prime, winning thirty games for the world champion 1934 Cardinals, plus two more in the World Series. Why, Diz got another $15,000 that year from General Foods for endorsing Wheaties, and he didn't even have to eat the stuff.

Rickey had also signed Robinson to a very miserly contract with the Montreal Club: a piddling $3,500 bonus, and only $600 a month salary. This came out when Jackie and his wife, Rachel, were living in a single room with bath at New York's McAlpin Hotel and had to hide all their young baby's things, as well as their pots and pans, under the bed when interviewers sought them out for a story.

Now, just when Rickey was trying to get out from under the "El Cheapo" image by treating his players generously, he got blind-sided by a man inside his own organization!

O'Malley was, of course, crying with a loaf of bread under his arm—both arms, in fact.

Shortly after that 1946 season ended, we got figures that showed the club made a net profit of $451,000, instead of being a half-step in front of the bailiff, as it had been for practically twenty years. The Dodgers drew 1,768,247 in Brooklyn with this young club. And Rickey had rounded up the talent: His Montreal club, with Robinson, had mopped up on Louisville in the Little World Series, and many critics came right out and said it was a better team than four or five in the major leagues. The Old Man had another dynasty under way.

On top of all that, the Mahatma was up to his old tricks, selling $239,000 in surplus players from his Dodger farm system—lemons, mostly—to the patsy owners of other teams that were left short of talent by the war.

Still, O'Malley moaned. Rickey was making too much money. There had always been a question about which was the real Almighty to the Big Oom: God, or the Dollar.

He kept undercutting the Old Man, dropping sly remarks where they would hurt the most. In 1947 Rickey would enter the last year of a five-year contract that they had all hammered out together when things were tough: $50,000 a year salary, plus a fat bonus on any Ebbets Field attendance over 600,000.

O'Malley didn't want that contract renewed; now that Rickey had the Dodger fish pond well stocked, the time had come to get rid of the expensive expert in the hatchery.

Rickey didn't seem to worry too much right then about O'Malley's boring from within, or the sniping of the MacPhails and Bramhams from without.

It was Durocher's didos that concerned him most.

He held up the "Love Thief" headline again and looked at me across his desk.

"Do you suppose," he asked, "our boy will *ever* settle down?"

⚒⚒⚒

24. MacPhail Declares War on Rickey

Baseball's biggest story of 1946, along with a record stampede of tourists from the North, was building to a climax when the Dodgers plunged into spring training that March in Daytona Beach, Florida.

Travel bans were lifted. Everybody north of Carolina, it seemed, wanted into Florida. There was a black market in train reservations going south, and to get a hotel room you had to know somebody with clout on the citrus circuit.

It wasn't just the Dodgers in Daytona; over at nearby Sanford, where the Montreal club was training, the Jackie Robinson story was emerging. Columnists, wire service newshounds, and all kinds of reporters, black, white, and even one yellow correspondent, swarmed over the Dodger base, trying to find what kind of game Rickey was playing.

Was Robinson for real, or was he just a minor league phony? Was this the start of something big, or was Rickey just planning

a quick ripoff of Negro fans at the boxoffice, like the old carpet-
bagger a lot of the half-asleep owners whispered he was? Would
the Mahatma leave Robbie in the International League all year
for "seasoning," or would he bring his stormy petrel up to the
Dodger varsity after a few weeks of breaking color lines in
trouble spots like Baltimore?

Every newshawk and his brother was buzzing around us, trying to find the answers to those questions, and more. I thought I
knew the truth, for it had come out one night—the very first time
the Old Man revealed his bold plans to the rest of his family. I
was happy to be counted in that family by adoption, you might
say, when I took the job as traveling secretary. We were all playing bridge—two tables—in the card room in the cellar of the
Twig's home in Queens. Rickey asked us, one by one, how we
felt about the "black experiment" he had in the works. We had
really thought he was just planning a black semipro team to play
at Ebbets Field while the Dodgers were on the road.

Mrs. Rickey was aghast when he had popped the real thing.
"Why *you*, Branch?" she said plaintively. "Haven't you taken
enough abuse, about being 'El Cheapo,' and about the chain
gang, and all that? This will be just more slander on your name."

His son, the Twig, voted against the whole idea, because he
said it would kill the Dodger scouting efforts among the whites
in the South; the Carolinas, for instance, had been the most productive source of playing talent for the Rickeys since the Cardinal days. Arkansas, Mississippi, Texas, and even Florida were
important sources, too.

The Old Man's charming daughters and Mary, the Twig's
lovely wife, were all against it, too.

Rickey looked at me next. I voted no, because I thought we
would be strong enough in 1946 to win without a black man. I
knew most of the problems would be mine if we brought in a
black ballplayer. Ebbets Field would embrace a Negro, or even a
Chinaman in a pigtail, if he could drive in runs for the Dodgers.
But road games would bring up many headaches, and Durocher
and I were the only members of the Dodger official family who
went on the road.

Rickey's soft answer to me told a lot: "Son, the greatest un-
tapped reservoir of raw material in the history of our game," he

said carefully, "is the black race! The Negroes will make us winners for years to come. And for that, I will happily bear being called a bleeding heart, and a do-gooder, and all that humanitarian rot."

I was convinced that Rickey *knew* Robinson was a super player, and who could doubt the Old Man's judgment on such things? I was convinced, too, that he was going all the way with his experiment.

The fact was, while some of the do-nothings among the owners were still debating the propriety of having Negroes in their parlors, and wondering how these creatures would smell and act on the bench or at a press conference, Rickey was already making plans for the second one he would bring up to the majors, and the third.

He had left all the other owners far behind him in rounding up young white hopefuls, because he gambled that the war would soon be over. Almost every other team had cut back to a skeleton scouting staff, but Rickey had quadrupled his bird dogs and talent sleuths. He rounded up and signed every fuzzy-faced prospect they could find. Some of these kids had gone to war, but now they were coming back. Others had been so very young that they hadn't even been drafted by the time Japan surrendered in August of 1945.

Rickey had gone further. He had set up farm teams in the high minor leagues so that they would have a place to play: Montreal in the International, St. Paul in the American Association, Mobile in the Southern League. While others were marking time, his pace was double-quick. He picked up Fort Worth and its ballpark in the Texas League for a mere $75,000.

He had the Dodger clubs in the lower minors going full blast. Jake Pitler, managing at Newport News in the Piedmont League, had fifteen boys of seventeen or under, and two of them were Duke Snider from Southern California and Clem Labine from Woonsocket, Rhode Island, to show how far the Rickey dragnet had stretched. "When we took off in our bus on a road trip," Pitler laughed, "we were loaded with comic books and candy bars; but we carried practically no shaving cream."

Even without his controversial black man, Rickey had lapped the field!

For all this, the Brooklyn boss had become very unpopular in the lodge, where the lords of the game, the standstills and the do-nothings, liked to throw darts at anybody who moved out ahead of them and their tortoise-like pace.

Already they had held a secret meeting and voted down the Negro experiment, fifteen to one. Had I been asked at the time if it were possible to keep such a momentous vote hush-hush, I'd have given an emphatic "No." But I might also have laughed off the idea of this bizarre secrecy, with its shredded evidence, which sounded to me like a rerun of an old foreign intrigue film or some flimsy spy plot that the Hollywood B-picture mill had rejected.

Rickey had begun to get heavy static about the signing of Robinson, even though it was only to a minor league contract. The ringleader of all the critics was none other than the Old Man's former protégé, MacPhail.

Larry charged that Branch had jumped the gun after the rest of baseball had voted to take an "orderly course" in handling the Negro question. MacPhail was chairman of a "Policy Committee," on which sat Yawkey of the Red Sox and Wrigley and Breadon from the National League. They had planned, they said, to include the Negro Leagues in the minor league system of Organized Baseball. But Rickey, that dastardly man, had spoiled all that by "raping" the black leagues and stealing Robinson and others. These stuffed shirts who were now so "worried" about the Negro Leagues had never even noticed them before.

What a joke! The Black Experiment would have died in committee, if Rickey hadn't pushed it on his own. MacPhail's own Yankees never even gave a black (Elston Howard) a chance until nine years after Robinson.

Why had MacPhail, of all people, taken to the warpath against his old mentor?

The success the Old Man had in Larry's old spot, Brooklyn, no doubt rankled. It was a personal thing, too, that the Mahatma had beaten him to another "first" that would have filled out an impressive MacPhail triple crown: The first to bring in radio, the first to start night baseball—and the first to bring in a black star.

If you're looking for more enemies, how about the way Rickey had stacked even more cards against himself by the course he chose at a meeting in April 1945 to pick a successor to old White-mane, Commissioner Landis, who had died? Rickey, a master at politicking, had gone to that meeting in 1945 at Cleveland carrying in his pocket four votes, including those of Carpenter of the Phillies and Stoneham of the Giants. Rickey's man was Ford Frick, then president of the National League. He knew Ford was honest, even if a bit of a milktoast, and there was no doubt he knew baseball inside and out.

Rickey's clique even had a backup candidate if the moguls failed to agree on Frick: Jim Farley, a great baseball fan, and a prominent New York politician who had been Postmaster General during two of Franklin Roosevelt's terms.

MacPhail helped beat down the Frick candidacy, admittedly because Rickey was pushing it.

But it was in the case of Farley that the muddle-headed Lords of Baseball showed their true stripes.

One of them did a hatchet job on Big Jim, reading a paper that attacked this man who had played the game in his younger days and who had been baseball's staunchest ally during the war, when some of the panic-pushers threatened to shut it down. Moreover, Farley had never been touched by the slightest breath of the scandals that had infected politics. He was undoubtedly an honest man.

Rickey was astounded at the attack and rose to ask the owner if he would personally vouch for the slanders and filth he was reading. This lightweight stammered a refusal, admitting the paper had been professionally prepared in Washington. Then he withdrew the document in a panic. But the damage had been done.

The owners fooled nobody but themselves when they settled on the pliable, deal-happy Chandler. Dan Parker, in his *Mirror* column, saw to that. Dan kidded the man from the fried-chicken belt unmercifully about a swimming pool the WPA had "misplaced," constructing it on the Chandler estate in Kentucky instead of the school where it belonged.

The owners had passed up other strong men besides Farley: They nixed Tom Dewey, the former crime-busting District Attorney from New York, and J. Edgar Hoover, the FBI bulldog. Perhaps they preferred somebody they could manipulate and make deals with. At any rate, when MacPhail waved the flag for the Kentucky politician, the other owners' fell in line like sheep. Chandler's only platform seemed to be three little words, which he repeated at every opportunity: "Ah loves baseball."

Eventually this small man proved how much he *really* loved the game—and MacPhail and the other owners who had made him king—by turning author in *Sports Illustrated*. The title of his contribution? "How I Jumped from Clean Politics into Dirty Baseball."

If only Dan Parker had still been alive to deal with that mess of twisted facts, omissions, and distortions when it appeared!

Anyway, the battle lines were being drawn even before we unveiled our controversial black ballplayers. It was very clear that it would be Rickey, backing Robinson as he was, against MacPhail and the rest of the ganged-up owners. And they had even increased the strength of their gang by adding a puppet commissioner.

This was pretty grim stuff. Rickey really feared that the Big Boys, led by MacPhail, were going to pass a special rule that would penalize him and keep him from launching his black player.

The Old Man had no idea, at that time, that they were going to rob him of Durocher, too. This was to happen at a time when the Lip was badly needed by the Negro as an icebreaker, a sort of loud-talking bodyguard, to take the heat off the muzzled black man.

⚬⚔⚬⚔⚬

25. The Betrayal of Robinson

The truth about how baseball's owners stonewalled it against Jackie Robinson, the first black—untold till now, as far as I know—is another totally weird chapter in the incredible story of how the Lords of Baseball run their show backward.

The gullibles in that owners' fraternity had been hornswoggled out of millions—yes, millions!—for junk ballplayers that super-salesman Branch Rickey palmed off on them.

Then, when the old spellbinder brought them the Black Beauty who would fill their ballparks, they fought him tooth and nail! They really believed that the Negro would spoil their Grand Old Game, and they fought him under the table as well as openly. In fact, they voted fifteen to one against Rickey's Black Experiment in a sceret meeting where the Old Man saw even the agenda and the ballots destroyed in a Watergate-type cover-up that was years ahead of its time. The lodge brothers insisted the meeting never happened; then, when I heard Rickey tell the whole story at Wilberforce University, they denied it again and again to press and radio.

I remember the Old Man telling me to pick up an extension telephone in his Brooklyn Dodger office less than a week before we—Robinson and the other players to whom I acted as confessor, valet, and nursemaid as the team's traveling secretary—were to make our first road trip of 1947.

We'd been looking forward to sleepy Philadelphia as a relief from the big-city pressure cooker that New York became when Robinson broke the color line.

After all, this *was* the City of Brotherly Love, wasn't it?

Nothing ever seemed to happen in Philadelphia, good *or* bad. The Futile Phillies, as the writers liked to call them in the quaint sports-page jargon of the day, had been the caboose of the National League for years—undistinguished and unnoticed, but quite necessary to fill out the eight-team league.

Robinson had never had any trouble when he played there before thousands of Negroes as the shortstop of the Kansas City Monarchs.

Even the Benjamin Franklin Hotel, the second-rate house the Dodgers had used for years, didn't figure to be a problem. They'd had my rooming list, with the black man's name on it, for almost a month, and they hadn't called me to complain. It all seemed to add up to a pleasant visit.

All these things were running through my mind as Rickey was motioning for me to pick up the extension phone. "Herb Pennock is calling from Philadelphia," he whispered, holding a hand over his own mouthpiece. "I want you to hear this . . ."

Pennock, known as the Squire of Kennett Square during his Yankee days as a southpaw pitching great, was now the suave, silver-thatched general manager of the Phillies, who were being revived by Bob Carpenter and the DuPont millions.

". . . just can't bring the Nigger here with the rest of your team, Branch," I heard Pennock saying. "We're just not ready for that sort of thing yet. We won't be able to take the field against your Brooklyn team if that boy Robinson is in uniform."

"Very well, Herbert," replied the always-precise Rickey. "And if we must claim the game nine to nothing, we will do just that, I assure you."

That was the official score of a forfeited game: 9 to 0.

When we arrived in Philadelphia and took cabs to the Franklin, I was bluntly told that there were no rooms for us. "And don't bring your team back here," the manager snapped, "while you have any Nigras with you!"

While the bellboys stacked our luggage on the sidewalk, I tried to call Carpenter and Pennock to see if they had any pull at the other hotels in town. No answer on either line, the Phillies' switchboard said. No, sorry, they couldn't be found anywhere.

I hired a truck to load the bags, got cabs to take the players and newspapermen to the ballpark where they could twiddle their thumbs for a few hours, and prepared to search for a hotel that would take in my homeless band. The thought crossed my mind that we might have to take the train back to New York after that night's game and become commuters for the rest of the series.

Higbe, the carefree Carolinian, didn't make matters easier when he asked Robinson in a loud voice if there weren't some of Jack's friends in town who'd take us in as boarders. Robbie managed a weak smile, but it was obvious he was smarting inside, knowing we were pariahs because of him. Worse yet, the other players knew the reason, and he knew they knew.

I very nearly didn't try the second hotel my cabbie took me to, because the fashionable Warwick looked too plush; but I brazened it out and asked anyway, mentioning our black problem boy. Delighted to have us, the manager told me. Of course the rates were almost twice those at the crummy Franklin, but any port in a storm, no matter how expensive. We stayed at the Warwick for many seasons after that one. The food was great, by a master chef named George Lamaze.

That night Pennock had the nerve to ask me if I'd found a hotel. I didn't tell him of our good fortune, just to see if he'd come up with any helpful suggestions, but he remained silent. All the talking for the Phillies was done a few hours later by their Southern-born and -bred manager, Ben Chapman, and at no time in my life have I ever heard racial venom and dugout filth to match the abuse that Ben sprayed on Robinson that night.

Chapman mentioned everything from thick lips to the supposedly extra-thick Negro skull, which he said restricted brain growth to almost animal level compared to white folk. He listed the repulsive sores and diseases he said Robbie's teammates would become infected with if they touched the towels or the combs he used. He charged Jackie outright with breaking up his own Brooklyn team. The Dodger players had told him privately, he said, that they wished the black man would go back into the South where he belonged, picking cotton, swabbing out latrines, or worse.

Chapman sang this hate song almost alone at first, but soon he picked up an infantile chorus behind him on the bench. These were guys who had acquired some bravery after listening to their fearless leader clobber the defenseless black, and who now hoped to make a hit with the boss man by parroting his lines.

Suddenly it dawned on me how many people whom I had previously regarded as normal and rational weren't about to give an even break to a black boy who wanted only to be a part of this thing all we "sportsmen" had always called the "Great American Pastime."

Meanwhile, there wasn't a peep out of Robinson. Everybody knew he had been muzzled by Rickey. The whole thing was as one-sided as a mugging.

I noted where Carpenter and Pennock sat, and I was sure they could hear just about everything that came out of their team's dugout. Certainly the fans in the stands nearby were in on this verbal lynching.

I felt sure that Chapman would tone down his attacks the second night, perhaps after some discreet hints from his embarrassed superiors. But no, Ben raved on without a letup. At this point Eddie Stanky, a gutsy little Dodger infielder who was out of Mobile, Alabama, himself, could take it no more. "Why don't you guys go to work on somebody who can fight back?" he barked. "There isn't one of you has the guts of a louse!"

But the jibes went on, even more vicious than before, if possible.

Years later, after I had written some of the details of this "riding" in the *Sporting News,* the paper sent a reporter to Chapman's home to check up on the story. They couldn't believe it, I guess.

Ben denied nothing. Rather lamely, he pointed out that Robinson had been a rookie when they worked him over. "We always gave rookies a baptism like that first time around the league, to see how they could take it. You wouldn't have wanted us to treat Robinson any different from the white boys, would you?"

On top of everything else, Robinson wasn't doing much on the field. He was pressing, trying too hard, and he had a sore throwing arm. It wasn't as bad as the spring before, when he had pulled a ligament trying to make a throw across his body from behind second base too early in training. Now he was playing first, and he could cover up the arm, because not many hard throws are called for there.

At the plate, he was popping everything straight up in the air. "It's a home run!" screeched one of the Phillies derisively when Robbie popped up right in front of the plate with two men on. "Yeah," cracked Puddinhead Jones as the ball dropped into catcher Andy Seminick's big mitt, "if you're playing in an elevator shaft!"

"You can't play ball up here, you black bum," came out of the Phils' dugout. "You're only up here to draw those Nigger bucks at the gate for Rickey—"

Chapman's tagline hurt worst of all: "If you were a white boy, you'd have been shipped down to Newport News long ago!"

After that first series in Philadelphia was over, we took the train back to New York, and I raced to Rickey's home in Forest Hills. I burst in on the Old Man and blurted out all that had happened in the City of Brotherly Love.

"Nobody can take vile stuff like this for very long," I said. "We'll have a nervous breakdown on our hands—"

"Ho, ho, ho," was Rickey's only reply. It wasn't just a chuckle, but a belly laugh; he doubled up as I poured out the shabby details.

I was hurt, and Rickey saw it. I guess I bit my lip and got red in the face.

"Don't you see what's happening, son?" he said, getting up out of his chair and putting a kindly arm around my shoulder.

Of course I saw. More than he did, I thought bitterly. I couldn't make out why Rickey was acting this way. What did he think I was, an imbecile?

"You and mother"—he meant Mrs. Rickey—"weren't very strong for this Robinson thing at the start," he began. "Now all of a sudden you're both fans of Jackie, and you're actually worrying about him. What do you suppose has happened?"

I thought it best to keep my mouth shut if I wanted to hang onto my job. I was seething inside.

"On this team, on any team," B.R. went on, "there are some fair-minded men of quality who will rebel against the treatment Robinson is getting, and they'll do something about it. There will be an incident, perhaps a small one, perhaps something big. But they'll be drawn closer to him and become a protective cordon around him. You'll see. . . ."

It occurred to me right then that I hadn't even told him about Stanky taking Robinson's side against the Phillies. I had wanted to make the situation sound as bleak as possible, I guess.

But something was to happen on our first trip to Cincinnati that bore out Rickey's prophecy almost to the letter. How could he have known such things in advance? All I can say is this extraordinary man was as wise as a country philosopher. Whether he had picked up his wisdom around the potbellied stove in the general store at Lucasville, Ohio, where all the problems of the farmer folk of Hog Wallow and Duck Run were argued and solved, or whether it had come in the college classrooms at Ohio Wesleyan and law school at Michigan, or from the long lonely hours he spent on his back fighting tuberculosis, I cannot say for sure. But he could read character and what went on in the minds of men as surely as I could read a railroad timetable.

At St. Louis, we ran into a threatened strike by Cardinal players who said they wouldn't go on the same field with the "Nigra."

We were running into this same white bigot fence everywhere. Sam Breadon, the Cardinal owner, didn't raise a finger to squelch the revolt, but Ford Frick, the league president, had to. All eyes were on him, and he threatened to slap a long suspension and big fine on any Cardinal player who went on strike.

Not all the Cardinals went along with Enos Slaughter and the other red-hots from the sowbelly and sorghum belt. Stan Musial gave Robbie some kind words of encouragement and even some tips about shifting his feet to take throws around first base. Musial's folks had been poor as church mice in the mine country around Donora, Pennsylvania, and the Polish boy remembered very well the putdowns he had received before he made it big.

Then the big thing happened in Cincinnati, without any warning.

By this time Robbie had started to knock the hell out of the ball. And even when he wasn't hitting, he had proved he could run; he had stolen the third game in that Philadelphia series from Chapman just as cleanly as a pickpocket lifting a farmer boy's wallet at the county fair. But now he had started spraying base hits to all fields, and they were shots that the players called blue darts or frozen ropes. Jack held both arms extended as far from his powerful body as possible, gripping at eye level the handle of a bat he carried high, almost proudly, and very still, above the level of his head. He looked almost like a big black bird about to take off, with those arms held that way. Every time I see Joe Morgan of today's Reds flap that rear arm of his while waiting to attack a pitch, I think of Jack.

They tried knocking him down, but the dusters only made him a tougher hitter, and the word on that soon got around. When he got up out of the dirt after a knockdown and rearranged himself with his eyes flashing, "ferocious" is the only word you could use to describe him as a hitter.

The news that Robinson was· "making it" spread fast, and the little ballpark in Cincinnati, Crosley Field, which then had less than thirty thousand seats, was jammed with whites who had come to see if this Nigra could really do it, as well as blacks there to cheer their new trailblazer on.

There had been a sack of mail for Robinson at our hotel, and I went through it the morning we hit town. Three of the letters

contained threats that Jack would be shot in his tracks if he dared
to take the field. I handed these over to the FBI, which got pretty
excited about it and searched every building that overlooked the
ballpark and would afford a sniper a shot at Number 42.

Usually I didn't show Robbie the hate mail, most of which was
scrawled and scribbled like the smut you see on toilet walls. But
this time I had to warn him, and I could see he was frightened. I
passed the word to Pee Wee, who was the captain, and to a couple of the other solid players on the club. I wasn't sure what was
going to happen in the Queen City, right across the river from
Kentucky. But all the folk from the hill and still country were
flocking into town for the big event.

Reese himself was in a tough spot. He had been born and raised
in Louisville, and his lovely mom had always brought fried
chicken and chocolate cake to Cincinnati for the boys on the
team. Pee Wee's two sisters came to the games a lot, and I seated
them in the club box whenever possible. Now I knew very well
the kind of flak they were catching from the crackpots who
thought their brother should refuse to put on the same uniform a
"Nigra" was wearing. It wouldn't have surprised me if some of
those nuts had marched up to Mrs. Reese and demanded that she
disown Pee Wee and scratch his name out of the family Bible.

Robinson had been pretty much of a loner so far. He wasn't
one to talk his way into a knot of white players as Campanella
would in the next year or two, with the funny stories Roy told
about Satch Paige and Josh Gibson in that high-pitched voice of
his. Even the guys from Alabama and Louisiana enjoyed Campy.

Robinson wasn't like that. Not that he was aloof. He was just
waiting to be asked in, and he hadn't really "made the team" yet.
A lot of the players, Reese and Hodges particularly, respected his
ability and what he was doing. They were polite and cordial, but
definitely not pally with him.

The record of our National Anthem they played that day had
the sound of bombs bursting in air, and the thought occurred to
me that that precise moment would have been the ideal cover for
gunfire, if someone were indeed going to take a shot at Robinson.
But we got through that all right, and through the top of the first,
too, in which Jackie was the third out. The crowd was still buzz-

ing from its first look at the black man in action when our team ran onto the field from the first-base dugout. Reese stopped at first for a few last-second words with Robbie. As he hid his mouth behind his gloved left hand the way ballplayers talk, Pee Wee put his right arm around Robinson's shoulders.

The silence that hit those stands where the fans had been buzzing a second before was truly deafening. Their boy had put his arm around the Nigra!

Robbie told me later that that gesture by Reese was the first big breakthrough and meant as much to him as any single bit of approval or acclaim that were to come to him in the ten years that followed.

Rickey had forecast it precisely!

I was to get corroboration, although it was twenty-five years late, of my fears that Robinson was close to a nervous breakdown in that trying first year. Chatting recently with Rachel, his widow, in their home in Stamford, Connecticut, I learned that Jackie never shared the load he carried in those breakthrough years.

"I tried again and again to get him to talk about the problems he was meeting," Rachel told me, "but he didn't want to burden me. He never would talk about those things at home. But I knew they were eating at his mind, for he would jerk and twitch and even talk in his troubled sleep, which was not like him."

Sharon, the Robinson daughter who sat beside her mother as we talked that day, added something significant: "Every time daddy went on one of those early trips," she said, "we had fears that he would be assassinated!"

Mind you, all this really happened, not in the Dark Ages nor the black days of the Spanish Inquisition or Atilla the Hun; nor was it some history-book tale of the Nubian slaves who were chained to their oars in the galleys of Egyptian princes. This was the year 1947 in supposedly civilized Philadelphia and St. Louis and Cincinnati and New York. By all means let us not forget New York.

The Polo Grounds was in the middle of Harlem, and even Frick wanted to back off when it came time for Robinson to appear there against the New York Giants. He suggested to Rickey that it might be unwise to press "too hard" by putting the black man in the very first series up there in such a highly inflammable black environment. How about leaving him at home in Brooklyn for a few days with a "sprained ankle"?

Rickey wouldn't hear of it. This was no time to pussyfoot, he said. He pushed boldly ahead with his Black Experiment and backed Robinson in every way he could.

But the rest of baseball did exactly nothing. Nothing, that is, but deplore this terrible, terrible thing that Rickey had inflicted on their Grand Old Game. The bumbling owners who were running the show in every city we visited never once appealed to their own players, coaches, and managers, or even to their fans, for sanity, or at least restraint.

My guess at the time was that they were ducking this issue because they were betting Robbie would cave in under all the heat he was getting. They figured he would just quit and disappear one day, for his own safety.

Of course the dum-dums among the owners who had been saying Robbie was just an ersatz ballplayer, a counterfeit who would be unmasked by a month or two of big league curves and fastballs, had already piped down. By now, even your Aunt Gertrude could have told you that here was a genuine ten-carat major league gem.

Even so, the other owners were still second-guessing Rickey.

If there *had* to be a black, they whined, why did Branch insist on this uppity type? Why couldn't it have been nice-guy Roy Campanella, that chubby light-skinned Negro the Deacon had hidden down there at St. Paul in the American Association? Everybody liked *him.*

I caught this kind of static in every ballpark we visited. Some of the Big Boys said nasty things to me they wouldn't have dared say to Rickey.

When I told the Old Man about the propaganda for Campanella, he just snorted. "Campy couldn't have pulled this off like Robbie," he said. "Oh, I know even Walker and Bragan and Higbe enjoy his stories . . ." His voice trailed off, and he stopped for a few moments. Then he added, "Son, Robinson is truly a colored gentleman. Compared to him, Campanella's a shoeshine boy!"

A few seconds later the Old Man added, with a touch of guilt, I thought, "Mind you, I like shoeshine boys, too!"

Rickey closed his ears to all the static and kept drumming it in to Barney Shotton, the manager, to make Robinson cut loose, to gamble for that extra base every chance he got, and to take those long leads that seemed to rattle even the oldest pitchers.

Manager *Shotton*, did I say?

Where was Durocher, the *real* leader of the Dodgers?

The Lip had been canned for a year by the comic commissioner of baseball, that corn-pone character right out of the hills of Kentucky. One strong owner, Larry MacPhail of the Yankees (who had a lot to do with getting Chandler the job), had stampeded Happy and enough of the weak-kneed brothers in the lodge into taking this drastic step, which was aimed against Rickey.

What difference does it make now that MacPhail regretted his whole antic when he sobered up and cooled off? It didn't help much when Larry announced that he really never wanted Durocher suspended, or even when the repentant Redhead put the machinery in motion that would eventually unseat Chandler.

The big thing was that Durocher was in drydock a continent away in California when Robinson needed him most as a shock-breaker and fighting leader.

Where was the Brooklyn Strongman, the Big Oom, the backroom politicker extraordinary, while his Brooklyn team was being so grievously hurt?

O'Malley was on the fence, that's where.

Walter knew full well he could not be a loser if he avoided taking sides for or against the Negro experiment, for or against his controversial manager. So he just deplored all the bad, bad things that were happening. The Big Oom had always been very good at deploring.

If Robinson were to flop in the majors as Bob Feller and a lot of very smart baseball men were predicting, O'Malley would have a nice booster shot for the power play he was even then starting to unseat Rickey as Dodger president.

If Robbie turned out to be a star, the Big Oom could prove he had never, never said a word against the blacks, cross his heart and hope to die! Hell, hadn't he flown all the way to Havana to scout a black power-hitter named Silvio Garcia, whom Durocher had called "a better hitter than Hornsby," even before Rickey dug up this Robinson boy? Walter would tell anybody that story at the drop of a hat.

O'Malley had it made both ways, by just doing nothing.

And nothing was just what he did to save Durocher when MacPhail and the others were bad-mouthing the Lip.

All the anti-Durocher noise had been started by a mildly eccentric Catholic priest who screamed at regular intervals in the newspapers and pulpits around town that Lippy's "immoral private life" was a bad example to the youth of Brooklyn.

Leo had just married divorcee Laraine Day against a judge's explicit orders. Father Vincent Powell announced that he was withdrawing the Catholic Youth Organization's "support" of the Dodgers.

"Support" was hardly the word. The CYO received four hundred thousand free passes for their youngsters each season, and this meant that it would turn down these Annie Oakleys.

Rickey, a thoughtfully religious man, was deeply hurt by the Catholics' public spanking of Durocher. During several long meetings with the Reverend Powell, the old psalm-singer had me sit in as a kind of Catholic interpreter or spokesman, for the Dodgers. In these debates the Mahatma badly outpointed the priest at every turn. He kept asking if the Catholics, like most other churches, weren't still dispensing mercy and forgiveness. And wouldn't it be better to use the colorful Durocher's appeal to youngsters, which was considerable, instead of blackening the man's character? "Can we ignore a tremendous force like this, and surrender it to Satan?" asked the Mahatma.

At one point Rickey went into one of the most dramatic speeches I had ever heard him deliver. "Fill Madison Square Garden with eighteen thousand youngsters," he boomed, closing his eyes to tune in the vision more clearly, "and on the main floor erect three boxing rings. In one would be you, Father, and I know full well what a force for good a man like you can be. I would be in the second ring, and if I do say so myself, there are those who say that I can capture a listener's interest . . ."

Here Rickey's voice trailed off, and he paused for the proper effect.

Of course, the old spellbinder had mentally positioned the Reverend Powell's villain, the swashbuckling, free-wheeling, devil-may-care Durocher, in the third ring.

Then Rickey shot the question: Who would win the kids' attention?

The Mahatma was at his very best this day.

It had been Tom Meany, the puckish wit of the New York *World Telegram*, who first hung the name "Mahatma" on Rickey. Meany had run across the word in a book about Asia by John Gunther, in which the author likened Mahatma Gandhi to a combination of "God, Tammany Hall, and my own father." This seemed to fit Rickey when the Old Man first came to Brooklyn, and was christened by Meany; eventually, just about every writer seized on it.

Never did the Old Man seem more of a Mahatma than when I heard him that day, as he pulled out all the stops trying to get the Reverend Powell off his sinning manager's neck. "Not a handful of youngsters in the Garden would notice me, nor even you, Father," the old Deacon roared. "Durocher would hold them all; don't you see what a terrific force we can make Leo *for* good, and *against* evil?"

The priest blinked but remained unmoved. All he wanted was Durocher's scalp.

O'Malley, the original Smiling Irishman when it came to blarney, carried a large prayerbook in the Catholic Church. He was respected by the clergy and was in all ways a powerful Catholic who could have stopped all this anti-Durocher nonsense had he wanted to. His best pal was Judge Henry Ughetta, head of the Sons of Italy and a Knight of St. Gregory, which meant his connections went all the way to Rome. One word from them both and the Reverend Powell, as well as Monsignor Edward Lodge Curran, another anti-Leo scold, would have piped down, and so would their Catholic Youth Organization.

But the Big Oom never gave the word.

Rickey had reason to wonder who had put the churchmen up to this. The Catholics had never boycotted Hitler or Mussolini the way they went after Leo.

Yes, there was indeed dirty work at the crossroads, the Old Man reflected.

Obviously, O'Malley enjoyed seeing Durocher revolving on the red-hot rotisserie, because Leo was Branch Rickey's favorite reclamation project, and that meant the Old Man would collect some of the critics' heat.

That was why it was a laugh to see the Big Oom turn up as "defense counsel" for Durocher and me at Happy Chandler's mock "Trial by Fury," as Dan Parker called it in the *Mirror*. O'Malley had to pinch-hit because Rickey had been called away by the sudden death of his wife's brother.

Walter could not find a single word to utter for our side of the story. He was happy to see Leo ridden out of baseball, even if it was only for one year.

All this five-and-dime intrigue wouldn't be worth the paper to tell it on if it hadn't happened just at the time the first black was due to join the Durocher-less Dodgers.

Lippy's stand-in, old Barney Shotton, was a good enough manager when it came to writing out the lineup or yanking a pitcher. But the old gent ran the team in a business suit with a Dodger windbreaker over it, so he wasn't allowed onto the field, even had he been spry enough. Barney hardly ever raised his voice enough to be heard at the other end of the dugout, much less by an umpire; and what he did say wouldn't have upset a Sunday School.

For Robinson, and the abuse he was catching from every enemy dugout, having a nice old guy like this on his side did not help. It was like taking an altar boy to a gang rumble.

What the black man needed behind him was Durocher's bark and brass and bellow—and in front of him too, to keep the umpires off him.

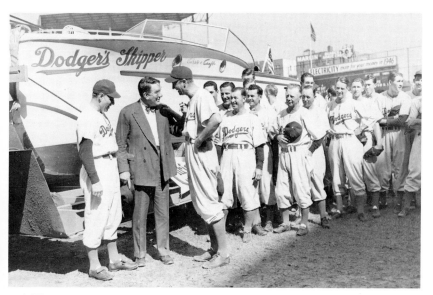

A First—and Last! Players Give Rickey a Boat   Dixie Walker (at Rickey's left, talking to him) presents a Chris-Craft speedboat bought by players' own contributions in appreciation for the Mahatma's generosity to the 1946 playoff team, to whom he gave Studebaker cars. A year later, when Jackie Robinson appeared in a Dodger uniform, Walker asked Durocher (at Rickey's right) and the Mahatma to trade him away. They did. The small man with the broad grin behind Walker is Charley Dressen; behind Dressen, to his right, is Ducky Medwick, and to his left, Vic Lombardi.   *Barney Stein*

Two Ladies Who Loved the Lip   Jan (Mrs. Branch) Rickey (left), who always worried about Durocher as one would a wayward child, and actress Laraine Day, who took a lot of the Lip. The man in the middle (as usual) was the Mahatma, the Brain of Brooklyn. Shortly after this Cuban spring training trip (1948), Laraine hung Rickey's picture over the toilet to show how she felt about her hubby's firing.

Barney Stein

"Nice Guys Finish Last" Started Right Here   "Nice Guy" Mel Ott (left) was deposed as manager of the New York Giants shortly after getting this glad hand from Durocher. Lippy had told New York *Sun* columnist Frank Graham that Giant players were walking all over Ott. Durocher, hated for decades in the Polo Grounds, moved into Ott's job and soon won the pennant there under Coogan's Bluff.   *Barney Stein*

Photo Finish   Ben Chapman (right), who had been the black man's most vicious rider in the 1947 season, begged Jack Robinson to consent to have this picture taken with him, to prove to blacks that they were pals. Walter Winchell had mounted a campaign against the Phils' manager as a racist. The picture didn't work. Chapman was fired anyway.   *The Sporting News*

Down and Out, but Far from Broke
Once the Dodger dynamo, Branch Rickey is a picture of dejection with head bowed after being short-circuited in a power struggle with executioner Walter O'Malley (partially hidden by fat cigar). Rickey took the count in O'Malley's famous gymnasium, Room Forty at the Hotel Bossert in Brooklyn. But there was also another count: the $1 million in Rickey's pocket (not shown in picture), which the old warrior shook out of the Big Oom in the famous Zeckendorf heist.

Wide World Photos

Pirate Owner's Wallet Safe—for the Moment!   Six hands are in full view here so Pittsburgh magnate John Galbreath (right) won't be frisked again. Rickey (center) sold Galbreath everything but the Brooklyn Bridge. The Mahatma took more than $1 million of Galbreath's cash for bum ballplayers, then sold himself to the famed horseman as general manager of the Pittsburgh team. The man at left who was kept busy writing checks to Rickey was Pirate treasurer Tom Johnson. *Wide World Photos*

At Top of O'Malley's Sucker List Dodger poobah Walter O'Malley (left, cupping hands) depicts the bag New York City's politicians would be left holding when he skipped town with his team. Nelson Rockefeller (center) and New York Mayor Robert Wagner were raising millions in order to build a stadium to keep the Dodgers in Brooklyn, but O'Malley had already made an under-the-table deal for defection to Los Angeles months before.

Wide World Photos

Sweet-talking Svengali O'Malley purrs, "Tell you what I'm gonna do for you today, Phil," to Wrigley, multimillionaire owner of the Chicago Cubs. By the time Big Oom stopped talking, the chewing-gum king was stuck with the shabby Ft. Worth franchise in an even-up swap for a Los Angeles gold mine, including a square block of the city.

Wide World Photos

The Greatest Catch in Baseball O'Malley takes bows as Hollywood greets the Dodgers with a luncheon arranged by Mervyn LeRoy and a bevy of actors and starlets. The Big Oom tried to duck this luncheon because he feared LeRoy was the lead of a klieg-light set that would "take over" his team. Later they became racetrack pals, and the famous director gave the baseball man some stock in Hollywood Park. O'Malley predicted a Dodger pennant, but the team finished seventh.

United Press International Photo

26. Robinson Scoops Bavasi— for $50,000!

Durocher had a voice that could shake chandeliers and a steel-trap mind that instantly supplied it with the sharpest words needed to put down an enemy.

This man swashbuckled his way through baseball—and life as well—pretty much as he cared to. If something went wrong, well, you could always talk your way out of it afterward, right?

To him there was no wrong, anyway. Things were always just right—right for the hit-and-run, right for the squeeze play, and right for a peek at the bottom card on the deck if your opponent was foolish enough to cut the cards carelessly.

Bang, bang, he made decisions, never slowing down a minute to think things over. What good would it have done to wait a minute, anyway? He never had one to spare.

In Leo's life the lights have always been all green. They locked him on "go" when they made him, and that's been his big word, whether for a double steal or for a leggy blonde on the other side of the street.

Fear? No room in the man for that, they had poured him so full of nerve and gall. Rattle the pitcher, then steal a base off him, see? Catch the shortstop chatting with an umpire and pull the hit-and-run!

The Lip was the sharpest bench jockey I've ever heard, and I've listened to them all, starting with Fresco Thompson forty years ago.

One day in St. Louis, Durocher started to climb all over a rookie Cardinal pitcher named Murry Dickson, hoping to rattle the kid, who was from a neighboring small town in Missouri. The youngster's parents, his high school coach, and his teen-age girlfriend were in the stands, and the Lip mentioned them all.

Between innings Beans Reardon, an umpire who was as tough as a motorman's glove, came over to the Dodger dugout to put in a good word for Dickson. "He's really a great kid, Leo," said the grizzled Reardon. "Whyncha give him a chance?"

"You gone soft or somethin', you old burglar?" barked Lippy. "Tonight I'll buy the kid the best steak dinner in town. Champagne too, if you say so, Beans—"

There was a pause, and the Loud One added, "—but right now, I wanna win this ballgame any way I can, see?"

Had Durocher been in the Dodger dugout backing Robinson up, it's doubtful that Chapman would have even opened fire on the Negro. Ben knew from experience the blowtorch that Leo could turn on you. The Lip was lightning quick, and sometimes very funny on the riposte, the verbal counterpunch. He would have turned the Philadelphia manager's filthy tirade around, and he would have given back, with full interest, the others like it that Robbie was forced to absorb in every city we visited.

So Jackie had to go it alone. He was catching it from all sides now, and sometimes from behind him, where the umpire stood.

There were thirty-five thousand in the stands at Wrigley Field in Chicago that day in 1947, and twenty thousand of them must have been black, come to hail their trailblazer. Nice-guy Gil Hodges, straight-faced, nodded up toward the stands and asked: "All your friends in on passes you left for 'em, Jack?"

In the seventh Robinson took a called third strike with men on. Angrily he grabbed the barrel of his bat with both powerful hands until it seemed that sawdust must surely pour out. Then he started striding back to the Dodger dugout.

Umpire Jocko Conlan, a feisty little rooster of a man, rolled out the *"steerrike threee"* just a little louder and longer this day, or so it seemed.

Then, to nobody in particular, Jocko added "—an' it was right down th' middle!"

That crack jerked Robinson out of his sullen reverie and back to the plate as if he were on some giant elastic band. They went to it, Jocko and the Negro, nose to nose. Robinson's eyes were flashing; worse, his arms were flailing, which is strictly taboo in the private code that all umpires live by.

Conlan threw Robbie out of the game. With so many blacks in

the stands who had come to see him, a tense situation was building, which could have added up to riot.

Robinson, no dummy, recognized the storm signals. Besides,
Rickey's repeated warnings about avoiding "incidents" flashed
through his mind. He spun on his heel, stalked to the dugout,
and got out of sight.

That night, to his credit, Conlan came to the Stevens Hotel,
where the Dodgers stayed. He rang Robbie's room and looked
everywhere in vain. Then he spotted me and gave me the
message.

"I made a bad mistake today, Harold," he began. "An umpire
should never be the first to open his mouth, and I did. I wanted
to explain that to Robinson tonight."

"That's nice of you," I said, "but you can't help yourself, Jocko."
We had been friends for years, even roomed together on some
spring trips.

The little Irishman looked hard at me. "What do you mean by
that?"

"I mean," I said slowly, "that you just hate Robinson!"

Conlan thought about it a minute. "If that were true," he said,
walking away slowly, "I would be a bad umpire."

I knew that, had Durocher been with the Dodgers that day in
Chicago, he would have been up to that plate so fast they'd have
thought he was shot out of a cannon. He'd have battled Conlan
nose to nose, and perhaps beaten a tattoo on Jocko's shins the
way he was to do in a later crisis in Los Angeles Coliseum.

Durocher had made no bones about wanting Robinson as a
player on his Dodger varsity right from the very first moment he
saw Jackie in spring training with the minor league Montreal
farm club in the spring of 1946.

Why? Was there perhaps a hidden streak of humanitarianism
running through this strange man who had been case-hardened
in the school of hard knocks and the pool halls of Hartford?

No, nothing like that. Leo probably wouldn't have been able to
spell "equality," much less preach it. He would be the first to tell
you that all men were *not* created equal, and that Robinson was
indeed a superman.

Then was it because the Lip had close Negro friends like Sammy Davis, Jr., Bojangles Robinson, and Nat King Cole?

Don't you believe it.

Money, that was the reason, pure and simple. Right from the very first time he saw this black man run wild on the bases and get up to rip the ball after they knocked him down with a duster, Leo had Jackie Robinson tabbed as a winner. The Lip figured Jackie could put them all in the World Series, the big dough, the endorsements and commercials, and all that went with winning.

I had heard him bark this at his unhappy Dodger players in a bizarre midnight meeting in an Army barracks in Panama, where we had gone to play exhibition games against Robinson and the rest of the Montreal squad in the spring of 1947. We were there because we daren't bring this black-and-white show into any of the Southern states.

By now it was a cinch that the Negro was too good to be kept off the Dodgers. When would he be brought up? That was the question.

Bobby Bragan and Dixie Walker and a few more of the hominy-grits boys decided to beat Rickey to the punch. They made up a petition saying they would not play on the same team with a Negro, and they were trying to get a few patsies like Carl Furillo to take it around and get others to sign it. The only south in Furillo's background was southern Italy; he wouldn't have known Mason and Dixon from the Smith Brothers.

Kirby Higbe, a strongarm pitcher, didn't like the aroma of the whole thing, even though he was from South Carolina. He tipped me off over a few beers in a Panama bar one night.

I phoned Rickey in Brooklyn, and the Old Man jumped into a plane within the hour, heading to Panama to quell the rebellion.

Rickey wasn't needed this time. Durocher handled the whole thing.

When I told Leo about the plot, he had exploded. He called the midnight meeting in the barracks, and I can still hear him as he challenged the mutineers. He was wrapped in a yellow bathrobe, and he looked like a fighter about to enter the ring. He stared down Walker and Bragan and started punching out the words.

"I don't care if the guy is yellow or black, or if he has stripes like a fuckin' zebra," Durocher rasped, glaring around the room. "I'm the manager of this team, and I say he plays. What's more, I say he can make us all rich." After a pause, the Lip added, "An' if any of you can't use the money, I'll see that you're traded!"

Money, that was it. Money to spend on clothes, beautiful women, horses, cards. Leo never had enough of the stuff. I remembered, as I listened that night in the barracks, how Leo had snorted when one New York writer had suggested in his column that the dandy little manager might retire rather than haggle with Rickey over a new contract. Durocher was rich now, insisted Arch Murray of the New York *Post,* and could make a career out of going on radio with Milton Berle and Jack Benny and Fred Allen.

"What's that Murray been smokin' lately?" Lippy had barked, tossing the offending newspaper into my lap. "Me, rich? Ain't he found out yet that I always spend more than I make?"

Leo hadn't meant it to be a wisecrack, either.

There had been dollar signs dancing in Durocher's eyes from the very first day he saw Robinson. Leo wanted the black man right then. He thought Jack could ring the cash register for us all.

But Rickey had stuck to his carefully planned timetable: slow, slow, get the boy ready with a full year in the International League.

Now, as 1947 Opening Day approached, Durocher was gone, sawed off by Unhappy Chandler.

Robinson was not to forget that. He had to face a tough year backed only by Rickey, who was way up in the front office, where you couldn't hear half of what they were saying.

Then, when Rickey himself was thrown out in a power struggle with O'Malley after the 1950 season, Robinson was left very much alone on the Dodgers. Oh, there were other blacks by then, but Campanella and Newcombe were pussycats, too timid to be openly pally with a hot potato like Robinson.

All these things fed the demon that was inside Jackie. Then, in 1953, he had to watch the same gang guillotine Charley Dressen, whom he liked very much and always called his favorite manager. The demon grew and grew.

So Robinson—and the demon inside—were quite ready for them when they tried to spring the trap door under him late in 1956.

He had filled their ballparks for ten great years with the Dodgers, made them all rich, and put the very dollars into the O'Malley pockets that the Big Oom used to sweet-talk the widow Smith into helping to ax Rickey. Jack's reward for all this? They traded him *up* the river to the hated Giants!

Would Robbie play for Stoneham, who he said had made him a very handsome offer? Or would he quit? For months it was the hottest topic wherever baseball was talked or written. It boiled and it stewed. The odor followed the Big Oom and Buzzie everywhere, like something they'd stepped in.

Robinson let them all wait. Big Oom seethed, but what could he do except climb all over Bavasi, who had milked in vain all his pipelines in the press? The headache they thought they had traded away now bugged them worse than ever!

Jackie wrote his own press release, finally. In sixteen paragraphs, for *Look* magazine exclusively, he quit baseball. And, oh yes, for a $50,000 fee, a sum I verified with those who worked on *Look* with editor Dan Mich. It was more than he'd ever made in his greatest years with the Dodgers!

This infuriated the Big Oom and his lieutenant, Bavasi. They tore into their ex-hero with the fury characteristic of the Big Boys of baseball, who seem to think only they should wield the scimitar.

I heard Bavasi goad the press against Robinson. "He scooped you all," Buzzie taunted. "That oughta prove you've been building up the wrong guy for years!"

"Never mind, fellows," he needled the press, in words that dripped with rancor. "You'll soon have him back to write about again. As soon as he cashes that check from *Look* he'll un-retire and play for the Giants. I'll bet on it!"

If Bavasi did bet—and he is a betting man—he lost his shirt.

Robinson told me the very evening that that quote from Buzzie appeared: "If there was a chance that I'd change my mind and play for the Giants, it went out the window when Bavasi said that."

"I'm through with them all!" he added.

They weren't through with Jackie Robinson, however. The anvil chorus of detractors never, never did let up on the man, even after his death following the 1973 World Series.

Of course they all—even the ones who let Jackie have it with both barrels—tell you piously today that they leaned over backwards to be "fair" in 1947.

The kindest words I could get out of Ford Frick when I took him to lunch in Toots Shor's shortly after Robbie's death were, "Robinson was no angel; neither was your man Rickey, although I see he gets all the credit for bringing in the first Negro."

I wrote Conlan in Arizona soon after that. Thinking that the retired ump might have some kinder second thoughts, I told him I'd like to come and chat. About Robbie.

"Don't come," said Conlan. "It would be a waste of time. I can't find one good thing to say about Robinson as a man. As a ballplayer, yes, but as a man, forget it." This was in a handwritten letter that was full of ugly words.

Conlan also blasted the dead Robinson in his autobiography, a book humbly titled *Jocko*. Nowhere in its pages are to be found the mistakes the umpire made, mistakes that sometimes made Robbie's road harder.

But I think it was *Sports Illustrated* that put Jackie down the worst after his funeral, in a few shabby paragraphs by a nameless staffer. Perhaps they were still carrying a grudge because of the scoop by *Look*.

". . . Even when Robinson was quiet, he seemed to bristle with truculence, to be inwardly steaming with repressed anger," this fellow wrote. "If you asked him something he looked at you directly, as if to challenge the motive behind the question. . . . He could be a bit frightening at times."

This was definitely not the Robinson I knew at all, at all. Or that Pee Wee Reese and Ralph Branca and Carl Erskine knew, and will talk about.

Of course the same *Sports Illustrated* writer added, in the very next grudging paragraph, that in his opinion "if Ruth, DiMaggio, Musial, and Ted Williams [and the writer here tossed in the fact that he had seen them all] were somehow playing on the same team with Robinson, *he* would be the dominating figure."

Why do we get only half this story? Why does it seem that all the good things this pioneer did were interred with all his plaques and awards, his steals of home, his .300-plus batting averages and RBIs, while only the bad-mouthing lingers on?

Robinson did not have a single friend—excepting, of course, Rickey—among the owners, and that includes O'Malley.

The ballplayers have a different view of history. Robbie gets praise from some unexpected quarters.

"I never saw him steal a base," Richie Ashburn told me, "unless it meant something." Ashburn, who now broadcasts the Phillies' games, has seen his share of hot dogs and showboats, black and white.

Pee Wee Reese said, "Put it down that I admired him as a man. Not that I agreed with everything he did. But he made up his mind to do the job as the first black man, and he got it done."

Durocher's praise runs in another direction: "If a war was gonna break out, I wanted to be on Robinson's side," Leo said. "*He'd* win the war, somehow. As you know, we had our spats, but he was a winner, through and through. I've never, at any time or place, never seen a player who could upset the other team like this guy. And you know," this last with a wink, "that was supposed to be *my* specialty!"

Ralph Branca told me a story that reveals a great deal about Robinson, the man. It revolved around the night Enos Slaughter, the Cardinal outfielder, came down hard with his spikes on the back of Robinson's leg as Jackie stretched out to take a throw at first base. Slaughter had crossed first base perhaps two thousand times before that and had never cut a defenseless first baseman. But hate was running high in that first Robinson year, and his career was close to ending at the moment Slaughter narrowly missed the Achilles tendon.

"I never thought I'd ever speak to Slaughter again," Branca told me recently, "but I ran into him at that Old-Timers' game in San Diego, and before I knew it there I was shaking the old buzzard's hand before I could help myself—"

Why did you feel so strongly about Slaughter after all these years?

"I can tell you don't remember I was pitching that game," Ralph went on. "I'm not likely to forget it, because I had a no-hitter going through seven innings. When I saw Slaughter step on Robinson with his spikes, I blew my top. Right then, I went over to Jack, where they were patching up his leg, and I said,

'I'm going to flatten that son of a bitch next time he comes up, like he's never been flattened before.' There were a few Cardinal players standing close enough to hear me, and they knew I meant what I was saying. I was raging mad.

"Before Robinson would let the game go on, he took me aside. 'Don't throw at Slaughter, Ralph,' he begged. 'I'll square the books some way. But not you. You've got too much going for you tonight. This no-hitter could mean a lot to you and your career. Don't mess it up.'

"How about that, for thinking of the other guy at a time like that?" snapped Branca. "How many ballplayers you ever met would talk the pitcher out of sticking a pitch in Slaughter's ear? That's the kind of man he was. I thought he was just great."

It was an opinion not shared by the thankless owners. These witless men seemed to prefer the likes of Charles Outrageous Finley and bankrupt Banker Smith.

27. The Black Ty Cobb Finds New Ways to Win

Robinson drew the fans to pack the ballparks wherever we went in 1947. In Chicago we had to hire a couple of black detectives to clear the way for us through the thousands of Negroes who milled around outside our dressing-room door and climbed all over our buses trying to get a glimpse of their hero.

National League attendance shot over 10 million, and it had never before touched 9 million.

It wasn't just that the man was a black novelty and filling the ballparks with his own kind; he was showing exciting new ways to win ballgames.

In Chicago, with the score tied at 1–1 in the top of the ninth, he led off and walked after a 3-and-2 count. Clyde McCullough, the Cub catcher, turned his head to argue with the umpire as Jackie trotted to first base, and—whoosh!—Robbie turned it on and slid safely into second base.

I had been writing baseball for a New York newspaper since 1928 and watching it from pressboxes everywhere since becoming the Dodger traveling secretary, and I had never seen that one. Neither had the Cubs, and they argued loud and long that a base on balls was just that, and no more, and that there was an automatic time out called before the next hitter.

Nobody could find it in the rulebook, and they lost that argument, of course. The ballgame, too, as we sacrificed Robbie to third and he raced home with the winning run on a short fly.

In Brooklyn, when we met the Phillies, he was on third base with the winning run, bouncing, always bouncing. Russ Meyer, the Phils' hot-headed pitcher, was close to going out of his mind, glaring at Robbie, trying to trap him off. Everything else was forgotten. Finally, Meyer thought he had Robinson picked off third, and they began the run-down. Routine, this would be. They would put this uppity Nigra in his place.

Five Philly players lined up on the third-base line for this simple exercise of trapping the runner: two of them behind Robinson, between him and third, the other three blocking his path to home plate, which was his target.

Back and forth went Jackie, feinting, darting, stopping, making the Phils throw the ball again and again, which is almost always fatal. Finally the third baseman, Puddinhead Jones, juggled it, and here came the black man. Andy Seminick, the catcher, made a swipe at him, but too late. As Robinson scooted across with the winning run Meyer, who became the losing pitcher at that moment, took a swipe at Robinson's face with his glove. Russ didn't even have the ball.

It was an ugly incident, the first time anybody had actually taken a swing at Robinson, although they'd all been shouting menacing, fight-provoking things. I sought to smooth the affair out right after the game, suggesting a picture of the two of them shaking hands for the next day's papers.

"I'll go over to their dressing room," said Jack, more than willing.

"Better let me see how they're feeling about losing that game before we go," I said.

As I opened the Phillies' door, Seminick was saying, "—an' I tell you it's impossible to catch him. What you need is a net!"

The Phils' catcher did not mean that as a cheap-shot animal joke, either. He was putting into words what they were saying all over the league: that Robinson, on pigeon-toed feet that turned in so badly he sometimes spiked himself, could stop and start so quickly that he was making the old "routine" run-down plays obsolete. Ordinary stuff just didn't work any more against this new black guy.

I remember that an ashamed Meyer came out of his clubhouse that night to apologize and shake Robbie's hand under the stands while our Dodger photog, Barney Stein, snapped the picture. Meyer gave the black man credit. But it was obvious Robbie was getting their goats.

He was now catching heavy static from the enemy dugouts wherever we went. I was getting some of it myself, so I knew the feeling.

In Philadelphia, Ben Chapman, the manager, cornered me under the stands for a heart-to-heart talk.

I knew him well, for he had pitched for our team in a fruitless and embarrassing comeback attempt after all those years of glory in the Yankee outfield. Ben was a charming man, intelligent, often witty. We had played a lot of bridge on the long Dodger road trips, and he had far-out bidding ideas, which he called the "Winslow System." I always called him Winslow after that.

"Poor Parrott," he said with mock concern as we stood there under the stands. "Know how you're going to end up?" We were alone as we chatted, for it was early. But Robinson had already stolen one game of the series with his daring running, and the ballpark would be jammed in a few hours to see if the black Ty Cobb was for real.

I begged my old friend to read my future for me: What did Ben use, a Ouija board or tea leaves?

He severely ignored my joke. "You'll be the nursemaid to a team of twenty-four niggers," Ben rasped, "and one dago." He didn't like Furillo, either.

Now it was my turn.

"If I was short a hotel room, and had the choice of bunking with you or with Number 42 [that was Robinson], know what I'd do?"

Chapman played straight man, just as I had, and waited for my answer.

"I'd room with Robinson, Winslow."

For a moment, I thought Ol' Ben was going to pop me, but he didn't.

It got pretty close to that sometimes, though, with some of the newspapermen.

In Cincinnati veteran reporter Tom Swope of the *Post* charged at me. "You New Yorkers are all alike," he said with a sneer. "You're exploiting the Nigras." It wasn't quite clear whether Tom and some of the other critics from the fried-chicken belt were slurring "Nigger" or just drawling "Negro" with a hominy-grits accent. They left that word "Nigra" in a sort of pronunciation limbo.

"You use the Nigra and then ruin him in Harlem," Swope went on, his agitated voice shrill enough to be almost a scream. "We know how to treat the Nigra in the South; why, I've had one of 'em as a maid at my house for thirty years, an' we love her."

Swope wasted none of that love on Robinson, however. In fact, he had loudly told everybody in the pressbox that he would never, never talk to Jackie, whom he regarded as some sort of fraud, a sideshow freak who would lure the curious to buy tickets to the games.

That vow of silence by Swope was one of the reasons I was catching some of the abuse; the bigots who wouldn't "lower" themselves to talk with Robbie were happy to corner me—and let me have it with both barrels.

It was laughable to watch Swope when the day of reckoning arrived. He had to eat crow and interview Robinson, who by then had become the batting champion and won the Most Valuable Player award that Swope's colleagues voted him. For Swope, it was a matter of eating his words or looking for a new job.

When that time came, Jackie was gracious and cooperative with Tom and made no allusions to all that had gone on before.

To those who still bad-mouth the black man, I would say he

was nicer to Ben Chapman than I could have been, after all the unspeakable abuse Ben had spouted his way. When Chapman was in a jam, Robinson even tried to save his job for him, and I am sure Ben would admit that today.

This all came up because Broadway columnist Walter Winchell, a year late as he was with most of his items on sports, had suddenly found out that Ben Chapman, from Alabama, suh, did not like black people, and particularly black ballplayers. The powerful peeping-tom columnist got a big anti-Chapman crusade going, and hardly a day passed when the Phillies' manager didn't get a jab as a racist in Winchell's syndicated column, which was big in Philly, with its large black population. Toward the end of Robbie's first season, it got so hot for Chapman in Philadelphia that he was about to lose his job.

On our last visit to Philly in 1947, Winslow sidled up to me and, with a sickly smile, got out something that was obviously very hard for him to say: "For old times' sake, will you do me a big favor? Ask Robinson if he'll agree to have a picture taken shaking hands with me?"

It was hard, but I resisted the urge to tell Ben that was the first time I'd ever heard him call Jack by a decent name. Usually, it had been something unprintable. I must have looked stunned, though, for Chapman added, as a humbling afterthought: "A picture like this in the newspapers may save my job. I'll come over to your dugout this evening to have it taken, if he'll agree."

Robinson smiled wanly when I told him of Chapman's request and—to my surprise—quickly agreed.

"Tell Ben he doesn't have to come over to our dugout, either; I'll meet him halfway, behind the plate during batting practice."

"I'll go with you," I said, thinking to make the chore easier. I had often been Jack's ice-breaker.

"No," said Robinson. "This is something I should do alone, not as if I'm being urged."

Dixie Walker, Chapman's pal from Alabama, and a fine man through and through, had listened to this whole conversation, from the moment I relayed the strange request to Robbie. Dixie watched wide-eyed—we both did, in fact—as Robinson and Chapman, each marching from his own dugout, met on the neutral ground behind home plate. Ben extended a hand, smiling broadly as if they had been buddy-buddy for a lifetime. Robinson reached out and grasped it. The flicker of a smile crept across his face as the photographer snapped away, getting several shots.

Beside me Walker gasped, groping for words.

"I swear," he said softly, "I never thought I'd see Ol' Ben eat shit like that!"

I've thought many times since then that Jackie gave better than he took. He got no such gracious treatment, even after death, from Ford Frick or Jocko Conlan, or *Sports Illustrated*.

There was only one time when I thought Robinson was close to saying the hell with it and quitting.

That was in the gloom of a deserted Greyhound Bus outside a roadside restaurant in Florida, during spring training for the 1948 season. Jackie and another black slumped dejectedly in their seats. All the other Dodgers were inside, wolfing their steaks after a hard game against the Yankees. Jackie and the other, who was Roy Campanella, had been refused admission to the restaurant even though the rest of the team, still in their soiled uniforms, were in a private dining room that was walled off from the rest of the establishment.

Getting the players transported, bedded down, and fed was part of my job, and now I tried to bribe a waiter, or even a busboy, to carry a couple of blueplate specials to the outcasts in the bus. Not a chance! They'd have lost their jobs, they told me, and been marked as "nigger-lovers."

As I juggled the tray of plates onto the lonely bus in the dark, I found a Robinson who was politely grateful—but seething at the put-down. Campanella was pleading to avoid a scene: "Let's not have no trouble, Jackie. This is the onliest thing we can do right now, 'lessen we want to go back to them crummy Negro leagues . . ."

Robinson's eyes were aflame, and I knew what was racing through his mind: He had played a big part in winning fat World Series checks for all those guys inside the restaurant, even the third-string bullpen catcher and the humpties who hardly ever got into a game. And there they were, all of them, stuffing the food down and seeming not to care that he wasn't part of it, wasn't one of them.

He had taken all the abuse without a whimper; the dusters and beanballs they threw at him didn't stop him from getting up from the dirt and socking the big base hits to prove that he really belonged. But what was the good of all the "big experiment" when here he was, still on the outside?

Carefully laying aside his fat cigar with all the éclat of an orchestra leader putting down his baton, the roly-poly Campanella tore into the meal I had brought.

Robinson didn't touch a bite as we chatted in the dark.

Other things had discouraged Jackie in the spring of 1948. He had come to camp twenty pounds overweight because of the banquet circuit he was forced into by his own exuberant people after the World Series. He had tried hard in camp, but the suet just wouldn't come off him now as it did for the rookies on the team. His next birthday would be his thirtieth, and his legs, which had taken a battering in college and semipro football, throbbed night and day.

In his heart, he was worried: Would he ever get into top shape again?

28. The Missing Paragraph

Robinson knew, because I had told him, that the Big Boys, Larry MacPhail and his hand-made commissioner, Chandler, had put Durocher away for the whole 1947 season on trumped-up charges he had hosted notorious gamblers in box seats in the Havana ballpark.

Jackie could hardly believe the $500 check I got back when Chandler rescinded my fine. He wanted to know the whole story, and he thought it was a pip.

I explained that I had chased Unhappy Chandler all the way to his home in Versailles, Kentucky, with affidavits from responsible newspapermen like Gus Steiger of the *Mirror* and Eddie Murphy of the *Sun.* They knew for sure, and they were willing to testify, that Memphis Engelberg and the other gamblers had received their tickets in Havana from MacPhail's club, the Yankees, and not from Durocher or the Dodgers.

As we chatted in the bus in the dark, I unwound the whole story. Campanella was chomping his food, but Robinson was eating only the details I was telling, how desperately unhappy the commissioner was about the fact that newspapermen with affidavits were now entering the case, and that there would likely be more bad publicity. The very thought made Chandler shake. He was in enough hot water already.

At that point, even the puppet commissioner seemed sickened by the lack of real evidence to support the charges brought by MacPhail, whose chief witness, Arthur "Red" Patterson, had suffered a bad attack of forgetfulness. It had been Red who actually gave the tickets to Memphis and his friends.

"I don't get it," said Robinson. "What was so bad about knowing Memphis Engelberg, anyway?"

He had a point. Memphis was just a garden variety horse handicapper who also handled large bets. Robinson had been around Brooklyn long enough to learn there wasn't a corner where you couldn't find a bookie if you wanted one, with as many as two or three at some busy newsstands.

Chandler wasn't that much of a dummy, either. Noting the flimsy evidence, he had called for a "cooling off" period before the "Trial by Fury" had even been set up; but MacPhail wanted blood and pushed for an early "trial." When the Redhead got what he had wanted—Durocher's spanking and suspension for a year—he changed his nimble mind in the face of the furor and said he never sought to have the Lip put in drydock.

MacPhail then blew up at Chandler and defied the commissioner's gag rule by holding a press conference at which he declared that the Durocher suspension was silly and unwarranted. That got MacPhail nicely off the hook with Dodger fans and Durocher partisans. But it left Chandler still in the middle. That's why he was less than overjoyed when I showed up loaded with the affidavits, hollering for my money back.

After promising to rescind the fine, Chandler threatened me again. "You will get a third-party check in an unmarked envelope," said the fearless leader of baseball, "but if you ever tell that you got your five hundred dollars back, I'll fine you five thousand!"

This troubled Robinson that night on the bus. What kind of

people *were* these, anyway, running baseball this way, and twisting things to their own advantage as MacPhail, O'Malley, and Chandler were? He had seen Durocher sawed off, and he had seen enough by now to realize that the Big Oom wasn't exactly leading a cheering section for Rickey inside the Dodger organization.

Jackie was to be even more puzzled years later, when the swiveling Chandler did another about-face, either to pick up a few bucks for a rehash article in *Sports Illustrated* or to have the last word on baseball, which had jilted him. His story never mentioned the return of my $500, and it was full of errors, omissions, and distortions. I wrote the magazine to correct these, and I had plenty of company.

The letter underneath mine in the "Nineteenth Hole," the magazine's readers' opinion section, was from Fred Saigh, an ex-member of the owners' fraternity whom the other magnates have not been too happy about. Saigh had sold pitcher Murry Dickson to Pittsburgh, and the large check had somehow wound up in his own account instead of the Cardinal treasury. Because of this, Fred eventually did time in the penitentiary on an income tax rap.

In his letter to the magazine, Saigh described Chandler as "The Bluegrass Jackass."

My letter appeared over my name, as follows:

> Sirs: My first inclination is to leave Unhappy Chandler and his bad memory to the oblivion he has earned. But the reference to the gamblers at the exhibition game in Havana, which is left hanging in the article like a dangling participle, needs a little laundering . . .

My letter ran for almost sixty lines farther, detailing the secret third-party check I had received from Chandler in restitution, and setting out all the facts, with one curious omission; there was one deletion that couldn't have been made in the interest of saving space, for it comprised only a very few lines. Here are the missing lines:

> Red Patterson was to say to me: "And if you had looked at the Yankees' room list at the Nacional Hotel, you'd have found that their [gamblers'] rooms were paid for by us, too."

That made me wonder: Did MacPhail somehow get wind of my letter and pressure the magazine to delete that telltale part? Or was it Patterson who got kittenish about seeing the truth in print?

As soon as Chandler's mysterious check arrived I cashed it and went to good friend Max Kase, sports editor of the New York *Journal American*. Kase spread the whole yarn under an eight-column headline and asked the obvious question: If Parrott was exonerated, wasn't Durocher in the clear also? Shouldn't the Lip be called back from his California exile?

O'Malley jumped me when the *Journal* ran the story. He said I should have warned him when I was going to give the papers anything sensational like that. I wondered: Would the Big Oom have forced me to kill the story, had I told him in advance? Didn't the affable Irishman want the truth to come out? Or was it that he didn't enjoy anything complimentary that was printed about Durocher, or Parrott, or any of Branch Rickey's men?

The whole thing was a tempest in the MacPhail-Chandler teapot. They had set out to hang Durocher but succeeded only in gaining friends for the embattled exile, who was paid his full $50,000 salary for lolling on Laraine's Beverly Hills estate.

If they had all been a bit more clever in their efforts to put Leo in hot water at that time, they could have tried a little harder and dug up the Anzac story.

Every ballplayer and newspaperman, even the Dodger batboy, knew all about Anzac!

29. Sleepout Louie and the Boat Race

Things were dragging one hot morning in Cincinnati when Durocher asked if I'd like to go across the river to Kentucky to see what a real horse parlor looked like.

There was nothing to do until we played that night, and I

jumped at the chance. I hadn't had much to do with bookies since Crist had sent me to Belmont Park. I wondered if these would look the same as the old guy with the slate who had growled at me.

There was no resemblance. I had never met anybody quite like Sleepout Louie before. He and his two partners, Cigar Charley and the Dancer, were right out of Runyon's *Guys and Dolls*. They were even more authentic than Nathan Detroit.

The three of them seemed delighted to have a visit from our dandy manager, and we swapped small talk until Leo informed them he was "carrying light," meaning he was short of cash. Did they have anything going whereby he might pick up a little "walking around money," as the Lip called the roll he liked to show off.

It was late in the meeting at Latonia, at a time when they ran what might be called a "benefit" for horsemen who had had a bad meeting and needed money for the feed bills or to get home on.

Sleepout told Leo to be on the watch for a horse named Anzac at Latonia.

"Write it down, kid," Leo said to me, "so we don't forget."

Turning back to Sleepout, he said, "How much should we bet?"

The three of them shrugged, with a knowing look. "Bet, and bet, and bet," said Sleepout, "till you ain't got no more."

Frankly, I forgot about the incident. We moved on to Pittsburgh, and on the second day there Durocher and I were having breakfast. Suddenly he jumped up as if he had been prodded by a pitchfork. Leo was so excited he didn't finish his food, or even the sentence. All I could make out was "Anzac."

I looked at the paper he had left in his haste, and there it was: Anzac. The nag was due to run in the fifth that afternoon at Latonia. Again I forgot all about it, for I was not much for betting or horses.

That afternoon we were on the third tee at the Pittsburgh Field Club—Roscoe McGowen of the *Times;* Connie Desmond, Red Barber's announcing partner; and Bob Cooke of the *Herald-Tribune*.

Casually I brought up the Anzac incident. Cooke, who was just about to tee off, showed more than normal interest. He asked me where I got the tip. When I mentioned Covington, Kentucky, his eyes lit up. Then I added, quite innocently, that there had been mention of a boat race, whatever that was. I had never heard the term.

That did it. Cooke dropped his club on the tee and sprinted back toward the clubhouse, leaving his amazed caddie and his three companions. We played on until the ninth hole and then went into the locker room, searching for Bob. He was still on the phone to New York, trying to get more money down.

By now I was impressed by the importance of the name Anzac. I called the bellman back at the Schenley and managed to get thirty bucks down on the animal.

By that evening I was $400 richer, and quite a bit wiser. Now I knew what a boat race was.

I never found out how much Durocher won, but it must have been a bundle.

A lot of ballplayers were aboard Anzac that day too. Leo could never keep a good thing like that to himself. He had no secrets whatever, unless it was his little black book of pretty girls' phone numbers. Even in that league he had to brag when he pulled off something extra good.

It was a silly brag that cost him five hundred bucks on that same road trip.

The brassy manager had been thrown out in the first inning of a game in Cincinnati for charging umpire Larry Goetz on a strike call. He had showered and dressed, and here he came into the club box beside me. Everybody in the park recognized him, and the three umpires glared in his direction. But he was within his rights, just as long as he didn't try to run the team.

"I'll give you the signs," he said under his breath, "and Dressen will pick them up from you. Just do as I say and we'll win this fuckin' game." He was talking through clenched teeth like a ventriloquist.

For the next couple of innings I was signaling for the "take" by putting my hand to my nose and giving the hit sign, which was rubbing both hands together. Dressen, in the third-base coaching box, had sharp eyes, and he didn't miss a thing, although we were clear across the diamond from him.

It was a tight ballgame, and in the eighth we got a man on

third with one out. Durocher had noticed the Reds' third baseman was gazing up into the stands at a blonde, and he decided
to put on the squeeze play.

"Pull your right ear, kid," Leo hissed.

The sign went to Dressen and then to Pee Wee Reese, who had
stepped out of the batter's box.

Pee Wee dropped a perfect bunt toward third and beat it out.
The run scored, and before the inning was over Reese scored as
well. That was enough to win the game.

That night, in the diner, Leo couldn't resist telling how he had
"outsmarted" the umpires and won the game by keeping his
mouth shut like Edgar Bergen.

One smart writer got off the train when the engine had to take
on water at Indianapolis and wired a box to his paper.

Ford Frick read it and slapped a $500 fine on Durocher. Me?
I had only played Charley McCarthy, the dummy, to Leo's Edgar
Bergen, so all I got was a reprimand.

But there was always some new adventure around the corner
when you traveled with this man. It was like living a special baseball version of the Arabian Nights.

But there was trouble in Paradise. Robinson was still fat and
couldn't run the way he had for Shotton in 1947. The team was
not far out of the cellar when O'Malley pressured Rickey into
dumping Durocher. Stoneham had to sack Mel Ott about the
same time, and he had wanted old Barney Shotton, who had
filled in for the suspended Durocher and won the 1947 pennant.

In one of his greatest flights of oratory, Rickey talked Stoneham into taking Durocher instead.

With Shotton directing the Brooklyn team, Robinson began to
run wild again, and Durocher now felt sure he had been lying
down. They went at each other hard whenever Dodgers and
Giants tangled.

Jackie made a crack about Leo's Chanel No. 5 and his "Hollywood wife." They had to hold Leo back when he started after the
black man, and it was well they did; Jack would have broken the
Lip in half. Before the next ballgame Leo sent a case of Lifebuoy
soap to Robbie in the Dodger clubhouse.

Lifebuoy, which smelled like a hospital ward, was a favorite insult in baseball in those days. There was a 30-foot-high sign on the right-field wall in Ebbets Field that claimed, "The Dodgers Use Lifebuoy." During a frustrating losing streak, a fan climbed the wall late one night and added, in bright red paint, "—And they still stink!"

Rickey had cornered the market in black ballplayers. He had brought up Campanella in 1948, and now he added a 240-pound Negro pitcher for 1949—Don Newcombe, who won seventeen as Brooklyn squeaked by the Cardinals to win another pennant for Shotton by one full game.

But O'Malley was far from happy. He redoubled his efforts to get Rickey out, and he bumped off the Dodger board of directors Jim Mulvey, the movie man, who had been there a generation before him. Mulvey and his family always came to spring training and loved the team.

"The time has come, my boy, to consider whether it is wise to say 'good morning' to Jim Mulvey if O'Malley is listening," Rickey warned me one day.

At this point the Mahatma reminded me of one of those old-time jugglers who usually opened the bill at a vaudeville house.

He was keeping three hot potatoes in the air at once: a scheming, ambitious O'Malley, who nitpicked at every move he made; a bitter Robinson, who was beginning to fight the umpires; and the Mulvey-O'Malley battle, which Rickey was trying to keep from erupting into a full-scale war.

On one extended leg and an outstretched arm, juggler Rickey was trying to keep two hoops rotating in the right direction: his own health, which was in precarious shape because of the dizzy spells that came without warning, and the frightening problem of his only son's diabetic comas. Young Branch, the Twig, had been out cold several times, once propped up against me as I drove most of the night in search of insulin.

Finally, on his own forehead the Mahatma was balancing his own chair, the president's throne of the Dodgers. It was spinning on one leg, and every time it got close enough, O'Malley made a grab for it. The Big Oom wanted very badly to plant his fat ass in that chair.

While this sideshow was going on, Robinson developed great empathy with Rickey, who had taken the place of a father Jackie never knew. He knew there wasn't one single thing the owners—and he included O'Malley—liked about the Old Man's Black Experiment, except the riches it brought them all. Had the other moguls pressured O'Malley into making things tough for Durocher, who had voted for Jackie right from the start, and also tough for Rickey himself? Why should he go on making these bigots rich, filling their ballparks for them while they were all undercutting his godfather? When would his turn come to face the ax? How would he fare when they did get Rickey out, and he had to face O'Malley alone?

I knew these were Robinson's thoughts, for I had gotten quite close to him, writing the radio program he broadcast every Sunday night live from wherever the team happened to be.

One Sunday, as spring training wound down, we found ourselves in Atlanta. I had our oldest son Tod on that trip, for it was during Easter vacation. At the game we sat behind two crackers who had come for their first glimpse of this Negro who could play ball. The place was packed; there could not have been more curiosity had we advertised we'd start an orang-utan who could turn the double play and steal bases.

"Theah he is," said the first fan. "Numbah foughty-two. Man alahve, is he black!"

"Black?" repeated his companion. "Ah say if you scratch on him wit' chahcoal, you'd leave a whaht mahk." And they laughed uproariously.

That night we took a cab to the radio station where I had arranged for us to broadcast. I brought my ten-year-old son along, for I wanted him to learn how radio worked.

The boy learned a lot more than that. It was a pretentious building, an outlet for the ABC network. The elevator operator, white, prepared to take us up when Tod and I stepped aboard. But when Robinson followed, he froze. "The elevator just went out of order," he said, "until *he* gets off." There was no doubt whom he meant, for he pointed a finger at Jackie. We three climbed four flights on the grimy back stairs together.

Later that evening Robbie took us to dinner at the home of the Negro family with whom he was staying. We had to make arrangements like that in every city we visited, for the black-only hotels were terrible fleabags.

When a Negro family entertained whites as they did us that night, they took a big chance. Uppity Nigras, if they were discovered, faced reprisals. Nobody ever bothered the white guests!

In Atlanta that night, Tod and I sneaked out of that Negro home under cover of darkness and walked the ten blocks to a white neighborhood where a white cab could pick us up. The black cabs wouldn't dare carry whites.

I couldn't believe all this at first, but when it seeped in, it made more and more of a Robinson fan of me.

Jackie was fed up with all this, and he played ball in that 1949 season like a man possessed. He hit .342 to lead the league. He ran with a new "I-don't-care" flair, and he led in stolen bases with thirty-nine. Every time he came up with men on, it seemed, he hit bingo with a base hit. He drove in one hundred twenty-four runs.

Robbie was starting to give it back now, and I understood why. He was like a sponge that could absorb only so much of that venom, and he had had more than enough. He was turning it around on them.

In Chicago one day Preacher Roe, the Arkansas control artist, wasn't getting the strike calls he deserved from the umpire behind the plate, who happened to be another Arkansan, a former great pitcher named Lon Warneke.

"Ball three!" said Warneke.

"That was a strike, Warneke," Robinson shouted from his position at second base.

"You can't umpire from away back here," challenged Jocko Conlan, the little rooster who was umpiring the bases that day.

Another inning went by, and Robbie thought the ump blew another key call. "That was a strike, Warneke," he shouted.

"It was low," came Conlan's voice from behind him.

"Oho," said Jackie. "I can't umpire from back here, but *you* can, I suppose?"

"One more word," threatened the umpire, "and you're outta here!"

Robinson clammed up. Next inning, when he returned to second, he said to Jocko, "I just want you to know it wasn't *you* who shut me up last inning. It was my wife."

"Whatever did he mean by that?" Conlan asked me after the game.

I explained that Rickey, who used to call Robinson after every tough ballgame on the road, had felt he was losing control of Jackie and had sent Rachel along on this important road trip. Jackie had promised her he would not be thrown out of any more games.

Robbie was a born leader. As the unappointed captain of the blacks on the team, he had his hands full with Newcombe, who was lazy and would coast on a lead.

One day in St. Louis Newk had an 8–1 lead, but the Cardinals were starting to get to him.

Robinson strode in to the mound, circled Newk, and confronted him. Six-footer though he was, Robbie had to look up to this giant. "You're just goosing the ball up there," he accused. "Start firing, or we'll blow this game!"

Newk threw hard for an inning or so, then started to coast again.

This brought a furious Robinson to the mound on the double. We could hear every word from the dugout. "Cut that ball loose," Jackie barked. "I think you're *yellow*, Newcombe!"

Newk blinked a few times, fell back a step, and delivered his answer in the same Negro jargon that I had heard a lot of blacks use from time to time: "Not only is you wrong, Robinson," he said slowly, "but you is *loud* wrong!"

Robinson's Dodger salary hadn't reached $25,000 yet, but he was worth twice that. He was doing the job in the engine room for Rickey, while the Old Man was battling topside to make things easier for the black ballplayers.

To do this, the Mahatma tried to place blacks all over both leagues, to make the Negro ballplayer accepted everywhere. He had the "black market" cornered, but he purposely let some of these gems that his bird-dogs had discovered "get away" to other teams.

We could have had Larry Doby, who had made the barnstorming trip with Charley Dressen and me to Havana. Rickey preferred to let Cleveland have the big guy. Junior Gilliam introduced me to Hank Aaron, then a second baseman playing with a black team called the Clowns as "the meal-money man," and that was long before the Braves got a string on him. Rickey sold Chico Carrasquel to the White Sox, where he became a distinguished shortstop.

The Old Man was a born auctioneer. The patsies among the owners and their general managers had always bought his surplus at inflated prices, as he played one baseball man off against another, jacking the prices up without mercy. You would have thought that they'd learn to keep the rubber band on their bankrolls after being bilked so often. But no, his 1949 "fall clearance sale" was the most outlandish ever, with millionaires like Lou Perini pushing and shoving to get to the bargain counter before Clark Griffith, the Old Fox of the Washington Senators.

The reason? Their ballparks were being picketed by minority groups who wanted a black ballplayer like Robinson or Campy or Newcombe for *their* team. Quite a few of the lords of the game now *had* to get a good black player, and who knew more about the breed than Rickey?

Greed played a part, too. The Lords of Baseball saw how the blacks were drawing for the Brooklyns. True, they had tried to bar the black man; failing that, they'd be happy to accept one, if he brought in the gold.

⚬⚒⚬⚒⚬

30. The Mahatma Auctions Off Some Clucks

Rickey had been collecting chocolate infielders and catchers and licorice pitchers and outfielders for four years now, while the magnates had been wringing their hands and moaning about the bad things the Old Man was doing to their Grand Old Game, taking the Nigras in.

Now it was funny to hear this same bunch bellying up to Rickey's counter like kids crowding a showcase full of candies.

Would he sell some of his black beauties, please? Can I buy that one you have up in Montreal, that Sam Something-or-other?

How about this one over here marked "Bankhead"? Will you sell, Branch?

Of course he would. "Sell" was his middle name. He had fun holding this auction by telephone, because he could move the livestock faster that way, and I swear he punctuated his chatter with a "Hurry, hurry, hurry" lingo that was right out of a carnival barker's spiel.

The Mahatma treated some of the millionaire owners like children, which indeed they were in the hands of an old horse-trader like him. "No, Mr. Perini, there's no way to tell how old Sam Jethroe really is. You could look at his teeth, perhaps. But Sam has no vital records; sorry about that. There's a story going around that Ol' Sam went so far back for a fly ball in some little cotton-pickin' village that he actually left town, and his records behind him, and never came back." Rickey had a different story for each Jethroe bidder. If half of them were true, this was the swiftest Grandpa the game had ever known.

I tried never to miss these "sales," but I was just an amazed and amused listener. The working staff consisted of Fresco Thompson and Rickey's son, the Twig; as well as Jane Ann Jones, the Old Man's faithful Girl Friday, who handled the jangling phones and put some of the biggest men in baseball on "hold," while Rickey was building his market, chiding another lodge brother for not spending enough money.

Here are my actual notes from one of the Old Man's extraordinary auctions:

JANE ANN JONES: Clark Griffith is on Line Two. This is the third time he's called.

RICKEY: Griff, you just cannot afford to miss this Danny O'Connell, who burned up the American Association with our St. Paul club. He is just a baby; but there is no doubt that Daniel is a coming superstar . . .

GRIFFITH (*cutting in*): I don't need a shortstop.

RICKEY (*purring*): But you did lose a hundred ballgames this year, didn't you, Griff? You need O'Connell to pull your infield together. He is still awkward because he is so young, but he can make every play. In another two years, he will be a two hundred thousand dollar star . . .

GRIFFITH (*weakening slightly*): How much do you want for him?

RICKEY: I could get a hundred thousand for him anywhere in our league, but I do not want to place this boy where he might hurt us, so I am offering him to you over there at a special price . . .

GRIFFITH (*impatiently*): How much, I said.

RICKEY: A paltry seventy-five thousand for a superstar of the future . . .

GRIFFITH: No kid shortstop is worth that much money. Let me ask around about the boy. I may call you back . . .

RICKEY (*sternly*): All right, but make it before four this afternoon. That is the absolute deadline on O'Connell, Griff, and I am doing this only as a favor for an old friend. We are moving fast around here today.

JANE ANN JONES (*waves a slip of paper with Frank Lane's name on it.* RICKEY *pushes the button and gets in the first word at the same split second.*)

RICKEY: Frank, how can you hesitate about this boy Carrasquel I am giving you a chance to buy? I don't understand you at all. The price is dirt cheap at thirty-five thousand dollars, but I will not accept your player Claxton as part of the deal. I need a minor league shortstop to replace Carrasquel if I sell him, but Claxton is too old. Why, he must be thirty-five by now——

LANE (*indignantly*): Claxton is *not* thirty-five.

RICKEY: All right, thirty-six, then. He can't bend over for ground balls. Don't try to palm off any of those Methuselahs you have on your White Sox roster, Frank. Some of them couldn't make my Montreal farm club. Gotta watch a sharp horse-trader like you Frank, or you'll take advantage of a poor old man . . .

LANE (*interrupting*): Carrasquel isn't worth any thirty-five thousand.

RICKEY: What? That boy is such a prize that my scout Fresco Thompson risked his life in a Venezuela revolution to get him out of there. And anybody who's worth a human life must be valued at more than thirty-five thousand dollars . . .

Reproduced with permission of *The Sporting News*, St. Louis, Missouri.

LANE: Let me talk to my scouts. I'll call you back.

JANE ANN JONES: Mr. Rickey, Roy Hamey is on the phone from Pittsburgh.

HAMEY: Branch, I've just got to get my hands on two . . .

RICKEY: I knew you needed pitching, Roy, and I believe I have just the two you need, a starter and a bullpen man. Let me tell you, this Bankhead can throw bullets . . . and did you realize he hit a home run in his first at-bat in the major league with the Dodgers?

HAMEY: No, no, no, you don't understand. I don't need pitching. It's two strips of box seat tickets for your World Series games in Brooklyn next week that I want. I am not interested in any more of your players. We had some bad experiences with that Marvin Rackley you sold us, remember? And Ed Stevens was a lemon, too. The press is on us here in Pittsburgh pretty badly about buying so many clunkers from you. Rojek has been terrible at short, and you told us he would be a star . . .

RICKEY (*sounding hurt*): Stan Rojek is a fine boy . . .

HAMEY: Maybe behind a counter someplace he would be O.K. He stands in one place all the time. He's playing on a dime. Why didn't you tell me he was dating that dame from the Ice Capades? He's been trying to learn to skate, and now I think his legs are gone. He left his whole game in some ice rink, that's what. Now, what about those tickets I need so badly for your World Series?

RICKEY: We are sold out, Roy. Oh, I have players to sell, but no tickets. But I may have a solution for you, Roy. This boy O'Connell would end your problems at short. He would put Rojek right on the bench. If you grab Danny O'Connell for seventy-five grand, you would have to give me Cassini, that second baseman you have at Indianapolis, and I will personally dig up those tickets you need . . .

HAMEY: I don't know about O'Connell. I'll speak to my manager and call you back. But be sure to hold those tickets for me.

JANE ANN JONES: John Quinn is on from Boston, Mr. Rickey.

RICKEY (*plugging Quinn in*): John, I do hope that you don't miss out on Jellico. This boy will make your whole outfield. I swear I have never seen a human being run as fast as Jellico . . .

FRESCO THOMPSON (*breaks in, waving his arms wildly*): Not Jellico, Mr. Rickey. Jellico was an English admiral, and he is dead. Happy Chandler will sock us all with fines if you take money for him. Sam Jethroe is the man you mean.

RICKEY: Ho, ho, ho, John, you know how I am with names. Jericho is the man I meant. You know him: He is black as coal, is a switch hitter, and can outrun his shadow . . .

QUINN: I hear Jethroe's arm is no good. But what is your rock-bottom price on him, so I can tell Mr. Perini . . .

RICKEY: Jemco's arm is all right, but it doesn't matter anyway. If he had to, he could run the ball into the infield quicker than most players could throw it there. I will take one hundred fifty thousand and two minor league players for him, and even then I am making a mistake. I should not let this boy get away . . .

QUINN (*gulping audibly*): Mr. Perini will never stand for that. Why, he would have to sell two of his steamshovels to raise that kind of money . . .

RICKEY (*cutting him short*): Tut, tut, John. Money means nothing these days, anyway. Now I cannot play that one hundred fifty thousand in center field, can I? And Mr. Perini cannot use those thousand-dollar bills to scoop out a foundation, can he now? Besides, you should tell Louie what he will be doing for the minority groups in Boston by buying this upstanding Negro boy. You know how the colored people buy your tickets when Robinson and Campanella come to town. Well, this Jericho is faster than Robbie, and twice as fast as Roy.

QUINN: I'll call you right back.

JANE ANN JONES: Mr. Griffith is calling back, Mr. Rickey. He is up to fifty thousand now for O'Connell, but he says he will not pay one nickel more than that.

RCIKEY: Tell that old tightwad to dig a little deeper. We cannot hold a fine Irish boy like O'Connell cheaply.

THOMPSON: Frank Lane is on Line Two. Says he will take Carrasquel. Now he wants a price on Bankhead.

RICKEY: Hold him off until Bankhead pitches tonight in Mon-

treal in the Little World Series. And tell him to get the
check for the thirty-five thousand for Carrasquel in the
mail tonight.

JANE ANN JONES: Mr. Hamey is on the line. Says he will take
O'Connell if you throw in six World Series tickets.

RICKEY: You have a deal, Roy. You sure know how to take advantage of an old man . . .

JANE ANN JONES: Mr. Griffith is on the other phone.

RICKEY: I'm awfully, awfully sorry, Griff, but I just sold that
boy O'Connell to Pittsburgh. You just waited too long . . .

GRIFFITH: Now I'm in an awful jam. I called a press conference for an hour from now; I told the newspapermen we
had bought a new player . . .

RICKEY: I know how disappointed you must be, so I will let
you have this fine young outfielder I did not intend to sell.
His name is Irv Noren, and he will hit .330 and plug up
your outfield holes for you. He is a regular churchgoer, too.
On top of that, I will knock Noren's price down to sixty
thousand dollars.

GRIFFITH: They tell me Noren cannot hit the high pitch . . .

RICKEY: Call your man Bucky Harris out on the Coast, and he
will give you the straight dope on Noren. But call me back
fast, or you will lose this boy like you lost O'Connell.

JANE ANN JONES: Mr. Perini just called and says he will take
Jethroe. He said they have been picketing his office and
will go on until he gets a Negro player.

RICKEY: Good. Keep notes on all this, or we will make a mistake and sell the same player twice.

THOMPSON: It just came over the ticker that Bankhead pitched
a shutout in Montreal . . .

RICKEY: Judas Priest, what a lucky thing we did not sell him
this afternoon! That will cost Lane an additional ten
grand. Fresco, call Hamey in Pittsburgh and tell him three
teams in the American League are hot after Bankhead at
fifty thousand dollars, so he had better move fast. We
sure are spending a lot of money on those telephone
calls . . .

THOMPSON (*with a wink*): It seems that every phone call costs the guy on the other end of the line more than it does you, Mr. Rickey.

RICKEY (*suppressing a smile*): Harrumph! I don't know what you meant by that, Tommy. I'm helping all these owners out. Don't you realize that?

Part IV

⚬⨉⨉⨉⚬

From Flatbush to the Freeways

31. The Cockroach That Stalled a Dodger Team

O'Malley snatched his Dodger dog and pony show out of Brooklyn on a dark night in late November 1957 and dropped the whole thing on Los Angeles. The move was about as well thought-out as a panty raid by a bunch of college freshmen who'd had too many beers.

First, the Blarney Man told me to start selling season tickets in a shabby bandbox of a minor league park called Wrigley Field, and we took in the money for a bushel of them. Then it was oops —hold everything, I think we're going to play somewhere else. We never came close to playing an inning in Wrigley.

The frantic fans bombarded us, and all were waving money. My average day went something like this: "Step aside there, please, and let the lady with that two-thousand-dollar check up to the counter. Yes, I know you were here first, sir, but we cannot accept checks for less than a thousand bucks, which will hold four seats for you. Where will they be? In the Los Angeles area somewhere, sir. Oh, you mean first base or third? Sorry sir, if you want a seat, you'll have to buy it for every game. No ma'am, the tickets aren't printed yet. No, I'm not sure where we'll play, and I can't tell you when opening day will be, but I'll be happy to take your certified check. You say you've never been to a big league game? Yes, I'll be happy to reserve four seats you wish behind second base—"

When the Smiling Irishman saw the way the gold was rolling in, he worried that too much of it would spill out of tiny Wrigley Field and went searching for a bigger spread, although by then we were looking right into January.

The Dodger leap to the Coast could have turned into a worse

fiasco, a bigger black eye for the National League than the Seattle muddle was for the Junior Circuit twelve years later.

O'Malley next made a pass at the Rose Bowl, and we were into 1958 before he reversed again and commanded me to have a rush print job on tickets for seventy-seven games at the Coliseum, a mausoleum that had 102,000 seats, every one completely unprotected from the searing sun. There is more shade on the Sahara.

Seats? Actually, there wasn't a single seat in this whole concrete pile. They were straight-backed benches, harder than a church pew and twice as long, and the numbers had been burned into them with a branding iron, presumably a hand-me-down from the first settlers to cross the Rockies—the place looked that old.

I remember taking O'Malley out among the benches to prove to him that four fans with fannies anything near his size couldn't squeeze into the spaces between four of the numbers. There went his dream of crowds of 100,000-plus. His face fell, but he agreed the Globe Ticket Company would have to pull and burn every fifth ticket. We'd have to settle now for houses of 92,000, which we had many times, once three days running in the 1959 World Series.

"Fix it up somehow," he sighed as he spun on his heel and left for Vero Beach, the team's Florida training base.

Canceling every fifth ticket led to some giant credibility gaps. A fan who had shelled out fifteen hundred bucks for six season seats would open his package and discover to his dismay that he had been mailed seats numbered 3, 4, 6, 7, 8, and 9. The guy next to him would get seats 11, 12, 13, 14, 16, and 17. No agency on earth could convince these good people over the phone that their tickets were side by side, and that the ticket office hadn't goofed.

On our first Sunday in the Coliseum, the temperature was up around 100. We were in the world's largest steam bath, and people were dropping like flies. We couldn't get enough ambulances to haul them away.

After the game a mild, almost apologetic gent begged me to change the location of his seats. He declined to say why, but he asked to have them moved slightly to the right or left, or even back a bit. He was in the twentieth row and didn't even request to be moved closer to the front.

When pressed for a reason, he hedged and insisted all the people sitting around him were very, very nice. Before I could move him, I had to pass on whether his reasons were important enough for me to switch all the other ticketholders around him so I could switch his seats.

Finally he broke down and confessed that there was a 250-pound Negro in the seat next to his, and on those hot days in the Coliseum this guy perspired so much that Freeman Gosden—that was the name he gave me—was afraid they'd all float away.

At first Gosden's name didn't ring a bell. Then it dawned on me that this polite white man was so upset because he had made a fortune broadcasting over the radio as a black in "Amos 'n' Andy."

The sides of the Coliseum slanted away from the playing field like some gigantic saucepan. As a matter of fact, we *were* frying our customers alive in this stone skillet, but that wasn't all: The holders of the best box seats had to descend twenty-four rows below street level, which means they had to climb back up forty-eight steps to use the rest rooms or escape when the game was over.

There were no elevators in the place then, and a climb to the cheaper pews really taxed the heart; by the time a fan reached the sixty-fifth row, his pump would have excited any cardiologist. It was no laughing matter to some, but the jokes flew thick and fast. One newspaper printed a letter from a fan who claimed he had climbed up from the diamond, as well as away from it, to the sixty-eighth row. When he then turned for a glance back, the ballplayers looked like pygmies. The fan asked a man already sitting up there what the score was.

"How should I know?" he guy said. "I'm flying the air mail to San Francisco!"

John Ford, the great director who had made John Wayne famous in Westerns, had only one workable eye, and it would have been a waste of his time to sell him tickets in the high rows. He could have done better staying home and listening to Vin Scully and Jerry Doggett on the radio. Ford wore a sinister-looking black patch over the bad eye; it was his trademark, and everybody knew him.

Ford was making *The Last Hurrah* then. Spencer Tracy, the star, always insisted on having old acting pals like Pat O'Brien and Jimmy Gleason in the cast, and all of them, including Ford, were great baseball fans. They even had a room on the set that carried a sign announcing it was "The Dugout" and was "for players only." They swapped baseball stories there while the grips and extras and subdirectors got ready for the next shot. Durocher was a regular visitor in their "Dugout," and one day he asked me to come along, because Ford wanted to buy four season tickets.

The old director begged me to get him as close to the action as possible, pointing sadly to his black patch over the bad eye. As a reward, he said I could use his 100-foot schooner, which he kept moored in Hawaii, any time I wanted. He had been a high officer in our navy during the war. But as this one-eyed character described his great schooner and its towering masts to me, he looked and sounded for all the world like John Silver in *Treasure Island*.

As a gag, O'Brien and Gleason got me to bring four tickets in the forty-fourth row, which they placed on top of the four stacks of season tickets in the boxes with little plastic windows, so you could read the locations.

When Durocher arrived to deliver the tickets the next day, Ford abruptly halted the scene he was shooting and grabbed for the box of tickets, even lifting the black flap from his bad eye the better to see where his seats were located. When he learned that they were in the forty-fourth row he let out a stream of words that would have scared off the cattle rustlers in one of his Wayne Westerns.

Eventually I got the old director some first-row seats a little beyond first base, where he sat every night with his well-known black eye-flap.

Soon I got a complaint from one of the umpires that Ford was crabbing at him on every close play, calling him a blind bat.

United California Bank, one of the big ones, had adopted us like a godfather when we landed in Los Angeles, lending us safes, ticket drawers, desks, and even typewriters. They also loaned me John Miller from the bank staff, and Miller became my shadow, following me everywhere, cutting red tape and solving problems.

E. John Burns, a comical colonel O'Malley had imported from his Room 40 cast in Brooklyn to do the bookkeeping, wanted to take our main account away from the United California and put it in another bank, which had some golfing crony of his on the staff. I fought this and won, for it is safe to say we would never have opened that first mixed-up season on time without the help of UCB, their furniture, and John Miller.

One day Miller brought me a check for ten thousand bucks of his bank's money for season tickets. That day he introduced me to an automobile dealer from nearby Alhambra, Bill Burch, who laid cash on my barrelhead for another forty season seats at two hundred and fifty bucks a pop. Burch then took everybody to lunch and offered to lend us all Oldsmobiles. I drove free Oldsmobiles for the next six years, and a lot of people, including players like Sandy Koufax, got them also.

This is a regular thing in baseball, although usually the auto sponsors of the radio broadcasts supply the free wheels. The Dodger front office later rode in Japanese compact cars, although as I remember Vin Scully would never accept one. Nor would Peter O'Malley give up his snooty Mercedes.

Even with the dirt-poor Padres in San Diego we had free cars; I remember Buzzy Bavasi posing beside one of the Lincolns wheeled out by Bob Townsend, the owner of the Lincoln-Mercury agency near the stadium. Peter Bavasi chose a wild yellow Cougar with a racing fin on the back, but when the car wasn't quite outlandish enough to please him, he blasted the whole courtesy-car program, which soon came to an end.

I slapped some sponge rubber covered with oilcloth in Dodger blue over the hard pews, easing at least that pain for the season ticket holders. The whole thing was rush, rush, rush, and the workmen were still putting on the seat numbers the morning of our opener.

Colonel Burns complained about the money for the seat cushions and threatened to have my job if I didn't stop spending. He had been imported to count the Big Oom's pennies and guard them, and he sure was overdoing it. If this guy ever was really in the military long enough to make colonel, it's lucky they never let him up near the shooting. He would have given our troops cap pistols to save money.

As a ballpark where big league games were to be played and records made that went into the book, the Coliseum was a bad joke. If there was a favoring wind at your back, you could stand on home plate and spit into the left-field stands. To take away some of the stigma of the Chinese home run that had to be hit only 251 feet, 42-foot-high girders were erected, and a chicken-wire screen was draped on these. This wire wall turned booming line drives by such as Hodges and Furillo into mere singles when they plunked into the wire and dropped like dead fish into the hands of waiting outfielders; but it couldn't do anything about the Little League pop flies that turned out to be home runs in the box scores.

The colleges, USC and UCLA, which had regarded the Coliseum as their sacred turf, where roamed the ghosts of Howard Jones and Morley Drury, Cotton Warburton and Buckets Waterfield, made O'Malley pay dearly for bringing his baseball circus into such holy precincts. They made him install an expensive drainage sewer under the hallowed gridiron, and they insisted that he take down his O'Malley wall in left field every time the Dodgers went on the road. This was a laugh, for the colleges had only track meets at that time of year, and the meager crowds they drew didn't have to look through the chicken wire if they didn't want to.

It took $4,500 worth of heavy cranes and ironworkers to take down the fence and the same amount to put it up again. Dick Walsh staged a dress rehearsal to see how long it would take to dismantle this erector set, and when O'Malley got the bill for this dry run he blew his top. This might have been what drove him to hire Colonel Burns as a watchdog for his treasury.

So much for the good news. After that, some really bad things began to happen to me in the Coliseum.

When I put in a requisition for a flashlight so that Frank Hess, the bulldog I had in charge of my vault, could poke around in the Stygian blackness there and find the right tickets, the colonel turned me down. When one of my salesgirls spilled ink on an expensive dress worn by a Pasadena lady who was buying two thousand bucks' worth of tickets, I had the dress cleaned. Burns refused to pay for that, too.

Not only that, this comical colonel sent me a full-page memo, single-spaced, explaining in elaborate terms why he was disallowing the total expenditure of $2.76 for the flashlight and the cleaning bill. I still have that memo. Even O'Malley would have to admit it was a classic exercise in muddleheaded corporate thinking.

Bavasi and Fresco Thompson had taken off for Florida even ahead of the Big Oom, and I couldn't blame them for wanting to get as far away from the mess in the Coliseum as they could. This left me alone with Colonel Bungle and Dick Walsh, who was charged with getting the Coliseum help lined up, the turnstiles checked, and the concession booths working. Walsh soon got into a battle with Bill Nicholas, long-time boss of the Coliseum, about garbage and cleanup. This made things even more sticky.

Nobody, including Bavasi and O'Malley, had stopped to think about lining up living quarters for the ballplayers and their families when they finished the usual spring training nonsense in Florida. The athletes themselves seldom take care of such minor details; they pranced around in Florida, blithely unworried until the moment came when they had to move into California.

Had O'Malley been smart, he'd have taken over a small hotel and put the whole tribe up until they could search for apartments. But that wasn't his speed. Nor was it the way Colonel Bungle Burns operated, either.

If you've ever been around a gossipy group of women, each striving for more status than the next because her husband hit ten points higher or made five thousand bucks more than the next one's, you must be able to guess what happened. And it occurred only because Dotty Reese, who had been the den mother and problem-solver in other years, wasn't around now. The captain was on his last legs, just playing here and there, and Dotty stayed home.

Joan Hodges, Gil's fussy wife, saw a cockroach in the apartment she got and fled all the way back to Brooklyn, never to return that season. The beast she saw must have been larger and nastier than a Brooklyn cockroach, for Joan took the pains to tell all the other wives, before she took off in a huff, about the perils of living in Los Angeles.

It's been said that an army travels on its stomach; a ball club is only as effective as its wives are happy. Our team was now most unhappy, with morale at an all-time low.

Of course this wasn't by any standards the same murderous bunch of Dodgers who had ripped the league apart for two pennants in the previous three years. Robinson was gone now, and Campanella, when he finally came to the Coliseum, would arrive in a wheelchair, after having his spinal cord all but severed in a freak auto accident near his home in the East. Podres was a .500 pitcher, Drysdale hadn't yet arrived as a star, and Koufax was driving everybody up the wall by walking two batters every three innings.

Who could get excited about a conglomeration of upset, over-the-hill veterans and question-mark rookies like this?

Nobody at all except the 78,672 who showed up for this team's first afternoon game in the Coliseum, against the Giants from San Francisco.

"They'll buy anything in Hollywood," Dick Young commented with some bitterness in New York. He deeply resented the kidnapping of the Dodgers out of Brooklyn, and he sneered at the crowds that went to see them.

The night of our opener, I was sitting on about sixty thousand bucks in cash, most of which had come in at the gate that day. I was having regular nightmares about a holdup, because we were in a really bad neighborhood, and any would-be stickup man could climb a tree in a nearby park and look right in on us as we counted O'Malley's greenbacks. You could jimmy open any window of our rickety office with a pen-knife.

Fearing a heist, I ordered an armored-car pickup. I wanted to get rid of that hot cash, which was all in small bills.

Colonel Burns canceled the armored car. Too expensive, because of the union rates for security guards after regular banking hours. The next morning would do just as well, he said.

A committee of show biz people officially welcomed the team at a luncheon, and O'Malley had to sit on the dais, although he didn't even want to attend. The organizer and toastmaster was Mervyn LeRoy, the famous director who had brought out classics like *Quo Vadis* and *Little Caesar*.

O'Malley had told us all that LeRoy was one of those Hollywood phonies we should have nothing to do with, and he sent me a note very similar to the one on Arnholt Smith. Mervyn was to get no preferential treatment for seats, and we were to fight against efforts by him and the rest of the Hollywood crowd to "take over" our Dodger players.

Next thing I knew, LeRoy was sitting almost every night in O'Malley's private box. Not only that, but as president of Hollywood Park and a kingpin of the dreaded "horse-race crowd" he had given O'Malley some stock in his track.

When no Dodger stock was forthcoming as a return gesture, the cronies fell out, but that came much, much later.

The big-name stars, like Doris Day, Spencer Tracy, Nat "King" Cole, and Gene Autry, attended almost every game, and that made the Coliseum the "in" place to go, where ordinary Joes could rubberneck at the celebrities from up close.

In addition, these Hollywood folk would fill O'Malley's ballpark once a year, climbing into baseball suits for the horseplay game against the disc jockeys or baseball writers that was always thrown in as a prelim to one of the less attractive games on the Dodger schedule. Red Patterson promoted this gimmick later, but the whole idea started when I offered Nat "King" Cole the manager's job on the celebrity team. Nat jumped at it, for he would have dearly loved to swap his days and nights in front of a big band for a life in the dugout, any dugout. Cole's agent was Carlos Gastel, who also handled Peggy Lee's bookings, and on their staff was Jack Leonard, another baseball buff who had once made it big as the featured vocalist with Tommy Dorsey's band.

This whole crew pitched in and called all the big names, asking if they'd play on Cole's team. Usually the stars responded eagerly; but if there was any convincing needed, Cole would call and twist an arm gently. The date for the game was set as early as possible, so the stars could have their agents book no appearances that would conflict. Cole himself arranged his whole schedule so that he would be at the Chez Paree in Chicago when the Dodgers were playing at Wrigley Field, where all the games were played in the daylight. The King would follow us like a shadow, and we'd find him at the Copa in New York when we were due to play the Mets. His dates at the Ambassador in Los Angeles always popped up when the Dodgers were on a home stand, and he would catch a few innings at the Coliseum before dashing to a waiting cab, performing, and then coming back to the ballgame, if it was a long one.

For one of the first celebrity games we had Dean Martin, who closed down the shooting on a big picture to play shortstop for Cole. Phil Silvers, who was big at the time in the "Bilko" series, was in the lineup, along with Mickey Rooney, James Garner, Pat Boone, and Dennis Weaver, who was really a fine athlete. Jack Benny was in one coaching box, and Doris Day and Dinah Shore were batgirls. Billy Barty, the midget, was always a big hit with the crowd, particularly when he walked between Chuck Connors's legs to take a pickoff throw. "The Untouchables" was big on TV at the time, and when an argument with the umpire broke out, Edward G. Robinson arrived on the field in a vintage car, whipped a machine gun out of a violin case, and mowed down the offending ump. These were the big Hollywood names O'Malley wanted to keep away from his players at first, although he warmed up to them later.

If the Dodger players had been able to adjust to Tinsel Town as well as the show biz people made themselves at home on the Coliseum ballfield, we'd have been all right. But the team, troubled by Joan Hodges's cockroaches, the freakish ballpark, the strangeness of the new city, and a different climate, fell apart with a loud clatter and dropped all the way into seventh place, twelve games under .500.

Only a paltry 1,845,556 paid their money to see this galling flip-flop by a team that had come to town billed as a contender!

In New York Dick Young, grinding his teeth, found it hard to explain this outpouring to see a loser. The enthusiastic writings of Bob Hunter on the Los Angeles *Examiner* and Frank Finch on the morning *Times* annoyed Young no end. Hunter and Finch saw no evil, heard no evil, and wrote nothing that would detract from the glitter of the newest and biggest show in town. O'Malley was the Great White Father; hardly an edition slipped by without some praise for the Big Oom.

Finally Young came up with the cause-and-effect explanation for the huge crowds that turned out to see such a lousy team: "Los Angeles fans are forced to come to the games in person just to learn what's going on," he wrote in his *News*, "because they can't find it out from the poorly written stories in the lousy sports pages there!"

After the team fell on its face, more than half our eight thousand season ticket holders canceled their seats.

O'Malley hit the panic button, fearing it would be epidemic. After all, a team just one notch above the National League cellar wasn't too appetizing.

Seeking every new avenue to push ticket sales, we all met with O'Malley. It was decided to seek out the ticket brokers and get them to peddle our tickets. Guys like Al Brooks in the Statler Hotel and Ben Creason and Alex Henig, the latter a fantastic character who carried his own boxoffice in his hat, could get our ducats into the hands of the carriage trade, which wouldn't think of going to an ordinary ticket window where the rabble lined up.

In addition, I got Mel Kahn, the owner of the Beverly Hills Health Club, to stock our tickets. His club was always full of high rollers who played high stakes gin rummy all day, and they bought plenty.

Murray Webber, the public relations director for Western Carloading, agreed to help, too. He had to take care of a lot of visiting firemen, and he also rewarded his truck crews with tickets.

Burch, the automobile dealer, increased his order, too. He had a string of customers as long as your arm, and he resold the tickets to them at no extra cost. Who cared, as long as the seats were full and Burch's money was in our till?

Nobody should have worried. The O'Malley magic was at work again, helped along by Wally Moon, whom Bavasi had obtained in a swap for a nobody, Gino Cimoli. It was Buzzie's best deal ever. Moon flicked left-handed fly balls over the O'Malley wire wall like a golf pro hitting wedge shots. And Larry Sherry, popular with the Jewish clientele in the City of the Angels, emerged as a magician in relief.

The team zoomed from seventh into a first-place playoff with Fred Haney's Milwaukee club, and it was the first time in baseball such a comeback had ever been made in one year.

We won the first playoff game in Milwaukee but were four runs behind in the second game, and I went in to rush the third game tickets out to the windows. Then the Dodgers rallied and blew the Braves right out of it. Now I had to get the tickets sold for our three World Series games in the Coliseum. Hank Greenberg predicted we'd have eighty thousand for the first game, on Sunday, but said we'd drop to fifty thousand for Monday.

He was all wrong. We were swamped, although you needed a transistor radio to "see" the ballgame from some of the four-buck seats we sold on the outlying shelves of our "Grand Canyon."

We had crowds of ninety-two thousand-plus for each game, and our three-game total, 420,784, just about doubled crowds at the three games in the White Sox park.

O'Malley had hit it big, with net receipts of $5.6 million, with $3 million more for television and radio, to make it the richest Series ever.

Now he crabbed because I had apportioned some World Series tickets to the brokers, to Mel Kahn in the health club, and to Burch, the automobile dealer.

We had begged these people for help in the spring, but now we didn't need them.

On top of that, when I told O'Malley we came up only two hundred seventy bucks short of $4 million in tickets on the combined Series and playoff handle, he scowled. "How come we never come out ahead?" he asked.

There was another bitter pill for me. Bavasi got the bright idea of "comping" more than a hundred tickets for the office help in some jury box stands we had built along the third base line. When Ford Frick's sleuth, Charley Segar, saw those Annie Oakleys in my ticket bins, he wouldn't let the Series go on until O'Malley coughed up the money for them. Everybody pays at a World Series.

It had been Bavasi's idea to save the Dodgers a few thousand bucks, and Colonel Burns was in on it, too. But they weren't around when Segar cracked down on O'Malley, and I had to do the explaining.

O'Malley made a scene before he grudgingly signed the check to square things. I knew in my heart my staff and I had done a fantastic job of getting the tickets out and the money safely in during the playoffs and the Series. Yet now the Big Oom was upset with me over a piddling thing I couldn't control.

How much longer, I worried, could I go on working like a dog for this man who treated you like one?

32. I Go to Work for a Pair of Red Cowboy Boots

Early in the 1959 season Lela Alston, the manager's wife, had their grandchildren in seats down front in the Coliseum's Aisle 10, which was where the big shots sat. The Dodgers were getting their ears beaten off, and the kids were restless.

"Could you get the youngsters' scorecard autographed by Roy Rogers, Harold?" Lela asked. "If I promise them that, I can get them to behave."

I protested that I'd never met Rogers and wouldn't know where to find him in the crowd.

"He's sitting about fifteen rows behind us, on the aisle," Lela put in eagerly, "and he's wearing a pair of red cowboy boots you can't miss."

Dutifully I crept up the steps, my head bowed as I scouted the footwear. Finally, there were the red boots, their toes so pointed they could have fatally impaled anybody who tripped over them.

I felt like a schoolboy as I presented my scorecard. "Mr. Rogers, would you please sign this for the grandchildren of the Dodger manager?"

"Dunno how he signs his name," drawled the owner of the boots, "but mine's Gene Autry, and I'll be glad to sign if you'd like."

After such an inauspicious beginning, I got to be good friends with Gene and his lovely wife, Ina, who attended most of the Dodger games. She was the one who had talked the Cowboy into recording a Christmas song he had rejected as too childish to fit his two-gun tumbleweed image, as he called it. To humor Ina, they stuck it on the flip side of a record they were sure would be a hit; Ina's "Rudolf the Red-nosed Reindeer" has sold a mere hundred and eleven million records, and is still going strong. Nobody can remember the name of the supposed "hit."

I liked to squeeze in beside the Cowboy for a few innings during the ballgames, and Gene always had some sharp questions about the strategy on the field, or my promotional nights, or the Dodger broadcasts, which he followed closely. Little did I suspect then that I would go to work for this amiable millionaire when O'Malley grew tired of me.

When we moved to brand-new Dodger Stadium in 1960 and began to iron out all the bugs the place naturally had, I scaled the whole ballpark, and the seat classifications have never been changed, although the prices finally went up for the 1976 season.

I also began the almost impossible task of moving boxholders over from the Coliseum so that they were given seats very close to their same locations in the new stadium and would have the same faces sitting around them as always. We gave the fans a chance to inspect their new seats in their as yet unopened park, and they could request a change if they so desired. This was a colossal task in public relations as well as merchandising, for many of the fans wanted to increase the number of seats they held to include their pals, and this was not always possible. Each case had to be handled individually, and of course they all wanted to talk to the head man.

O'Malley was still paying me less than $15,000 a year for this backbreaking job. On game nights I couldn't wrap things up and balance out until close to midnight, and the Big Oom wanted you in there, if he buzzed you on that snarling intercom, by nine-thirty the next morning.

I had the season-ticket total up to nearly sixteen thousand by now, and there was positively not another seat in the place that was good enough to sell on an every-day-every-night basis. Selling more than fifteen thousand season seats, some of them de luxe jobs in the sunken dugout section and the press level at five and a half bucks each, put $4.5 million in O'Malley's till for every upcoming season before a ball had been pitched!

What more could I accomplish in this thankless job? I was expendable, and I knew it.

I had had that gut feeling since Rickey lost his power struggle with the ambitious O'Malley. The Old Man had offered me "a better job than I'd ever had" with him in Pittsburgh, but Josephine and I chose to stay in friendly Brooklyn surroundings at that time. We had no idea we'd eventually be uprooted anyway.

O'Malley's hatred for all Rickey's staff ran very deep, and most of them got out when they could. Of course the Big Oom's feelings did not seem to include Bavasi and Fresco Thompson, although they had been very close to Rickey. They had been with the Dodgers in the MacPhail era, preceding the coming of the Mahatma. Moreover, the Irishman needed them both very badly right after Rickey's exit, and I guess I was vain enough to think he needed me as well.

Even though we had now moved into Dodger Stadium, the anti-Rickey demon was still nagging at the Big Oom. It often surfaced in a new eating and insulting room Walter had opened behind the sumptuous new pressbox. This new circus where the Dodger ringmaster liked to put his animals through their paces was similar in many ways to the original Room 40 at the Bossert back in Brooklyn, even to the lettering on the door.

I thought many times of the story, current at that time, about the Dodger fan who was skeptical about going to Heaven unless there were ballgames there.

At the gate, Saint Peter assured the fellow that there was indeed baseball, complete with all the trappings, even dugouts. Just then the fan caught a glimpse of a portly gentleman pacing one of the dugouts. He was wearing a baseball cap with the "LA" monogram above the bill.

"Isn't that Walter O'Malley?" asked the breathless fan.

"No," said Peter with some scorn. "That's God. He just *thinks* he's O'Malley!"

That was the way the Big Oom presided over his new saloon, where the luncheons amounted to command performances for the staff. The top Dodger brass quickly found it was wise to attend, for the Big Oom's court jesters and sycophants, frequently led by the incredible Colonel Burns and Red Patterson, would tear an absent brother limb from wisecrack if he wasn't there to defend himself, and often even if he was. This sort of daily assassination seemed to delight the big man, and nobody was exempt, not even the late Harry Walsh, O'Malley's own brother-in-law, about whom he moaned endlessly because of having to keep an extra lawyer on the payroll when we moved West.

The routine was well rehearsed. The Big Oom would take a backhand rap at Rickey and glance for my reaction. Was I still loyal to the Mahatma, or would I laugh uproariously with the rest of the Room 40 chorus?

Next, Buzzie would harpoon Durocher, who was then a coach for the team and a problem for Alston, the manager. They all knew I often defended Leo when something said about him was off base. How would I react to the newest barb?

After a while, I began to feel like a dartboard.

One night after a game a sudden shower hit just as I tooled one of Burch's big Oldsmobiles onto the Hollywood Freeway, heading home to Malibu. After a long dry spell, a flash rain in California will float the engine oil and grime out of the pores of the concrete roadway and turn it into an iceless skating rink. A lady who was unprepared for the sudden squall, the skid conditions, and the heavy on-ramp traffic from the ballpark, plowed through everybody at eighty miles an hour—so she tearfully apologized later that night—killing one and sending many to the hospital.

My face was badly sliced up and spurting blood, but I struggled out of my battered car, which was still being hit like a gymnasium punching bag as others coming onto the grisly scene spun out of control and into multiple crashes. I crawled out of the car, up into the ice plant bordering the Freeway, and lost consciousness. I could have bled to death there had not a passing fireman, who had spotted me from all the way across the Freeway, came to my rescue.

This was Colonel Burns's chance, and he pounced, calling in his troop of auditors while I underwent plastic surgery.

I remember the whole timetable well, for the next night Bob Hope, phoning from Washington, reached me at home in Malibu.

I had been released from the hospital, but every muscle in my body was screaming, and I could not even turn over in bed. Hope's first question was, "Are the Dodgers ahead?" He was calling to tell me our second son, who had been a lieutenant in the U.S. Air Force, and had served three full years in North Africa without once coming back to the States, would be sprung as I had requested. It took a man like Hope, who had the muscle because he had done so many shows for the Air Force in foreign countries, to break the incredible red tape and bring the boy and his wife back with their two children who had been born in Africa.

While I lay in misery, the colonel's bloodhounds ransacked my private papers and records, as well as the club's ticket drawers. I felt as if a pickpocket was going through my pants while I lay there powerless. But due only to my bulldog in the ticket vault, faithful Frank Hess, not a ticket nor a dollar was found out of place. Colonel Burns invented a few problems that were quickly disproved by Hess's figures, and O'Malley had to fall back on his complaints about the brokers and agencies who were selling our tickets. These were the same people we had begged to help us when things looked black in 1958.

The Big Oom was particularly derisive toward Webber and Kahn, both of whom were fine gentlemen. Scornfully he asked Kahn, the Beverly Hills Health Club owner: "Where is that bathhouse you run, anyway?"

Burch had been doling out his string of season box seats to his customers, but he had a habit of not releasing them in April until each one signed up to buy a new Oldsmobile. I didn't know of this polite blackmail marketing technique at first, but some of the people Burch had on a string had written in demanding that they be allowed to buy their box seats directly from the Dodgers instead of through the tall, handsome ex-navy flight instructor, who really had the gift of gab. Burch was selling every moment he was awake. One night at a championship bout in the Coliseum, I stood beside him in the rest room and listened to him peddle a Toronado to the man at the next urinal. He was a salesman right down to the last drop.

Technically, there was nothing wrong with what Burch was doing with our seats. He had signed up for his string of locations when we desperately needed fan support after flopping to seventh. He was far and away our largest single ticket-buyer, and his check was always among the first in our till. Burch alone took the risk of collecting from his own customers. At no time did he ever charge a dollar more than he paid, and he was actually doing our work for us, "selling" the Dodgers to the fans and at the same time using the tickets as his own selling tools.

But the ball club was prospering now. O'Malley no longer had any use for the likes of Burch, and he had the gall to call him in for a conference with me in Room 40. When we sat down, O'Malley suggested that I go to work for Burch. It was the most outlandish proposition I had ever heard; the Big Oom was asking me to throw out twenty years of blood, sweat, and tears I had put in for the Dodgers, and push Oldsmobiles instead of Drysdale, Koufax, and Duke Snider. The Irishman blandly offered to pay my first two months' salary with Burch's organization!

Up until that moment the most bizarre, insane deal I had ever heard of was the one in which Rickey had talked Horace Stoneham into taking Durocher, who had been top villain in Horace's ballpark for a generation. Maybe O'Malley was trying to top the Old Man with this one.

Burch was willing to make the deal, but I declined with thanks to him and no thanks at all to O'Malley. That was when I went to work for the Cowboy in the red boots, and glad of it, thank you! I took a solemn vow never again to involve myself in the thankless, nerve-racking ticket end of baseball into which O'Malley had trapped me back in 1951, and the Cowboy and Horse Reynolds agreed. They wanted me to concentrate on promotions and pushing season tickets in their new ballpark in Anaheim. It would be the third new stadium I would open.

Autry was undoubtedly lucky with the Red-nosed Reindeer song, and with some of the oil wells that spouted for him, and with the instant success of the Western potboilers he made for RKO Pictures at the rate of one a week for $25,000 a picture in an era when there were few taxes. He is a fabulously wealthy man and a pal of Jimmy Grainger, whom we had known at Belle Harbor on the East Coast with his producer-son, Edmond.

The Cowboy is a compassionate, extremely generous man and often a clever talker, in a witty way. Why he feels he must juice himself up with a few drinks before he delivers a speech, I will never understand; but I shudder when I see him down that first one, for in his case it means that he is only a scant step away from oblivion, like walking into an open elevator shaft.

The man knows his problem, and once he told me the greatest embarrassment of his life was falling off his horse, Champion, and onto his nose, which he broke, in front of a Madison Square Garden audience of close to eighteen thousand kids. He deprecates his own wealth, which is so great he sold a half-interest in his chain of radio and TV stations to Signal Properties not long ago for $24 million in cash. He laughs modestly when Johnny Grant, one of his long-time disc jockeys, introduces him at banquets as "the Cowboy who, at the close of each picture, used to ride into the sunset. Now he owns it."

Perhaps Autry has been lucky, as he says, but never have I met a man, inside baseball or out, who more richly deserves his good fortune than the Cowboy; nor has deserved less, I might add, the rousting he got from O'Malley or the faithless performances from some of the types who eagerly snap up his salary checks.

The day I signed on with Autry and Reynolds, I ran into Fred Haney, the Angels' general manager, whom I had thought of as a long-time friend. This was in the press room at the 1963 World Series, at the Sheraton on Wilshire Boulevard in Los Angeles, and eargerly I reached for Haney's hand. "Fred, I'm happy to be with you and want to do all I can to help the ball club," I offered hopefully.

"Don't thank me," said the little man coldly. "I had nothing to do with it."

It was a tough beginning, but I was soon to learn Haney had a built-in dislike for any new face Autry and Reynolds brought in, even though they owned the team. Fred apparently hired nobody but former ballplayers, like Johnny Lindell, who had pitched for him in Hollywood after completing his days in the Yankee outfield, and Jimmy Piersall, the Red Sox eccentric who was the hero of the book and movie *Fear Strikes Out*, which was about his own nervous breakdown. Piersall was a good-looking chap with piercing eyes, and he loved to perform on TV, selling tickets and appealing to the housewives to support the Angels. Around our office, Jimmy was a dashing, romantic figure who excited all the secretaries. At that point, Jimmy was divorcing the wife who had borne him nine or ten children and was living with the brood in Hyannisport, Massachusetts, while dashing Daddy cavorted around Southern California. Piersall used to pester me continually to write him a few paragraphs he could use as a spiel to the ladies from in front of Autry's cameras.

Ted Bowsfield, a broken-down southpaw pitcher, was another Haney asked me to put to work selling tickets. But Bowsfield really wanted to work and learn front-office methods, and he rose to become stadium manager of the new Kingdome in Seattle.

Another thing I learned very soon at the Angels was that Haney wanted nothing to do with radio and TV. He looked down on all the electronic people, supposedly because he had once been fired by Tom Gallery as broadcaster for NBC's "Game of the Day." Haney had a folksy way on the air, although he was no Dizzy Dean. He liked to wind up his broadcasts by saying, "This is Fred Haney, rounding third and heading for home," and it got to be a very popular tagline. But Fred spoke in a monotone, sometimes so low you had to strain to catch his words, and Gallery had to bow to a flood of adverse fan mail.

If I was to get the Angels into the kitchens and living rooms of Southern California, Autry's TV and radio arms at KTLA and KMPC were going to be by far my best tools, and I began to work on thawing out the cold war that kept these properties of the Cowboy at odds with the Angels.

I began to work with Stan Spero, a promotion-minded radio man, and we cooked up games featuring the KMPC disc jockeys against a team of airline stewardesses, which were talked-about prelims to the Angel games. Dick Whittinghill, the station's mischievous morning deejay, dropped in a lot of double entendres, like saying he had heard the shapely pitcher for the stewardesses had a good move with a man on, and things like that. It caused a lot of talk.

Spero helped me with radio publicity when Walt Disney, who was still alive, agreed to bring all his Disneyland characters, headed by Mickey Mouse and Snow White and her dwarfs, over to the ballpark to help us sell out our Stadium opener against Minnesota. Then we started the unique Disneyland Doubleheaders, in which one bargain ticket got you a seat at a Sunday Angel game, plus unlimited rides at a special Sunday night session when Disneyland was open only to Angel fans.

This was all good for attendance. Once or twice it got out of hand, as when we had a "Pony Day" at the ballpark, with Autry giving away a Shetland, as well as bikes, kites, and cowboy hats. Fifty thousand kids and parents showed up, ten thousand were shut out, and we had to have a second Pony Day for the disappointed ones.

All this got me in a crossfire between the radio people and Haney, as well as Haney's yes-man, bookkeeper Frank Leary. At one time Reynolds had to step in and declare that Pony Day had been a success, and that he didn't want to hear another word of criticism about it.

But the Horse did not make many of those forceful decisions, which could have cleared the air. He preferred to let the wars within the Angel organization, like the feud that grew between Haney and his manager, Bill Rigney, rock along without stepping in. A man high in his radio arm called this amiable giant "a sheep in wolf's clothing," because he looked so imposing but chose to act like a milktoast.

When publicity director Irv Kaze left the Angels, Haney was miffed at me because I turned the job down. Reynolds came to me and asked my advice about getting a new man. I told him I thought Tom Seeberg, then an assistant to Red Patterson on the Dodgers, was the very best in the field.

I met with Haney, Reynolds, and others in the Angels' organization, and it was agreed I should try to get Seeberg at a $10,000 salary after getting permission from Bavasi to talk to him.

I made the deal that night with Seeberg, who was happy to come over.

The next day Haney called me over and said, "Tell your friend the deal is off, and we will have somebody inside the organization do the job." Somehow Haney had managed to kill the appointment. Reynolds was so embarrassed that he wrote Seeberg a letter and apologized as Angels' president for not being able to hire him after all his high recommendations.

The whole organization in Anaheim was run like an old ladies' sewing circle. O'Malley took advantage of the Seeberg mixup, saying it would now cost him more money to keep Tom happy, and bidding the Angels to stay away from his employees.

Ironically, Seeberg became an Angel a few years later, after a detour via the Cincinnati Reds. Haney wasn't able to block him a second time. He's now assistant to the president, Red Patterson.

In my third year with the Angels, a shortage occurred in their ticket department. Reynolds came to me and said he was aware of my desire to stay away from tickets, but would I please make an exception and install the ticket control system that had worked for us so well for the Dodgers?

I agreed, which made Leary and Haney both furious, for I was being brought into it over their heads.

I explained to Reynolds no system would work without the right man to enforce it. He told me to get whomever I needed, and I brought over Frank Hess, my old vault bulldog from the Dodgers. Hess had been with the Dodger organization forty years, the last ten with O'Malley, and was making a big, fat $8,000 a year. I couldn't believe it at first.

In the ticket department I inherited all the old ballplayers whom Haney had put into soft jobs. If it came down to a choice between two ballplayers for one job, he would hire both of them.

Leary got even with me one day when Reynolds, the president of the ball club, was not looking. Boarding the Angels' plane to go East, I sat by chance beside Dick Foster, an assistant in Anaheim Stadium. He got flustered when I asked him where he was going but finally blurted it out: Leary had talked Haney into training him as the new ticket manager, succeeding me. He was going to poke around other ballparks in the East to find out how to handle tickets! Haney had never breathed a word to me about his plan.

With all the sniping and backbiting, it was little wonder that the Angels made little progress; nor did the good people who tried hard to do a job there. Three Angel graduates went on to jobs as major league general managers, and two of them were outstanding: Roland Hemond with the White Sox of Allyn and Veeck, and Cedric Tallis with Kansas City and later with the Yankees. Marvin Milkes ran the ill-fated Seattle-Milwaukee franchise for a while, but he never really had a chance. But it was strange that Haney never praised and seldom mentioned these lieutenants to Autry and Reynolds; that is why the Cowboy and the Horse brought in an outsider when the time came to nudge the old broadcaster out to pasture.

Ironic it was, too, that it turned out to be Dick Walsh, another ex-ballplayer, who did Haney in, and that Dick was sold to the Cowboy and Horse by two of the TV and radio men whom Haney despised so: Spero at KMPC and Bert West from Autry's station in Seattle. One or both of them had gone to school with the Smiling Shark.

After they had handed the job to Walsh, an uncomfortable Reynolds called to ask me for a description of their new GM.

"In one word, Bob, he's efficient," I answered.

After a pause, Reynolds asked if I could expand a bit.

So I used two words: "Coldly efficient."

Reynolds laughed, but admitted to me later it worked out that way. It was a long time before the Angels could defrost their organization and unload the teutonic Walsh, almost a heel-clicker in his severity. Dick succeeded in putting the whole organization into the deep freeze.

It would doubtless have helped had Autry and Reynolds collected opinions *before* they invited Walsh into their parlor. But that is how the poobahs of the national pastime do it, just as they leaped into Seattle without testing the market—or the huckster they were installing there.

Walsh is out of the Angel organization, along with Tallis and Milkes and Roland Hemond, at one time all hopeful vice-presidents. Harry Dalton, hired away from Baltimore for an Autry ransom, now sits in Haney's old chair as general manager.

In Reynolds's former office, at the extreme other end of the building, Red Patterson, one-time "LAD VPI" and ex-assistant to the nonexistent Dodger GM, sits over Dalton, or perhaps on him, as president of the club.

How is it all working out? Well—

Let me give you John Hall, columnist in the Los Angeles *Times:* "Harry Dalton and Red Patterson sit in suites at opposite ends of the Angels' offices in Anaheim. Last week, three secretaries were wounded by the crossfire!"

XⓄXⓄX

Epilogue

Did an advance copy of this book fall into the hands of the moguls of The Game?

If so, they seemed bent on making a piker out of history, bizarre as theirs already is.

It's almost as if these addle-brains said "Come on boys, let's top anything this Parrott has written about our dumb didoes of the past. So he thinks we underrated Marvin Miller and botched the players' strike of a few seasons back? Let us show how we can really bungle things when we put our heads together!"

Their churlish response to the arbitration they had agreed to in the cases of Andy Messersmith and Dave McNally sounds like something out of "Can You Top This?"

Peter Seitz, the experienced judge in the case, has revealed that the owners literally forced him into a decision he was extremely reluctant to reach. "I begged them to negotiate," he said. "I had no deadline. I could have withheld my decision indefinitely had the owners shown the slightest inclination to adjust their differences. But they rebuffed me completely and said they wanted my decision now. Right now!"

What was the magnates' answer to the resulting Messersmith-McNally catastrophe that put another crack in their cornerstone, the Reserve Clause?

They fired Seitz as arbitrator!

This had all the logic of a loser who destroys the coin used in a flip that went against him.

It equates with the petulant little boy who lost a toss for first-up in a stickball game; he then demanded a two-out-of-three decision. Losing again, he begged for three-of-five.

When you come right down to it, the baseball owners are really little boys with big wallets.

You may have gathered from the pages of this book that they are sometimes peevish (Wrigley, Veeck), overbearing and vindictive (Finley), gullible (Autry), vain (again Finley), childish (Galbreath), and cruel (O'Malley).

But the ultimate put-down came not from this pen, but from the mouth of Marvin Miller and it was delivered in spades, doubled and redoubled. Miller was talking about community ownership of big-league teams, as first proposed on a nonprofit basis by the Carlson-Douglas combine, would-be saviours of the Seattle Pilots (pages 61–62), and hastily vetoed by the moneybags of baseball's Inner Sanctum.

"The owners," quoth Marvelous Marvin, "are unnecessary!"

That is something the lords of baseball will never be able to say about their players.

Finally, in appreciation

To a very thorough mother, who made sure her only child learned to spell, and then to read, and then, perhaps, to write . . .

To Jimmy Murphy, the old workhorse of the Brooklyn *Eagle,* who cultivated and nurtured in me the love of newspaper work that was always there in my heart . . .

To Taylor Spink, the fire-breathing dragon of *The Sporting News,* who drove me to pursue many a good story he had ferreted out—and drove me up the wall, as well. To his son, Johnson Spink, now the publisher, and his managing editor, the extremely capable Lowell Reidenbaugh, a headline writer from the old school, and a baseball brain . . .

To a boyhood chum, Joe Gorevin, who romped through many of the aforementioned episodes with me, and was always at my shoulder when need arose . . .

To Branch Rickey, the most brilliant and articulate man I've met . . .

Last, **to Red Barber,** the Verce of Brooklyn, who seems to be happy writing a cool column for a Tallahassee newspaper and living the life of a southern grandee with his lovely Lylah in their charming home—but who still seethes inwardly at the manner in which some baseball moguls strove to make him a nonperson. It was Barber who first said to me: "There's a good book in you, Harold; why not let it come out?"